# ONE
# FOR
# JOY

**One for Joy:**
**An introvert's guide to the**
**secret world of solitude**

Written by Tom Albrighton (www.tomalbrighton.com)
Editorial support by Liz Dalby (responsiveediting.com)
Cover illustration by Mat Saunders at Handsome Frank
Internal illustrations by Irina Burtseva at PeoplePerHour

Text, design and internal illustrations
© ABC Business Communications Ltd 2023.
Cover illustration © Mat Saunders.
All rights reserved. The moral rights of the author have been asserted.

All intellectual property rights in the third-party materials and works reproduced in this book vest in their respective owners. These works have been reproduced for the sole purpose of criticism and review pursuant to s30 Copyright, Designs and Patents Act 1988. The owners of the third-party materials and works have not endorsed this book or been involved in its development.

Except for acts in the course of private research or study or criticism as permitted under the Copyright, Designs and Patents Act 1988, no part of this publication may be reproduced, stored or transmitted, in any form or by any means, without the prior written permission of the publisher, or in the case of reprographic reproduction in accordance with the terms of licences issued by the Copyright Licensing Agency. Enquiries concerning reproduction outside those terms should be sent to the publisher.

ABC Business Communications Ltd accepts no responsibility or liability for any decision a reader may make, or refrain from making, based on the content of this book.

All URLs were correct at the time of publication, but online content may have been moved, changed or deleted since then. The author and publisher accept no responsibility for the content of third-party websites.

ABC Business Communications Ltd
100, George Borrow Road
Norwich NR4 7HU
United Kingdom

ISBN 978-1-7399154-3-8 (paperback)
ISBN 978-1-7399154-4-5 (hardback)

# ONE FOR JOY

an introvert's guide to the secret world of solitude

TOM ALBRIGHTON

**for Adele**

our one and only

# contents

ONE

# HAPPY ON YOUR OWN

Introducing solitude
and its many joys.

# what is solitude?

The best things in life happen to you when you're alone.
AGNES MARTIN

The word 'solitude' comes from the Latin *solitudo*, which in turn comes from *solus*, meaning 'alone'. So solitude is simply being on your own. But that's not the end of the story. It's just the beginning.

Solitude can be many things to many people. Your experience of solitude depends on where you are, how long you stay and what you do – as well as the thoughts you think and the emotions you feel. Your own character, plus your mood in the moment, defines what you want from your solitude, and what you get out of it.

Solitude can be mindful and focused or daydreamy and diffuse. It can be diligent and hardworking or laid-back and relaxed. It can be disciplined and ascetic or it can be luxurious and self-indulgent.

Solitude is as long as a piece of string. It might be a few moments snatched in the midst of a busy day – taking a shower, perhaps, or gazing through the window of a train. It might be a stint of highly focused work, either on a task you choose or one you've been given.

It might be a day or more spent home alone, doing whatever you want. Or it might even be an extended solo trip, finding yourself as you discover the world.

Your solitude might be such a humdrum, everyday thing that you don't even think about it that much. It could be simple downtime, spent doing nothing in particular. It could even be a bit boring – in a good way. But equally, it could be your ticket to a luminous, unforgettable experience that far outshines anything you do with other people, and is all the more memorable precisely because it can't be shared.

You might find your solitude in wide, wild spaces, or in a cosy little room. You might explore unseen horizons, or you might never leave your sofa. You might yearn for perfect isolation, with no-one around for miles. But you could just as easily find solitude when others are nearby. You can even experience a kind of solitude when you're in company.

Solitude is where the life of the mind is lived. You can explore new knowledge or learn more about yourself. You can immerse yourself in the work of a poet, novelist, artist, songwriter or filmmaker you really love. You can explore fantastical other worlds, or look at this one through other people's eyes. Solitude is the natural home of both writing and reading, and a place where creativity thrives.

Solitude can be an oasis of self-care. It can be a secluded haven where you rest up, recuperate and regain your energy. Free of distractions, you can gather in your scattered attention, making your mind whole again.

When people get too much for you, solitude is where you can take refuge. It brings you back to a state where you can give others the help and support they need. And it's where you regain your strength for the busy times ahead.

Solitude can be a time machine, transporting you to revisit your past and imagine your future. You can zoom out and survey the big picture of your life: where you came from and where you're going next. You can hatch plans, devise schemes and dream dreams.

In solitude, you can be yourself – and be *with* yourself, too. You can take all the time you need to think things through. You can ask your own opinion and await the answer. You can remember who you really are, and listen to an inner voice that may have been unheard for a while.

Finally, solitude comes in every shade. It can be sad and blue. It can be beige and neutral, a blessed relief from emotional extremes. And as the title of this book suggests, it can be a place of bright and bursting joy. What's more, although solitude has strong associations with religion and philosophy, it doesn't have to be serious and solemn; it can be fun and playful too.

As you can see, solitude encompasses everything from a week of mountaintop meditation to a five-minute spell of Wordle in the bathroom. So what's the common thread?

In my view, there are four vital ingredients. The first, and most obvious, is the *absence of other people.*

> Solitude is, most ultimately, simply an experiential world in which other people are absent: that is enough for solitude, that is constant through all solitudes.
>
> PHILIP KOCH[1]

The word 'experiential' here hints that other people may be *physically* present – but if they are, you need to be able to disengage from them. Whatever else is going on, you have to *feel* alone.

The second ingredient is *quietness*. Solitude often has a still, calm quality that marks it out from the time we spend with others. This quietness has two sides: the quietness around you, and the quietness within you.

External quietness results from the absence or silence of others. But it can also be a quality of a particular place – anywhere from a bedroom to a forest. And this outer quiet brings inner quiet. As distractions fall away, your thoughts and emotions become deeper, calmer and more focused. Now you're no longer reacting to people and events around you, you can 'hear yourself think' and get a clearer sense of how you really feel.

However, the peace you experience might not be physically quiet at all. You might use your solitude for an activity that's fairly noisy, like playing electric guitar, or energetic, like mountain biking. But because you do these things alone, they still bring you a certain quietness and stillness in your mind. You find a certain balance between your inner and outer reality, as if you and the world are perfectly in tune.

The third ingredient is *reflection*: a change to a different way of thinking that only happens when you're alone. Your attention will often turn to your own thoughts and feelings – although you might also lose yourself in a book or a film, immerse yourself in the beauty of nature or become absorbed in a task or activity. Or you might just space out and let your mind wander where it will. But whatever you do, your solitude lets you enter a certain frame of mind that is far harder to achieve when other people are around.

The fourth and final ingredient is *choice*. Solitude is a positive state that you choose to experience. It's not just a default option that you end up with if there's nothing better going on; it's something you create for yourself.

Having said that, solitude might sometimes be imposed on you – as it was during lockdown, or as it might be if you make plans and someone bails out. But even then, you can still choose how you *respond* to being alone. You can make a conscious decision to lean into it, to explore it, to enjoy it, to squeeze every drop from it. Even those in solitary confinement may be able to make that choice.

This positive engagement is what distinguishes solitude from loneliness. While solitude is a state of being that can take many different forms, and generate many different emotions, loneliness is a very specific emotion that people feel when they're alone: the longing for some kind of human contact. And unlike solitude, loneliness isn't something that anyone would willingly choose.

Similarly, solitude is different from isolation (feeling cut off from other people), privacy (wanting to conceal certain things from others) and alienation (feeling disconnected from a person, group or culture). All these other things involve some sort of 'consciousness-of-other'; when we experience them, our minds are always on other people and places somehow.[2] But in solitude, we're centred on ourselves in the here-and-now. Instead of looking 'out there', we're focusing 'in here'.

## who needs solitude?

Different people have different needs when it comes to company and solitude, and the easiest way to understand them is through the distinction between extroverts and introverts. Extroverts are sociable, talkative and outward-looking, while introverts are solitary, quiet and tend to focus inwards.

Introverts prefer to work on their own rather than in groups, and dislike being the centre of attention. They're cautious about meeting new people and usually form just a few deep attachments rather than having a wide circle of friends. Reflection is vital for introverts, and they're generally good at concentrating. They limit their interests, but explore the few they have very deeply. And last but not least, introverts need their private space and time, and are happy to spend time on their own.

In fact, solitude isn't just a preference for introverts – it's a need. While extroverts gain energy from company, introverts get theirs from being alone. The feeling an extrovert gets on walking into a party is how an introvert feels about the prospect of an evening curled up with a book. An extrovert stranded on their own soon gets bored and lonely, while an introvert trapped in company for too long becomes irritable and stressed.

Introvert and extrovert aren't rigid categories, but two ends of a scale. Some people, known as ambiverts, combine both extrovert and introvert traits. And we all have different moods at different times, whatever our underlying character might be.

So far, so good. We're all different and we all have different needs. Nobody can argue with that. But the problem is that not everyone's needs are seen in the same light.

Basically, we live in an extrovert world – in Western society, at least. It's a world that favours sociability over solitude, speaking over silence and action over reflection. It's obsessed by sharing, teamwork and togetherness. It encourages us to define ourselves in relation to others, and to see almost every problem in terms of relationships. It tells us to celebrate our uniqueness and independence, yet insists we do so in the social sphere. Self-reliance is laudable, but solitude is questionable.

Here's how author Susan Cain puts it:

> We live with a value system that I call the Extrovert Ideal—the omnipresent belief that the ideal self is gregarious, alpha, and comfortable in the spotlight... We like to think that we value individuality, but all too

> often we admire one type of individual—the kind who's comfortable "putting himself out there."[3]

The prevalence of the Extrovert Ideal means that introverts face many challenges, everywhere from the classroom to the boardroom. Their needs are often misunderstood or simply ignored, and they have to deal with many situations they find hard. Some introverts end up pretending to be more extrovert than they really are, or hiding their discomfort, because they've learned that it's easier than trying to explain what they really want. Growing up introvert is sometimes hard, and so is parenting a child who's on the same path.

## the choice to be alone

When you live in an extrovert world, choosing solitude can be tough. It's hard to say you want to be alone, or you don't want to talk to anyone right now, without causing offence. You can end up feeling bad twice over: yearning for solitude on one hand and feeling guilty for wanting it on the other.

But seeking solitude *doesn't* mean you dislike other people. It just means that what you want for yourself, right now, is to be alone. Why is that so hard to understand?

As a lifelong introvert myself, I can only speculate on others' state of mind. But I think extroverts probably see solitude as the absence of experience. Being alone is a state of unbeing or not-doing. It's a blank space that should be filled, or a need that should be met. Life is what we do with other people, while solitude is just the gaps in between. So for an extrovert, actually *choosing* solitude seems like a perverse act of negation; a heretical turning away from the light.

If there's one thing I'd like to get across in this book, it's that solitude is real and good in its own right. It's an experience, just like all our other experiences, with just as much substance as the other aspects of our lives. And it can be just as vital to our happiness as company is.

Solitude is the flip side of company. Being alone and being with others are complementary opposites, like yin and yang. Where one ends, the other begins, as surely as night follows day. And everyone – even the rowdiest, most gregarious extrovert – needs both sunshine and moonlight in their lives. We just differ in how we feel about them, and how much of each one we want.

If you like to be alone, you're in good company. The list of notable introverts, shy geniuses and solo achievers includes writers like Emily Dickinson, Marcel Proust, Philip Larkin, J.D. Salinger and Dr. Seuss, composers like Frédéric Chopin, musicians like Kate Bush, Prince and The Weeknd, scientists like Isaac Newton, Charles Darwin and Albert Einstein and world-beating sportspeople like solo yachtswoman Ellen MacArthur. Being an introvert is no barrier to success, and neither is being on your own.

## before we begin

What follows in these pages is a celebration of solitude, for anyone who chooses to be alone and enjoys it.

You don't have to live a particularly solitary life to enjoy this book. You don't have to be single, live alone or work on your own. You don't have to spend weeks in isolation or retreat. You don't even have to spend that much time alone – in fact, you might wish you could spend more. All you need is a love of solitude, whatever that means to you.

We'll be looking at solitude from every side. We'll explore different ways to reach it, and what to do once you arrive. We'll explore all the reasons why we love solitude, and all the ways it helps. And we'll look at some of the ideas and stories people have spun around solitude, from the distant past to the present day.

As its title suggests, this book is about chosen solitude that brings you joy. So if your solitude is actually loneliness, and you've come to this book seeking solace, I hope you find it – but please bear in mind that wasn't my goal. I'm also aware that solitude has special significance for many neurodivergent people, and if that applies to you, I hope you find some interest here.

Along the way, we'll be exploring the thoughts and ideas of many thinkers and writers smarter and more eloquent than me. If you want to explore further, check out the notes at the end of the book. My aim here is to roam wide rather than dive deep, but there's a great deal more to discover beneath the surface.

Finally, I should point out that this isn't a serious psychology book or a self-help guide. I'm not on a mission to convince extroverts of the pleasures of being alone, or help introverts deal with company. All I really want to do is cook up some verbal comfort food for those who love to be alone.

So if that's you, let's bolt the door, light the fire and get on with the wonderful business of being on our own.

TWO

# WAYS TO BE ALONE

Solitude is a friend
with many faces.

## shades of solitude

> It is possible to be solitary in one's mind while living in a crowd, and it is possible for one who is solitary to live in the crowd of his own thoughts.
>
> Syncletica of Alexandria[4]

As we saw in chapter one, there's more than one way to be alone. First, we can be *socially* alone, or alone in body. Here, our solitude is the simple objective fact that no-one else is around. What constitutes 'around' can vary, and the guide is our own perception: whether we're aware of other people at that moment.

We're normally aware of the transition into or out of social solitude. Solitude begins when other people leave, or we leave them, and it ends when they return, or we return to them. On the other hand, it's rare, and unsettling, to unexpectedly find yourself on your own – and even worse to suddenly realise that someone else is there when you thought you were alone.

Solitude is also determined by the inner world of our subjective experience, where we can be *psychologically* alone. In other words, we enter a state of mind where we're centred in ourselves, with no-one else's consciousness impinging on our own.[5]

As we'll see, many distractions can follow us, even when we're physically alone. So getting into a state of psychological solitude may take some time and effort, and is less likely to 'just happen' than social solitude. Henry David Thoreau, author of *Walden*, the classic book on finding solitude in nature, found that removing himself from other people didn't necessarily remove other people from him:

> I am alarmed when it happens that I have walked a mile into the woods bodily, without getting there in spirit... I cannot easily shake off the village.[6]

If we turn the levels of social and psychological togetherness into the axes of a simple graph, we can plot four different 'flavours' of experience:

| | Psychologically alone | Psychologically together |
|---|---|---|
| Socially together | **Abstracted solitude**<br>Alone in the crowd | **In company**<br>Present and engaged with others |
| Socially alone | **Perfect solitude**<br>Alone and present with ourselves | **Networked solitude**<br>Alone, yet connected |

Being psychologically and socially together is the experience of being in company (top right). For example, you're with some friends at the bar, or at a family gathering, and you're actively engaged.

Then there is being socially together while feeling psychologically alone. This is a state of *abstracted solitude*, or 'alone in a crowd' (top left). For example, maybe you're still at the bar, but you fall silent and drift off inside your head for a while.

On the other hand, we can be psychologically together but socially alone. This is *networked solitude*: we're physically on our own, but still connected to others somehow (bottom right). Reading, writing, records, films, TV and the internet can all give us this sense of connection – but we can also create it in our imagination.

Finally, if we're both psychologically *and* socially alone, we're experiencing *perfect solitude*, where we're physically on our own and also present with ourselves (bottom left). (The word 'perfect' doesn't necessarily mean that this type of solitude is better than the others – just that it's a kind of ideal form.) We might experience perfect solitude through meditation, work focus or just deep thought.

These four categories are a useful first step, but our experience is too complex and subtle to fit into neat boxes. There are many shades of grey between the extremes, and one type of experience might blend into another over time. So it can be hard to pinpoint exactly where and when our solitude begins and ends.

For example, imagine you're walking on a deserted beach, with no-one else around for miles. You feel an intoxicating sense of isolation, as if the whole world exists only for you, and you're savouring being alone with your thoughts. In other words, you're in perfect solitude.

But wait. Over there, in the distance, another walker has appeared up on the clifftop. Even though they're just a tiny silhouette, a stick figure, you can still sense that they're looking down at you, as you look up at them.

In a way, nothing has changed. They're too far away to talk to, or even yell at. Whatever route you take, you'll be able to keep many yards of sand and shingle between you. By any reasonable measure, you are not in each other's company. So are you still socially alone?

Arguably. But the questions run deeper than that. Psychologically, some sort of link has been forged between you and the other walker, simply because you're sharing this experience, right now. You're aware of them, and they *must* be aware of you, since you're the only thing moving on all these miles of sand. Against your wills, this moment has brought you together.

What's more, your whole experience has now been reframed. The walker has appeared in 'your' landscape, while you have appeared in theirs. Previously, you were the lord of all you surveyed – the absolute centre of everything, the sole audience for the spectacle. But now there's *another* centre, another viewpoint on the scene. Before, you were the director of your own play, but now you've flipped into being a character in someone else's.

So does this mean the end of your solitude? The answer, like the solitude itself, is in your mind. You could take it all in your stride and firmly tell yourself you're still alone, or you could accept that your solitude bubble has irrevocably burst. If solitude has indeed gone, you might feel furious that your walk's been ruined, or you could be grateful that you enjoyed as much solitude as you did. Then again, you could reason that although your solitude may have been dispelled *just for now*, it will surely return very soon.

Now rewind and consider a different scenario. Once again, a figure comes into view – but this time they are not on the cliff, but in your mind. Like the hiker, they seem to come from nowhere, since there's no conscious cue for you to start thinking about them. But whatever their reason for appearing, there they are.

They could be someone you're glad to see, like an old friend, or someone more objectionable, like an irritating work colleague. Either way, they come to mind so vividly that you launch into an imaginary conversation with them, in which you feel you can actually hear their words and see their mannerisms. In other words, psychologically speaking, it's as though they were really there on the beach with you. So are you still alone?

The same idea works in reverse. Imagine you're having coffee with a friend and you're deep in conversation. You want to be there and listen to them. But even as they're speaking, and you're looking directly into their eyes, your mind spontaneously wanders to the solo cycle ride you've got planned for tomorrow. Socially, you're still present – but psychologically, you're miles away.

Or you might still be thinking about your friend, but in a self-centred way. Instead of being fully present for them, you're thinking about what *you* want. You're regarding your friend as a means to an end – not in a cynical or exploitative way, but just with a view to a mundane, everyday transaction. In everyday life, our interactions are always partly aimed at gaining something we want – information, entertainment, solace or just a willing ear. A conversation focused exclusively on just one of the participants is rare outside a job interview, the confessional or the psychotherapist's couch.

Whatever the reason, it's easy to slip into abstraction when we're with other people. We can even be in abstracted and networked solitude at the same time, such as when we go on our phones in someone else's company. So, where are you in such moments, and who are you with? Are you still in company, or somewhere else?

Human consciousness is rich, deep and complex. Our perceptions, thoughts, feelings, memories, imaginings and impulses all come together to create our experience in the here-and-now. And our minds can work at multiple levels at the same time – some above our conscious level of awareness, and some below.

Abstract concepts like solitude are simple labels for complex phenomena. You know solitude when you're in it, but sometimes it's hard to say where and how it begins and ends, or why. You can also experience it to different degrees, shifting between presence and absence, both mental and physical, from one moment to the next.

The problem is that none of these shades of meaning are really captured by a word like 'solitude'. Because it's an abstract noun, it objectifies and reifies the experience. But solitude isn't a solid thing we can make or a possession we can own ('a solitude'). It's not even an activity we can do ('solituding'). Instead, it's a mode of experience that we can sometimes purposefully bring about, and other times just happens. And it depends as much on what's going on internally as on events out there in the world.

## be mindful

There is a solitude of space
A solitude of sea
A solitude of death, but these
Society shall be
Compared with that profounder site
That polar privacy
A soul admitted to itself—
Finite infinity.

EMILY DICKINSON[7]

In the previous section, we looked at some types of solitude whose borders were hard to define. But what about the other end of the scale – pure, unadulterated, solid-gold solitude?

Perfect solitude is a state where you're definitively alone, both socially and psychologically. You're separated from others by distance or physical barriers and fully aware of yourself as a person and your thoughts and feelings in the here-and-now.

That state is close to the Buddhist practice of mindfulness meditation: a state of awareness and concentration where you maintain your focus on the present moment, while calmly acknowledging and accepting your feelings, thoughts and bodily sensations.

Buddha himself was big on solitude. Having abandoned his aristocratic origins and then rejected a life of asceticism, he retreated into the forest alone to meditate, eventually attaining enlightenment while sitting under a large fig tree (known from then on as the Bodhi Tree, or 'enlightenment tree').

> Apply yourself to solitude. One who is given to solitude will see things as they really are.
>
> GUATAMA BUDDHA

In Buddhist practice today, withdrawing from others is known (in the Pali language) as *pañisallàna*, *pavivakà* or *viveka*. If done with the right spirit, it can lead to *pavivekasukka*, or 'joy of aloneness'.

Buddha drew the same distinction between social and psychological solitude that we saw above. He considered physical seclusion to be the most important, and saw psychological solitude as a state of non-attachment where the mind was kept free of negative thoughts and emotions.[8] For him, the 'good' reasons to seek solitude were to reflect or examine yourself, to support spiritual growth or simply for the contentment of being alone.[9]

Anyone can try mindfulness meditation. It's simply a non-judgemental, non-interfering awareness of your experience. When you're mindful, you concentrate all your attention on what is actually happening: the things you can see, hear and feel, and the thoughts arising in your mind. The idea is to separate your actual experience from the ideas, emotions and judgements that pop up in normal daily life. If you practise it regularly, mindfulness can bring you more contentment and composure in the face of life's problems and provocations. As Buddha said, 'Mindfulness is helpful everywhere.'[10]

We introverts have a natural tendency to reflect deeply on the events of our lives. But if we take that too far, or do it in the wrong way, our precious solitude can curdle into brooding, sulking or fuming. We can end up worrying about past events we can't change, or what might happen next. Or we can start second-guessing what other people might be thinking and feeling.

Mindfulness offers a way out of this trap. It allows you to be alone, in a quiet and thoughtful way, without going into a spiral of anxiety and judgement. Through mindfulness, you can fully think things through, then let go of them and move on – so they don't take root as what Shunryū Suzuki calls 'mind weeds'.[11]

The simplest way to practise mindfulness is to focus your attention on your breathing: *in and out*. When your attention wanders, which it inevitably will, just gently bring it back to your breathing. Instead of being ensnared by your thoughts, just watch them. Thoughts arise, hang around for a while and then pass away, like clouds. That is just your mind doing what it always does. For now, there's no need for you to get involved.

Many people take up a certain position – sitting cross-legged or in the lotus position with a straight spine, eyes closed or half-closed, hands held gently in the lap. You don't necessarily have to do that, but it does help to have a controlled, alert posture: mindfulness is about focus, not just spacing out.

Mindfulness can also help you let go of judgements about your solitude itself. Maybe you could be doing something 'better' or more 'productive' with this time – reading a book, learning a skill, taking some exercise. Through mindfulness, you can let your experience be what it is, without wanting it to be anything better or different. This is sometimes called *radical acceptance*.

Try it. Just a few minutes can transform your thoughts and feelings. It's an ideal way to mark the transition into solitude: when you're first alone, just take five minutes to sit with your breathing and watch your thoughts. You'll find you feel much more centred and aware, and prepared to get the most out of your time alone.

Even though mindfulness is simple to imagine and describe, it can still feel a little weird, because it's so different from our normal experience. In everyday life, if we're offered a shot at distraction, we generally take it. We probably have a dozen chances to sit and do nothing, at least briefly, every day – but we very rarely do so. In fact, researchers have found many of us dislike being left alone with our thoughts, and would rather do almost anything else.[12] So you might have to push through some internal resistance to discover what mindfulness can do for you.

Focused contemplation isn't exclusive to Buddhism. In the fourteenth century, an anonymous Christian mystic wrote a work called *The Cloud of Unknowing*, encouraging the faithful to pursue reflective solitude and contemplative prayer as a way to get to know God better. For this writer, contemplation wasn't something that just happened, but an 'exercise' that had to be worked at:

> Ask yourself what will most strengthen you, what will best meet your needs, and what will most help you and all humanity mature. Blind, ordinary contemplation will. When with purity and integrity you practise this spiritual exercise, it's always better for you than any thought, no matter how holy.[13]

In other words, it's not necessarily something you can 'just do', however much you might enjoy it. It's something you have to work at. Just as a physical exercise helps your body get stronger and fitter, so this mental exercise is training for your mind.

## alone in the crowd

> Whether we are in a crowd, on a journey, or even at some festive gathering, our thought should make for itself an inner sanctuary.
>
> QUINTILIAN[14]

Our country-dwelling ancestors probably wouldn't have understood all this fuss over solitude. If they wanted to be alone, they could just step out into the fields. But as cities expanded rapidly in the eighteenth century, and living spaces became ever smaller and more crowded, people began to feel their solitude and tranquillity slipping away – and, perhaps, to appreciate it more and more.[15]

However, as we've seen, solitude isn't just physical isolation; it's a state of mind. You can enter a solitary mindset even when you're physically close to other people. This is *abstracted solitude*: the feeling of being alone in the crowd.

Robinson Crusoe, who knew a thing or two about being alone, was perfectly happy to enjoy some solitude alongside others:

> All the Parts of a compleat Solitude are to be as effectually enjoy'd, if we please, and sufficient Grace assisting, even in the most populous Cities, among the Hurries of Conversation, and Gallantry of a Court, or the Noise and Business of a Camp, as in the Desarts of Arabia and Lybia, or in the desolate Life of an uninhabited Island.[16]

As we saw earlier, it's easy to slip into abstracted solitude without realising it. During a conversation, your eyes glaze over and you drift off inside your mind. Indeed, active listening, where you consciously focus your attention on other people as they speak, is a skill that takes time and effort to develop. It's a kind of mindfulness of other people.

Another way to become abstracted is by becoming absorbed in a task. Other people are around, but your attention is completely focused on your work. Or you might just drift off into a daydream. We'll come back to these mental states in chapter seven.

If you're feeling drained or overwhelmed by company, a quick burst of abstracted solitude can often give you just the mental holiday you need. However, it's fragile, and easily dispelled by noise or someone else's words. And it can also be a symptom of your yearning for a deeper solitude. That's often when you feel the strongest pull towards solitude: when you're strung out by too much company, and you realise that the presence of others is actually making you feel lonelier than you would if you were on your own.

## alone together

Just as you can feel alone in a crowd, so you can stay in touch with others, even while you're physically alone. This is known as *networked solitude*,[17] and you can achieve it by reading, watching TV, talking on the phone, going online or using social media. We'll take a closer look at some of these later in the book.

Staying networked isn't necessarily an inferior form of solitude; it's just a different way of being alone. It's about deliberately letting other people's words, voices or presence into your aloneness, in a way that you control. Networked solitude retains the vital element of choice: you decide which connections you to make, how long to maintain them and when to let them go.

The connection might even be completely in your mind. For example, we often 'play back' remembered conversations in our heads to process past events. Interestingly, these 'recordings' are really just fragments we piece together in our minds – we only recall around one-tenth of our conversations accurately, even immediately afterwards.[18] Moreover, we're often remembering our own reactions, rather than the actual spoken words.[19] But wherever these 'memories' come from, we still have to retreat into solitude to get them straight in our minds.

Going a step further, you might imagine a conversation with someone you know, furnishing their responses as well as your own. Sometimes, it's comforting to reflect on the advice a much-loved friend or family member might offer, even if they can't be with you.

Or you could bring to mind someone who inspires you and reflect on how they would respond. Christians sometimes ask themselves 'What would Jesus do?' – but you can do it with anyone you 'know' but haven't met. How would Samuel L. Jackson deal with your annoying boss? What relationship advice would Taylor Swift give you right now? And since you're now well into the realm of imagination anyway, you may as well go the whole hog and consult someone completely fictitious. What would Katniss Everdeen do now? Or Black Panther?

It can even be helpful 'talking' to someone you *don't* get on with. Some research suggests that imagined conversations could help us work through disagreements, or uncover implicit knowledge.[20]

The only problem with networked solitude is that it can pull your solitude out of shape – particularly if two-way communication is involved. Being alone is a chance to get back to yourself, feel rooted in a particular place or experience your own subjective flow of time. But networks threaten all those things, by drawing you into other thoughts, places and times. And that can threaten both your mental focus and your emotional balance.

A little bit of that is OK. If you're reading a novel, immersion in the story is the whole point. If you're listening to music, you want to be transported by the sound. If you're reading a letter from a friend, you want to feel as if they're right there with you.

But other types of networking are less helpful. For example, distressing news coverage can evoke feelings of sympathy, concern or anger that then have nowhere to go, leaving you feeling powerless and despondent. Social media is a reliable distraction, in both senses of the word: a good way to fill the time, but also a destroyer of focus. Plus it can confront you with views that you really don't want to let into your solitary state of mind. We'll explore this important point in chapter eight.

## from the beach to the bedroom

> And I'd say to myself as I looked so lazily down at
> the sea:
> 'There's nobody else in the world, and the world was
> made for me.'
>
> A.A. Milne

How much space do you need to be alone? Sometimes it's a whole beach or a mountain, and other times it's no more than a tiny room. And there's a real difference between these indoors and outdoors ways of being on your own.

Outdoors solitude is all about the wide-open spaces. It's expansive, elevated and exposed, and sometimes barren and bleak. It's swimming in the open sea while the wind whips up the wavetops. It's striding along a ridge, seeing the land roll away for miles around. It's tracing a winding track through thick trees, sunbeams piercing the canopy here and there. It's standing alone in a field with the big sky stretching from horizon to horizon.

When you get this deep into nature, you're not just alone, but isolated too. To be isolated in space is also to be isolated in time: technology aside, if anyone wanted to reach you, or if you wanted to reach anyone else, it would take a while. It may be that no-one knows exactly where you are. So your solitude has a certain weight: it's not something that can be easily dispelled or tossed aside.

At times like these, you have the feeling that the whole world is yours. Right now, no-one else is seeing these sights, or hearing these sounds. This moment in your life, and in the life of the world, has been given to you alone.

However, while you may feel that you own the world, you also have to respect its power. To be out in nature inspires a sense of awe, reminding you that you're part of something greater than yourself. The ego is tamed by the earth.

At times like these, you may have a sense of replenishing your mental reservoir of solitude memories to draw on in the future – just as William Wordsworth did:

> While here I stand, not only with the sense
> Of present pleasure, but with pleasing thoughts
> That in this moment there is life and food
> For future years.[21]

He reflected on the same idea in his famous poem 'Daffodils':

> I wandered lonely as a cloud
> That floats on high o'er vales and hills,
> When all at once I saw a crowd,
> A host, of golden daffodils;
> Beside the lake, beneath the trees,
> Fluttering and dancing in the breeze.[22]

On one level, the poem is a hymn to the beauty of nature. But it also contemplates abstracted solitude, drawing a contrast between being alone in a landscape and recollecting that same experience while alone in a room.

At the start of the poem, Wordsworth is 'lonely' – although in his time, the word meant simply 'alone'. As a 'cloud', he's a part of the natural world, yet also detached from it. Floating high and out of reach, he can observe everything beneath, but never touch it. In the same way, the 'jocund company' of the daffodils brings him deep joy, even though he himself is excluded from their 'crowd'. Towards the end, he explains how he only fully appreciated the 'wealth' of this outdoor experience when he was indoors later on. He takes his memories of nature back home with him, to his 'couch', so he can recollect them in tranquillity:

> For oft, when on my couch I lie
> In vacant or in pensive mood,
> They flash upon that inward eye
> Which is the bliss of solitude;
> And then my heart with pleasure fills,
> And dances with the daffodils.

This is a double solitude that echoes across time: an outdoors solitude recollected during an indoor one.

When we're in a big space, we feel open to big ideas, and a belief that things could change. The further we go from our day-to-day lives, the easier it is to imagine how they could be different.

> We all need space. Unless we have it, we cannot reach that sense of quiet in which whispers of better things come to us gently.
>
> Octavia Hill, co-founder of the National Trust[23]

When you're far removed from society, no-one can demand anything of you. But since nature prompts reflection, this may also be where you see your everyday life in the clearest light. For example, you might feel your duty to others most keenly, or come to big decisions about your future.

> True solitude is found in the wild places, where one is without human obligation. One's inner voices become audible... In consequence, one responds more clearly to other lives.
>
> Wendell Berry[24]

Nature isn't only good for the mind and emotions; it benefits the body too. The Japanese practice of *shinrin-yoku* – literally, 'forest bathing' – involves spending long stretches of time deep in natural environments, connecting with them through all five senses. Unlike the Western habit of 'going for a walk', forest bathing is not about conversation, exercise or reaching a destination, but rather a mindful, meandering immersion. Now calls are growing for doctors to prescribe it as a preventative medicine, since it boosts immunity, reduces stress, improves sleep, enhances mood and fights a range of illnesses from high blood pressure through to cancer and stroke.[25]

At the other extreme is indoors solitude. This is the solitude of cosy rooms, locked doors, secretive seclusion and reassuring security. It's curling up in an armchair with a cup of tea and a good book. It's snuggling under the covers while the wind howls outside. It's soaking in the tub with the bathroom door safely bolted. If you want to get Freudian about it, inside solitude reprises the solitude of the womb: returning to the soft chamber where we all began, when we were as close to our mothers as we could be, yet still completely isolated in our own little room.

Because it takes time to move into an outdoor space, exterior solitude comes on slow. But when you enter indoors solitude, the transition is instant, like switching on a light. As soon as the door clicks shut, you feel the change of state. You may even think to yourself: *Now I am alone.*

People might have some idea where you are, and what you're doing. But within the chamber of your solitude, you are essentially unknowable. Like Schrödinger's cat before the box is opened, you exist in an indeterminate state that only you know for sure.

Inside solitude usually has a hard physical border, delineated by walls and doors. And while the outside world will usually change as you move through it or just watch it, indoors spaces are more static. However, sitting by a window offers the best of both worlds: the still and stable comfort of the room allied with a sense of shifting nature outside. Clouds scudding silently across the sky, the light of the setting sun slowly tracing the wall or flowers waving in the breeze all help to bring the outside in. The movement outside highlights the stillness inside – both inside the room, and inside the self.

> I am sitting at my desk and looking out the bay window at some swaying trees and those bright autumn leaves that have not yet fallen to the ground. It is quiet, and I am alone. At this moment I choose to allow the quiet to surround and penetrate me. I can feel the concerns,

> and plans, and details of an ordinary, busy day recede for a time.
>
> OLIVER MORGAN[26]

## time alone

> Solitudes are not to be measured by miles; they are to be numbered by days.
>
> ALICE MEYNELL[27]

Just as you can be alone in different areas of space, so you can be alone in different periods of time.

At the shortest extreme, there's the solitude of fleeting moments. At a party, you step out into the garden to take a break from making conversation. Riding in a bus or taxi, you have a chance to look out of the window for a while. A five-minute trip to the bathroom provides psychological as well as physical relief. For an introvert, these brief snatches of solitude can feel like coming up for air.

Sometimes, these moments arrive when we're least expecting them. I once had to visit one of my clients, and when I arrived, I was left in a meeting room to wait. And since this client was in Switzerland, the window opposite did not overlook a car park or a shopping centre, but a rocky, snow-capped mountain ridge.

As I sat quietly, gazing at this unfamiliar sight, I had a sudden, still sense of *now-ness*. I knew I was floating in a unique bubble of time that would soon burst, and would never come again. So instead of checking my phone, or fiddling about with some papers, I did my best to savour it. Maybe that's why I still remember it so clearly now: because I made a conscious effort to live it fully at the time.

Moments like these usually come to an end because we're on a schedule. We can't just sit around all day; there are things to be done. But there is also solitude that is unbounded in time. It's the temporal equivalent of a wide-open landscape, when you have hours, days or even weeks of solitude stretching out in front of you.

For an introvert, this stored-up solitude is the ultimate luxury. It's like contemplating a full sock drawer, a well-stocked larder or a healthy bank balance. All that solitude is just sitting there, waiting for you to use it however you wish – and nobody is going to spoil it.

This knowledge brings deep joy – not the epiphanic burst of a solitary moment, but something deeper and more mellow. May Sarton describes the feeling of contemplating a wealth of winter days in which to write stretching out before her:

> We are one, the house and I, and I am happy to be alone—time to think, time to be. This kind of open-ended time is the only luxury that really counts and I feel stupendously rich to have it.[28]

Sometimes, it takes time to get into your solitude, as if you really are travelling to a particular place. The further into solitary time you go, the deeper the experience gets. And this can even apply to unchosen solitude: Terry Waite, who was kept in solitary confinement for three years by his captors, puts it this way:

> Each day, each month, each year, I was left alone with my thoughts. I discovered then that solitude needs to be approached gradually and experienced calmly. It is not just a matter of being quiet for an hour or so. Like a journey to a remote region, it takes a long time to reach the location and even longer to begin to appreciate the positive benefits of the experience.[29]

Clock time makes society tick. Bound by the social contract, we all submit to having our lives carved up into minutes and hours and governed by the almighty clock. But when you're alone, with nothing to do, no-one to meet and no place to be, you can return to your own internal, subjective time, or 'self-time'. This is when you can feel you're truly living life on your own terms, rather than 'being lived' by other people.

Self-time is closely intertwined with our emotions, which is why it's so wildly impractical compared to clock time. For example, we perceive intervals with more changes as being longer than more stable ones. If we're motivated to do a task, it seems shorter – but if we're constantly interrupted while we're doing it, it seems longer.

Self-time changes with age, too. To a young child, a dull afternoon can seem a lifetime, while an adult will barely notice it. The more vivid or emotional events we've experienced during a stretch of past time, the longer it seems in memory. Conversely, if we settle into a routine where nothing much happens – that is, we become middle-aged – everything blends together, and the days seem to fly by. Intriguingly, this effect seems to be even stronger if you have children: the days are long, but the years are short. [30]

If clock time is a metronome, self-time is a melody. Instead of marching, it dances and sings. And it refuses to be measured out or boxed in. You-time is free to flow wherever your mind wants to go – encircling the present, probing the future or doubling back into the past. It descends into sleep and rises into wakefulness, allowing both states to combine and complement each other as they will.

> This flowing personal time is not metrically regular: sometimes swift and sometimes slow, it rushes through emotional narrows, settles down into widening pools, sinks slowly into unconsciousness.
>
> PHILIP KOCH[31]

The busyness of our day-to-day lives, along with constantly refreshed daily news and social-media feeds, can make us feel

trapped in a permanent present. Something new is always going on, right now, that seems to demand our attention or concern. But no sooner have we got to grips with one event than some new distraction or revelation comes along to replace it.

The antidote is what Thomas Pynchon called *temporal bandwidth*. In his novel *Gravity's Rainbow*, a character explains that temporal bandwidth is 'the width of your present, your now… The more you dwell in the past and future, the thicker your bandwidth, the more solid your persona. But the narrower your sense of Now, the more tenuous you are.'[32]

Temporal bandwidth is useful in thinking about history, politics, literature, music and much more. Applied to our own experience, it brings personal perspective, revealing where we are within the landscape of our lives. As we look forwards and backwards along our personal timeline, we can spot deeper themes and connections that we might otherwise have missed. Sometimes, the decisions we make – the job accepted, the invitation declined, the friendship rekindled – only make sense in retrospect. What turning did we take back there, perhaps without even realising, that ultimately brought us here? And what crossroads are we approaching now?

Seen from up close, our lives are a meaningless mosaic, all fragments and no whole. Every day is a jumble of connections and coincidences, mixed up with our own memories and make-believe. It's hard to read the story of your life when you're trying to write it at the same time. But in solitary reflection, you get your chance to see the wood for the trees – to contemplate life through the eyes of the playwright rather than a character. You can sit back from the work and consider where to take it next. And however much has already been written, maybe you can still devise a different ending, even now.

# THREE

# WHY WE LOVE SOLITUDE

How do I love thee?
Let me count the ways.

## when the curtain falls

> All the world's a stage,
> And all the men and women merely players;
> They have their exits and their entrances,
> And one man in his time plays many parts…
>
> WILLIAM SHAKESPEARE[33]

If life is a play, solitude is the intermission. It's when the curtain falls on our social performance and we no longer have to play our role.

Solitude allows you to see yourself through your own eyes rather than those of other people. Instead of impressing others, or catering to them, or envying them, or fighting them, or simply trying to understand them, you can let go of self-consciousness and just *be* – unseen and unheard, like the proverbial tree falling in a forest.

Introverts are often fairly serious, guarded people, and we take a while to warm up in company. If your face naturally falls into a frown when relaxed, solitude allows you to stop worrying about how you look to others (and, if you're a woman, to escape those idiots who call 'Cheer up!' or 'Give us a smile!' as you walk down the street). Now you're alone, you no longer have to feign a cheeriness that you don't feel, and you can relish the *inner* happiness that doesn't have to force a smile.

The need to manage impressions is more than skin deep. Social anthropologist Erving Goffman analysed how we interact with each other face to face.[34] He suggested that social life is always about putting on a mask, stepping out on stage and playing a role.

Like actors, we're finely attuned to the audience's reaction. In fact, that's the whole point of our performance. Whenever we go out into the world, we're constantly trying to project a certain impression of ourselves to other people. Meanwhile, they're doing their best to peek backstage and find out what we're really like.

Sometimes, we take on particular roles, like those of a friend, partner, parent or colleague. These roles might have their own 'scenery', like a classroom or an office, or 'props', like a laptop or a

pram. We might play different roles throughout the course of the day, or we might find ourselves obliged to play two or more roles at the same time, depending on who's around. Our roles can even clash – like that awkward moment when you bump into a work colleague while you're hanging out with friends.

Throughout all our performances, our most important aim is to avoid being embarrassed, or causing embarrassment to others – that is, to *save face*. We don't want to look stupid, or cause offence, or put our foot in it. So we walk a high-wire of social expectation, etiquette, politeness and moral judgement where one false step could mean a nasty fall.

We feel relieved in solitude because this effort to control our image and behaviour is exhausting. Now there's no need to play a part, you can take off your mask and resume being the real you. In fact, as Goffman points out, to be perpetually on stage would destroy us. Without the choice of what to reveal to others, we would have no individuality at all. Privacy is essential to sanity.

Being 'always on' is the exact scenario explored in Jean-Paul Sartre's *Huis Clos* ('No Exit' or 'Behind Closed Doors').[35] The play presents a vision of hell where three damned souls, Joseph, Inèz and Estelle, must inhabit a single room together for eternity. As they learn about each other's foibles and failings, and how they all torment one another in different ways, they realise that all three are both actor and audience, or torturer and victim, at the same time.

More recently, Mike Schur revealed that *Huis Clos* was an inspiration for his hit TV comedy *The Good Place*. In the show, new arrivals in heaven are dismayed to find themselves matched with supposedly ideal 'soulmates' who actually drive them crazy.[36] What's more, heaven isn't just a single room, but a bright and breezy holiday village where guests must plough through an endless succession of relentlessly 'fun' group activities. No wonder most of the characters get so tired of having a good time that they wind up choosing another path.

I'm sure every introvert, after too many hours in company, has felt like they're stuck in a torture arena designed for them alone. Unlike extroverts, we don't get such a thrill from putting on a good show, or hearing the audience's applause. We're perfectly happy spending most of our time backstage, only stepping into the spotlight now and again. For us, a five-line cameo, even within the drama of our own lives, is more than enough.

## alone and free

> A man can be himself only so long as he is alone... if he does not love solitude, he will not love freedom; for it is only when he is alone that he is really free.
>
> Arthur Schopenhauer[37]

Being in company is like a contract. You have to put something in, or you don't get anything out. Even if you don't speak that much, you still have to invest your attention. And whenever you're in company, you have to deal with being observed, evaluated or judged – or, at least, the *feeling* that you are. Whatever you feel self-conscious of, or insecure about, you're sure to see it reflected in the faces of those around you, no matter what they're actually thinking.

Intimacy offers some relief. As long as your relationships with friends, family and partners are strong and healthy, you can relax around them. You know they like or love you, unconditionally, so you don't have to worry so much about what they think. And yet, you still have *some* obligations. We want our loved ones to be happy, and even if we take on that burden quite willingly, it's a burden nonetheless. Having children, in particular, means being permanently shunted to the side of your own life; in later years, we may find the roles of parent and child reversed.

In contrast, solitude means freedom. Freedom from wanting things from others, or having them want something from you, or second-guessing what they might want.

> Freedom is the possibility of isolation. You are free if you can withdraw from people, not having to seek them out for the sake of money, company, love, glory or curiosity, none of which can thrive in silence and solitude.
>
> FERNANDO PESSOA[38]

When no-one can see you, no-one can judge you. You don't have to explain or justify yourself. Whatever you want to do, you can do it. Nothing gets between your desires and their fulfilment. Nobody judges, or comments, or even knows what's going on. It's just you.

## going goblin

> You do not have to be good.
> You do not have to walk on your knees
> for a hundred miles through the desert repenting.
> You only have to let the soft animal of your body love
> what it loves.
>
> MARY OLIVER[39]

Solitude can be a rare and precious thing. And that can raise the problem of over-burdening it with expectations. When solitude feels so valuable, you want to make the best possible use of it, so you don't regret squandering it later on.

In my day-to-day life, I'm always thinking that I should get into such-and-such a book or film the next time I'm alone. But when the time comes, I find myself gazing at the bookshelf or TV, paralysed by indecision, and then I end up doing nothing much at all. I'm like a child at a fairground who can't decide how to spend their one remaining coin, and hesitates for so long that the rides close down for the night.

Maybe I should give myself a break. In one sense, you can never really waste your time. It was yours to use as you wished, and that's what you did. Whatever you did was what you wanted to do at that time, by definition. Even worse than judging yourself, though, is catering to the judgements of others – for example, spending precious alone-time on a self-conscious, curated experience that only exists to be posted online.

No wonder people rebel against the tyranny of opinion and decide they'll just do whatever feels good to them. There's even a phrase for it: *goblin mode*. It's when you stop worrying about how you look, what you eat or when you sleep, and allow yourself to slump into the slobbiest, most decadent lifestyle you can imagine: living in sweatpants, binge-watching Netflix and gorging on pizza.

The phrase 'goblin mode' suggests that you're degenerating into some repulsive, subhuman creature that no-one even *expects* to be pleasant. You can't blame a goblin for its actions; that's just how goblins are.

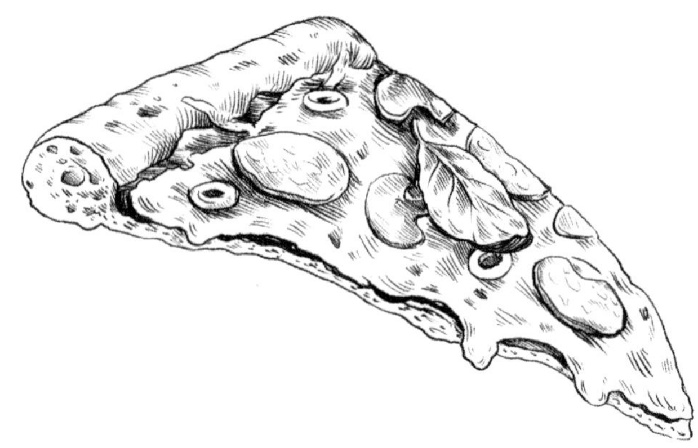

Actually, it's not a new idea. In 1855, French dramatist Émile Augier coined what he called *nostalgie de la boue*, or 'mud nostalgia'. Author Marion Goodman called it 'pig consciousness' – 'wallowing in the mud and loving it'.[40]

The term 'goblin mode' first surfaced in 2009, but it really came into its own during the pandemic. In the early days of lockdown, we were bombarded with perky pep-talks about using this time *productively* – to freshen up our homes, tutor our kids, bake sourdough bread or take up basket-weaving.

But as lockdown dragged on, it felt less and less like an activity holiday and more like a prison sentence. Even those who had it good started to feel the emotional toll. Soon, people lost patience with the wholesome-yet-tiresome idea of 'cottagecore'. They realised that nobody was watching, and nobody really cared – not even themselves. And they started asking themselves if self-care might be less about self-improvement and more about self-indulgence.

When you go goblin, you stop trying to live up to an external ideal and tune in to your own wants. Instead of aspiring to be your best self, you accept being the worst. Goblin mode isn't necessarily solitary, but that's probably the best way to experience it – because it's something that focuses your gaze inward rather than outward, and it involves doing stuff that you may not want others to see.

However, just as solitude is more than the absence of others, so goblin mode is more than the absence of self-discipline or self-respect. It's a *different kind* of self-respect, when you choose to honour your solitary self rather than your social one. It's when you say, 'This is who I really am, and what I really want.' And that's a whole lot deeper than merely slobbing out.

# still waters

> You talk when you cease to be at peace with your thoughts. And when you can no longer dwell in the solitude of your heart you live in your lips, and sound is a diversion and a pastime. And in much of your talking, thinking is half murdered. For thought is a bird of space, that in a cage of words may indeed unfold its wings but cannot fly.
>
> KHALIL GIBRAN[41]

We might not like to admit it, but introverts need extroverts. There are times when we need someone chatty and cheerful to breeze into our lives, blow away the cobwebs and lift us out of despondency. They need to open up, and we have become too closed. Even the quietest introvert needs what Mary Oliver calls 'smilers and talkers' in their life.[42]

However, this is one good thing you can definitely have too much of. And one of the clearest signs that you need solitude is the desire to stop talking. You don't want to make conversation, or share the ins and outs of your life, or formulate an opinion on stuff you don't really care about. You don't want to ask or answer any questions. You have no wish to betray your experience by forcing it into language. All you want to do is be silent and alone.

Conversely, you don't want to be spoken *to* either. When someone speaks, you can't help but listen, and decorum demands that you reply. Conversation is obligation.

Even if you make no spoken reply, you still respond in thought. That's why overheard conversations, or people thinking out loud, are intrusive: they're hijacking your cognitive resources. It's the sonic equivalent of passive smoking or fly-tipping: verbal pollution pumped out with no regard for the sonic ecosystem we all share.

I don't think extroverts appreciate how heavily their words can fall on the introvert ear. To them, I'm sure it's just having a friendly chat. But to the introvert, every word is another pebble needlessly flung into the lake of the mind. Chatterers deny the introvert's most basic need: to hear themselves think.

You know how it feels when you've been trapped by someone talking at you against your will. Having your attention yanked towards some footling question, rambling anecdote, unsought opinion or unsolicited advice. Feeling that you're swimming against someone else's relentless verbal tide. Worst of all is when you finally chip in to share a thought or story of your own, and your interlocutor *talks over you* to drone on about some loosely related thing that happened to *them* instead. Naturally, the conversation never returns to your sad little offering, and you watch forlornly as it drifts off downstream, disregarded and forgotten.

What you need is hard to ask for. While it's fine to say, 'Let's have a chat,' it is absolutely not fine to say, 'Let's have a silence.' Luckily, I've never snapped and said something completely unacceptable like 'Please stop talking'. Instead, I become gradually more withdrawn, or make terse, tetchy responses that are clearly intended to close down conversation rather than sustain it.

But at least listening is passive. You don't have to actually *do* anything, apart from sit there stoically as the words wash over you, and there will be no uncomfortable silences. Sometimes, you can even switch off and escape into abstracted solitude, as long as you give the appearance of attention. Since many talkers only want to hear their own voices, this approach might earn you a reputation as a *really good listener*.

Even in company, I'm often silent. It's not because I feel shy or awkward, or because I don't want to be with the people who are there. It's just that I'm happy to let the conversation go back and forth over my head, like the net judge in a tennis match, without the need to be involved at every turn.

Now, you could say that's selfish. It's like 'lurking', where website users read everyone else's comments but never post any of their own. In one sense, I guess I am 'taking' from the situation without giving. But my taking doesn't really leave anyone else worse off. And you could equally argue that I'm *giving* the space for others to speak. If company is all about give and take, I'd rather give what is most valuable – not just what's mine.

Besides, the more you say, the more of your own mystery you dispel. By saying less, you turn yourself into an intriguing puzzle.

> In dramatic narrative, nothing is more powerful than the withholding of information. It's only inexperienced performers who ask for more words.
>
> DAVID HARE[43]

## solitude for two

> He who does not understand your silence will probably not understand your words.
>
> ELBERT HUBBARD

For most people, company *means* talking. That's its essence, its *raison d'être*. When we say we're looking forward to 'seeing' someone, we mean talking to them. Just to be with them would not be enough.

Conversation is reassurance. When it stops, we usually assume that something has gone wrong. If all the world's a stage, a break in dialogue means we've forgotten our lines. Or, if conversation is a transaction, silence means the deal is off. Better to toss out the blandest banality, the tiniest small talk, than risk any implication that we're not enjoying ourselves, or that we dislike the other person, or that we're just too dull to think of anything to say.

This anxiety may have its roots in our evolutionary past, when our animal ancestors used 'contact calls' to stay in touch with the rest of the group. Noise and movement from others meant safety, while freezing and going silent indicated danger was close by.

Very rarely, however, there are people with whom you can share a comfortable silence. That's where you bring your two silences together, fusing them into something like shared abstracted solitude. And when there's no speech, there's no judgement either. Instead of demanding interaction, you simply accepting the other person for who they are in this moment.

If only you could ask for a comfortable silence, instead of just waiting for one to arise somehow. Etiquette should permit a request like 'How about we take a break from talking?' or 'Hey, let's just sit quiet for a while.' But you'd need to know the other person pretty well to be sure of the right response. Comfortable silences are like diamonds: the most precious ones grow naturally.

However, if you find the right provider, you can buy comfortable silence by the hour. In Japan, Shoji Morimoto has built a thriving business as a 'do-nothing guy'. Wherever you need to go, and whatever you need to do, *Rental-san* ('Mr Rental') will come along for a very reasonable seventy pounds/dollars a session.

With *Rental-san*, there are no expectations, no judgement, no pressure to speak or interact. All he does is *be there*. People have hired him to eat dinner with them, watch them compete in a race or make sure they keep working on their thesis. Sometimes, he helps his clients through difficult events like leaving home or getting a medical diagnosis. In a previous job, Morimoto was told he lacked initiative; now he's turned his inaction into a vocation.[44]

# sounds of silence

> For almost all of us, truth can be attained, if at all, only in silence. It is in silence that the human spirit touches the divine.
>
> IRIS MURDOCH[45]

Solitude and silence go hand in hand. Other people mean noise and conversation; being on your own means quiet and reflection. In silence, you can 'hear yourself think'.

As we've seen, your chosen solitude activity might actually be pretty loud. But for most people, quietness is part of the texture of solitude. Many introverts are 'quiet' people by nature, and we want our solitude to reflect the way we are.

The good news is that silence is extremely good for you. It boosts relaxation, improves mood and alters the perception of time, focusing attention on the here-and-now. In bodily terms, silence lowers diastolic blood pressure, heart rate, breathing rate and levels of cortisol, the main stress hormone.[46] Excessive noise, on the other hand, is thought to increase city dwellers' risk of developing mental disorders like schizophrenia, depression and anxiety.[47] Indeed, continuous noise is a brutally effective way to break the will of prisoners, or to oppress citizens in general. In *Kundun* (1997), the Dalai Lama (Tenzin Thuthob Tsarong), hearing loudspeakers blaring Chinese propaganda over occupied Tibet, laments that 'they have taken away our silence'.

In *A Book of Silence*, author Sara Maitland recounts her quest for long-lasting silence in an isolated cottage. She explains how, for her, solitude and silence are so close that they're effectively the same:

> For me, from the beginning, silence and solitude have been very closely linked… I have noticed that I tend to

> use the words almost indiscriminately… they both refer to that space in which both the social self and the ego dissolve into a kind of hyper awareness where sound, and particularly language, gets in the way.[48]

It's usually in silence where you become most acutely aware of your solitude. Just for a moment, you raise your eyes from the page, sit perfectly still, and appreciate what a wondrous situation you are in. *It's just you. No-one else is here!* The realisation brings a rush of euphoria – the sheer joy of being alone.

However, most of the time, what we call 'silence' isn't really silence at all. There's always *some* sound of one sort or another. Perhaps you're sitting in a quiet place right now. What can you hear? The whirring of a refrigerator, a buzz of traffic, muted voices?

In John Cage's composition '4' 33"', a pianist sits at their instrument for four minutes and thirty-three seconds without playing a note – hence its reputation as 'the silent piece'. But in fact, there is always something quite unique to be heard at every performance. Recalling the premiere in 1952, Cage pointed out:

> There's no such thing as silence. You could hear the wind stirring outside during the first movement. During the second, raindrops began pattering the roof, and during the third people themselves made all kinds of interesting sounds as they talked or walked out.[49]

As Cage wryly acknowledged with 'walked out', many concertgoers felt short-changed by a recital that was so short on, you know, actual notes. But his motive in creating '4' 33"' was not to confront the audience with silence, but to make them listen to what was already there. The piece encourages you to listen to all the sounds you usually ignore with fresh ears. It puts a frame around the moment and turns it into art.

Why don't you listen to – indeed, perform – the piece right now? After all, you don't *really* need the piano; all you need is a timer and four and a half minutes. I'll wait.

Obviously, silence is the absence of sound. But the *experience* of silence is also a state of mind. Like the mindful meditation in chapter two, it's about being fully present in the moment and paying attention to the quiet things behind the loud.

In 1975, musician Brian Eno was confined to bed following an accident. Music was playing on the stereo, but the volume was set far too low. Unable to rise and adjust it, he was obliged to listen to the music at the very threshold of audibility. The effect was entrancing: instead of blotting out the silence, the half-heard music twined around it, enhancing it while leaving it mostly undisturbed:

> This presented what was for me a new way of hearing music – as part of the ambience of the environment, just as the colour of the light and the sound of the rain were parts of that ambience.[50]

Seeking to replicate his experience, Eno created what he called 'discreet' or 'ambient' music. Designed for low-volume listening, ambient features drones and loops that gently phase against each other over time, like drifting clouds or intersecting waves.

Ambient is introverted music: music for solitude. Instead of grabbing the listener's attention, it willingly places itself in the background. Rather than demanding to be heard, it 'listens to' the space in which it's played, or to the listener themselves. Its message is that it has nothing to say. As Eno explained, ambient was 'intended to induce calm and a space to think'.[51] His *Music for Airports* was designed to help air travellers relax before boarding their flights.

Silence can have its dark side too. If taken to excess, or in the wrong situation, it can become oppressive or disturbing. It can be ominous, like the calm before the storm or a tense atmosphere where you can 'hear a pin drop'.

Sara Maitland describes several powerful effects of prolonged exposure to silence: intensified sensory experience (the taste of food, the sound of the wind, the feeling of the body), a physical disinhibition and a disregard for social norms, hearing voices (often singing), a sense of connectedness, a blurring of the boundary between the inner and outer worlds, losing track of time, a feeling of ineffability and a profound state of bliss.[52]

For Maitland, who had willingly sought out silence, these strange happenings weren't alarming signs of madness, but rather an exhilarating glimpse of the divine. However, it's easy to see how some of them might be far more upsetting to someone else, in a different situation. That's why interrogators use sensory deprivation – no sound, no sight, nothing – to break down prisoners' will. The figments of the captive's own imagination are far more terrifying than anything their tormentors could think up.

A few years ago, I developed tinnitus, which means a constant ringing in my ears. Around one in ten people suffer from this most invisible, most solitary condition, hidden from view inside their heads. Now silence is something I deeply crave, but can never quite attain. (The best compromise is a low-level background noise, like the sea or a dishwasher.) So if you can still hear silence, enjoy it while you can – through times like early mornings and late nights or places like libraries, galleries, gardens and the natural world.

FOUR

# HOW SOLITUDE HELPS

On the many kinds of good that being alone can do.

# hey, remember you?

> Wanting to be someone else is a waste of the person you are.
>
> KURT COBAIN

Humans are social animals. We evolved to live in groups, sharing tasks and creating complex social rules and structures to govern our interactions. That's why we're often preoccupied with our relationships to other people.

> We're drawn to identity-markers and to groups that help us define [ourselves]. In the simplest terms, this means using others to fill out our identities, rather than relying on something internal, something that comes from within.
>
> MATTHEW BOWKER[53]

However, there is so much more to us that others will never see. When you're alone, you return to the one true constant in your life: your own indivisible sense of self. Events pass, emotions fade and people leave, revealing what has always been there underneath:

your own continuous experience, stretching on through time like an unbreakable thread.

> Think for a moment of the immeasurable solitude of self. We come into the world alone, unlike all who have gone before us, we leave it alone, under circumstances peculiar to ourselves. No mortal ever has been, no mortal ever will be like the soul just launched on the sea of life.
>
> ELIZABETH CADY STANTON[54]

It's easy to forget your inner self when you're busy doing other things. But whether you're aware of it or not, it's always there, just as your heartbeat and breathing are always there. Your selfhood is like a river running through a tunnel: always flowing onward, constant and unseen, until it bursts into the light once more.

> Once more
> Uncontradicting solitude
> Supports me on its giant palm;
> And like a sea-anemone
> Or simple snail, there cautiously
> Unfolds, emerges, what I am.
>
> PHILIP LARKIN[55]

## one's company

> It should no longer be your concern that the world speaks of you; your sole concern should be with how you speak to yourself.
>
> MICHEL DE MONTAIGNE[56]

All of us have two selves: our social self, which we present to the world, and our solitary self, which no-one sees. Thomas de Quincey described the solitary self as 'that inner world, that world of secret self-consciousness, in which each of us lives a second life apart and within himself alone, collateral with his other life, which he lives in common with others'.[57]

In solitude, you can pay a visit to this inner self. Hannah Arendt defined solitude as 'being together with oneself', or a state of being 'two-in-one'.

If you've been spending a lot of time in company, solitude can feel like catching up with an old friend. So much has happened, you need to talk it over with yourself to make sense of it. You might even be surprised to find out what you really think.

We all talk to ourselves all the time, inside our heads. It's called intrapersonal communication, internal monologue or simply self-talk, and it helps us make plans, solve problems, self-reflect, think critically and deal with emotions.

Talking to yourself out loud is sometimes seen as a sign of 'going crazy'. It's true that people with schizophrenia will sometimes speak aloud to themselves, or hold conversations with voices in their heads. However, for most of us, there's nothing wrong with a bit of 'private' or 'self-directed' speech (as psychologists call it).

Saying our thoughts out loud can help us to feel more aware and alert. Because we're speaking rather than thinking, we have to slow down and really listen to our words. That helps us get a clearer sense of what's happening, what we're doing and what to do next.

When we're working on something difficult, talking to ourselves helps us concentrate, track our progress and focus on the next step. In one study, two sets of people had to find a list of products in a supermarket. One group was allowed to say the items out loud, but the other wasn't. The self-talkers finished first.[58]

As young children, we speak to ourselves all the time, gradually learning to sub-vocalise (silently form the words with our mouths) and finally to keep the words inside our heads. (It may be this association with childhood that makes us feel so embarrassed when we're overheard talking to ourselves out loud.)

When talking with yourself, it's important not to be hurtful or discouraging in a way you never would with someone else. Apart from being upsetting, negative self-talk can become a self-fulfilling prophecy. In contrast, sportspeople who talk positively to themselves ('You got this!') tend to perform better.[59] Even neutral remarks and questions like 'What would be most helpful here?' are better than talking yourself down. Interestingly, self-talk seems to work best when we address ourselves as 'you' rather than talking about ourselves as 'I'.

One step on from talking to yourself is having someone else play the same role – that is, an imaginary friend. Many children develop 'pretend' or 'invisible' friends, either by infusing a favourite doll or toy with personality or by mentally conjuring an entire being.

Most pretend friends are regular humans, but they can also be animals, robots, ghosts, monsters or angels. Some stand in for 'real' people, perhaps offering a preview of connections that the child has yet to form, while others allow them to fill out their knowledge of the world through imagination. Imaginary friends can also act as advisors, confidants and protectors – like the animal-spirit familiars who were once thought to stand guard over witches and featured so memorably (as 'dæmons') in Philip Pulman's *His Dark Materials*.

To an adult, it might seem fanciful that a 'made-up' being can have thoughts and wishes of its own, or teach us anything we don't already know. Yet that's exactly how many writers describe the experience of creating a fictional character: their creation takes on a 'life of its own' and seems to 'speak' with its own voice. By knowing our creations, we come to know ourselves.

Now, all of this is not to say we can do *everything* ourselves. There are times when we need the kindness of a friend, the wisdom of a confidant or even the expertise of a therapist to put us back on track.

These helpful others can help by showing us how to speak to ourselves with a kinder voice. Or they can set us 'emotional homework' by guiding us towards fruitful thoughts and productive ideas that we can pursue when we're alone. The right kind of company doesn't frustrate solitude; it enhances it.

## solitary strength

> To understand the world, we must sometimes turn away from it.
>
> Albert Camus[60]

The language used to describe solitude can be revealing. For example, words like 'retreating' or 'retiring' highlight moving *away* from something we dislike, rather than *towards* something we love. The implication is that solitude is the refuge of the weak. Instead of 'facing' social situations, we're fleeing from them.

However, there are inner battles, as well as worldly ones. Solitude can also be a source of inner strength, because it brings self-knowledge – and that knowledge is power.

Sociologist Jack Fong says that solitude brings 'existentialising moments', when we discover important truths about ourselves. Through moments like this, we get a new perspective on our life with others, and how social context affects us. Then we can choose which parts to keep, and which to let go.

> When people take these moments to explore their solitude, not only will they be forced to confront who they are, they just might learn a little bit about how to outmaneuver some of the toxicity that surrounds them in a social setting.[61]

Through solitude, you learn that other people do not define you. You develop a strong and stable sense of self that will keep you grounded and centred, no matter what life throws at you. Based on that, you can choose to be with other people in a deliberate and conscious way. You know that you're not using company as a distraction, an escape or an excuse. You're being with others on your terms – not out of need, but out of choice. You're the oak that stands firm, not the ivy that clings.

To know ourselves fully, we have to give up some control. Sociologist Kurt Wolff calls the technique 'surrender and catch': we have to let ourselves go with the flow, then catch hold of revelations as they arise. Some of our discoveries might be uncomfortable, or even upsetting. But however difficult the learning may be, at least we know it will allow us to turn the page.

> There is a you
> telling you another story of you.
> Listen to her.
>
> PÁDRAIG Ó TUAMA[62]

## recharging

> I find it wholesome to be alone the greater part of the time. To be in company, even with the best, is soon wearisome and dissipating.
>
> HENRY DAVID THOREAU[63]

Most people find solitude restful. One survey of 18,000 people worldwide found that most saw time alone as an opportunity for rest, particularly when they spent it on low-key activities like reading, being in nature, listening to music or just mooching about.[64]

This recharging effect is even stronger for introverts, because of the way our energy works. While extroverts are energised by company, introverts draw energy from the time they spend alone. That's where we recharge our social batteries.

In solitude, you regather the energies that you've spread across all the different areas of your life, and draw them back into yourself, making yourself whole again.

> At this moment I allow the quiet to surround and penetrate me... I can sense that my "person" is pulling back from its scattering into the details and plans of today, like a wave rolling from sand and shore back to its ocean source...
>
> OLIVER MORGAN[65]

When extroverts have to spend too long on their own, they start to feel despondent, frustrated or just bored. An introvert deprived of solitude, meanwhile, becomes irritable and withdrawn. The longer you spend in company, the more your energy dwindles. All that energy that extroverts are constantly soaking up has to come from somewhere, and part of it comes from *you*. Eventually, you end up feeling 'thin, sort of stretched, like butter scraped over too much bread,' as Bilbo Baggins puts it.[66]

It's a bit like knowing your limit for alcoholic drink. Just as you learn how many glasses will tip you over from merry into messy, so experience teaches you how much company you can deal with, and the tell-tale signs that you've probably had too much.

Sometimes, you need to be strategic about your social energy levels. You know company will drain your reserves, so you have to schedule in a spell of solitude to build them up in advance. Guard your energy so you have plenty to spend when you need it.

## healing

> Melancholy can be overcome only by melancholy.
>
> Robert Burton[67]

Is solitude a sad thing? Does it make you sad, or is there something inherently sad about it?

Extroverts would probably say so. For them, happiness is bright, loud and sociable, while sadness is drab, quiet and lonely – the feeling of being left behind or left out. That's reflected in the slang meaning of 'sad' as unfashionable, undesirable or socially inadequate – a word for someone who spends time alone because they have no choice.

That seems to be what scares extroverts about spending time alone. They fear that without other people to buoy them up, they might slide down into a deep, dark pit. They might also have to face up to thoughts they usually ignore – and might not like.

For introverts, it's the other way around. Being alone rarely makes us sad – but when we're *already* feeling sad, we *really* need to be alone. Solitude is our cure for sadness: the place we retreat to when we need to heal. We know that certain emotions have to be thoroughly felt before we can move past them. The only way out is through – and it's a path that we can only tread alone.

Solitude makes life make sense. It's where you press pause, step back and reflect on what's been happening, or what you've been doing. However much life may be 'out there', your deepest understanding of it can only be found 'in here':

> I am here alone for the first time in weeks, to take up my "real" life again at last. That is what is strange—that friends, even passionate love, are not my real life unless there is time alone in which to explore and to discover what is happening or has happened.
>
> MAY SARTON[68]

Dwelling on your memories doesn't mean you're 'stuck in the past' or even indulging in nostalgia. You're just catching up on all the thinking and feeling that you didn't have time for in the moment.

If someone else has hurt you, it's only natural to retreat inside your shell. When you're feeling bent out of shape or knocked off balance, solitude allows you to regain your emotional equilibrium. If interaction has left you feeling rough around the edges, solitude smooths them over and makes them new again.

This has been borne out by research. In one recent study, solitude was shown to reduce 'high-arousal effects' – strong, sudden, uncontrollable emotions – in a way that being with somebody else just can't.[69] It doesn't really matter what you *do* while you're alone; whether you read a book, listen to music or just sit there, the effect is the same.

Some people might unfairly describe solitary sadness as 'wallowing in misery'. That makes introverts sound like lumbering beasts stuck in the mud. But solitude isn't a swamp that drags us down – it's a river that washes us clean.

Psychotherapy puts a strong emphasis on 'the talking cure'. But while talking through negative feelings is certainly helpful for many people, it's not the only way. Around a hundred years ago, people with mental health problems were encouraged to go for a 'retreat' or 'rest cure' where they withdrew from society to recuperate on their own. The word 'asylum' literally means 'place of refuge'.

These days, the focus is mainly on talking and interaction as means to get better – for example, through Cognitive Behavioural Therapy (CBT). The possibility of therapeutic solitude is rarely considered – probably because 'isolation' has connotations of confinement, loss of liberty and sensory deprivation, while conversation suggests togetherness, belonging and support.

But we're all different, and we all experience sadness and solitude in different ways. As psychologist Anthony Storr points out, 'Coming to terms with loss is a difficult, painful, and largely solitary process which may be delayed rather than aided by distractions.'[70] For some people, a nurturing period of time alone, free of obligations and anxiety, could be just what the doctor ordered – or, indeed, what the patient themselves would prefer.

Working through sadness on your own is like holding a sympathetic conversation with yourself. This is beautifully illustrated in the Disney animation *Inside Out* (2015). The movie tells the story of Riley, a young girl who has to adjust to life in a new town with help from her emotions – Joy, Sadness, Fear, Anger and Disgust, all personified as characters who live inside her head.

During the emotions' adventures, they meet up with Bing Bong, Riley's former imaginary friend, who becomes downhearted when he loses the rocket the pair used to play with. Joy is anxious when she sees anyone feeling bad in any way, so she bounces around, chattering manically, trying to distract Bing Bong with happy thoughts and exciting things to do. But Sadness knows that Bing Bong's feelings must be felt before they can be overcome, setting up the most moving moment of the film:

Sadness: That sounds amazing. I bet Riley liked it.

Bing Bong: Oh, she did. We were best friends.

Sadness: Yeah. It's sad.

*Bing Bong puts his head on Sadness' shoulder and CRIES. Sadness keeps her arm around him until he's done.*

Bing Bong: I'm okay now.[71]

At first glance, the scene seems to be saying that a problem shared is a problem halved – and you can certainly read it that way. But for me, the real point is this exchange takes place *inside Riley's head*. It's not a conversation between two people, but a dialogue between a memory and an emotion about letting go of the past. Riley – an only child – can be her own counsellor if she needs to.

Another important aspect of the *Inside Out* scene is the *naming* of the emotion. While Joy wants to sweep Bing Bong's sadness under the carpet, Sadness brings it out into the light. Just by saying 'It's sad' out loud, she gives him permission to feel what he's feeling, and to see it for what it is. A lesson here for introverts is that even if we're going to sit alone with our feelings, we still might need to put them into words, whether to ourselves or to a sympathetic listener.

While I was writing this book, a member of our family suddenly died, giving me a heavy, pervasive sense of melancholy that lasted for weeks. But I was surprised to find that I didn't want to talk about it. I honestly didn't feel I had anything to share with someone else, or that talking to them would help.

Instead, it was enough to take the dog out walking on my own. The blackthorn was coming into flower, white flowers on bare branches, and that was all I wanted to hear or say. As I walked, I felt a sort of internal settling or drifting, like snow. I knew that if I stayed with that feeling for long enough, things would eventually come right. Time would heal – and time alone would heal best of all.

In his book *Solitude*, Terry Waite recounts his meeting with John and Terry Underwood, who live alone at Riveren Station, near the head of the Victoria River in the Northern Territory of Australia. Early in their marriage, their firstborn son, Daniel, died at the age of just nine months. As Terry Underwood explains, she could only deal with her grief in solitude; for her, there was no other way:

> The fact that I could come back here and work my way through it, and not be distracted, and not be interrupted, and simply let this powerful country absorb me and me absorb it – that is how I was able to work through it. Solitude has been the greatest gift that I have been given.[72]

Relationships with people can be vital. But so can those with places, with nature or with yourself. Healing is where you find it.

## growing fonder

> We cannot find ourselves within ourselves, but only in others. Yet at the same time, before we can go out to others, we must first find ourselves.
>
> THOMAS MERTON[73]

Everybody needs their space. However much we love our friends, partner or family, we can't be with them all the time. Wanting some time alone within a relationship doesn't mean you've stopped liking or loving the other person; it just means you need to give some love to yourself, too. Without some time apart, the time together becomes a torment – as lockdown made very clear.

As we've seen, time alone puts you back in touch with yourself and your energy. You realise what you want, and don't want, from other people. You get a strong sense of where you need help and where you can stand alone. If you've had an argument, solitude restores your perspective. You can decide if you want to take every word to heart, or stand by the things *you* said. Then, when your head is straight, you can return to the relationship and do the right thing.

In her book *Alonement*, Francesca Specter proposes the idea of 'standing in love'. The traditional idea of 'falling' in love can imply surrender: giving up part of yourself to make yourself more 'lovable', or folding yourself into the other person to become a single united whole. In contrast, *standing* in love is about entering a relationship as an independent equal: respecting yourself, standing on your own two feet and stating what you want and need – including time alone.

> Having discovered alonement [positive solitude], it's almost impossible to practise it without making it a value within your relationship, too. If you consider yourself whole in the first place, romantic analogies to do with 'completing' one another no longer seem so, well, romantic…[74]

On the face of it, the best way to improve your relationships with other people is to spend time with them. 'Working on a relationship' means a constructive partnership where two people try to find a better way forward together.

No doubt, that sort of collaboration can be crucial. But you have to be in the right frame of mind to do it. And for introverts, solitude is the only way to get there. Returning to the relationship in a little while, once you've got your head together, will be far more constructive than trying to 'work on it' before you're ready.

Henry David Thoreau felt that we should spend time away from other people to improve the time we spend together:

> Society is commonly too cheap. We meet at very short intervals, not having had time to acquire any new value for each other… We live thick and in each other's way, and stumble over one another, and I think that we thus lose some respect for one another.[75]

Instead of being bought too 'cheaply', Thoreau argues, our company should be paid for with the 'value' we can bring to the meeting. That includes the experiences we've had in the meantime, and our reflections on what has happened since we last met. It's the flip side of the extrovert's desire to hang out with others all the time by default because, well, why wouldn't you? For Thoreau, it is solitude, not company, that is the default option, and he needs a good reason to give it up. That may sound arrogant, but it's actually humble: Thoreau wants to give value to his friend as much as receive it, and solitude is the best way for him to do so.

As airline safety briefings explain, you should always put on your own oxygen mask before you try to help anyone else. Sometimes, we have to help ourselves before we can help others. If we don't yet have the right knowledge or mindset to help, it might be better not to try – for the moment, at least.

There are parallels here with Buddhist thought. Buddhism encourages us to share freely with others, and give what we have to them – our material possessions, and aspects of our selves too. However, we may have to purify our selves before we can help others to be pure. Buddhist teachers say, 'Save yourself first.'[76]

For introverts, the thing that purifies the self is solitude. We have to finish being with ourselves before we can start to be with other people. If you're feeling strung out and unbalanced, or you're longing for some time alone, it's hard to be your best self. At the extreme, it becomes difficult to even focus on what people are saying, or maintain basic standards of courtesy, because your desire to get away has grown so strong.

Your mind is like a container with a limited capacity. If it's full of other people's words, thoughts and situations, there's no room for your own. Time alone lets you empty all that stuff out, and replace it with the things you choose. Christian hermits used prayer and penance to attain *kenosis*: an 'emptying of the self' that represented a complete submission to God's will.[77] In the same way, you can use solitude to 'empty yourself out' so you're ready to receive whatever life will bring you next.

## wise counsel

> It is always important to have something to bring into a relationship, and solitude is often the means by which you acquire it.
>
> CARL JUNG[78]

When someone asks you for advice, you need to follow three steps: listen, consider and respond. But in a face-to-face conversation, it's all too easy to skip the middle part. You listen, hesitate for a second and then blurt out some impulsive suggestion, or something you just remembered that might be relevant. After all, you have to say *something*, right?

This hasty pronouncement then crystallises into 'your opinion', even though there may have been hardly any thought behind it at all. Even as the words are leaving your mouth, you may be thinking, 'Hang on, where did this come from? Do I really think that? Is it even true?' But now it's out there in the world – and it will be hard to take it back.

> Why, words, did I let you get out? I have often been sorry that I have spoken, never that I have been silent.
>
> ARSENIUS, DESERT FATHER[79]

No doubt extroverts like being asked their opinion because it gives them an immediate, gold-plated opportunity to talk at length about themselves. But introverts don't like being put on the spot, because we prefer to think things over before we share our thoughts – and solitude is where we do it. When someone brings you a problem, you just listen, without even trying to offer an answer. You take it away, examine it alone and work out what you really think. Then, when you next see the other person, you have a far better answer to give them.

## time to think

> My mind to me a kingdom is
> Such perfect joy therein I find,
> That it excels all other bliss
> That earth affords or grows by kind.
>
> SIR EDWARD DYER

You don't have to be alone to think deeply, but it helps. Solitude is where distractions, interruptions and self-consciousness fall away, giving you the chance to *just think*.

Thought brings clarity to how we live, what we want and what we value most. If we never step off the hamster wheel of day-to-day activity, we can never reflect on what our lives are really about. As Socrates said, 'The unexamined life is not worth living.'[80]

'Just thinking' sounds like a simple, basic activity that anyone can do – and in theory, it is. But how often do you actually do it?

How many times a week do you just sit there and think about something, without reaching for your phone, a book or the TV remote? In practice, what we call 'thinking' is usually mingled or overlaid with something else – and not always in a helpful way.

Computer scientist David M. Levy saw this as a real and pressing issue. He first became concerned when he noticed that his students never took the time to sit and think about their work. Technology had put the whole of human knowledge at their fingertips, saving many hours on research – yet they never seemed to have a second to spare. As a result, they rarely attained the state of deep contemplation that great minds use to discover new insights. To help them, Levy researched how we can resolve 'the challenge of achieving contemplative balance—how as individuals and as a society we might live healthy, reflective, and productive lives while participating in an accelerating, information-saturated culture'.[81]

The ancient Greeks may not have had smartphones, but they still grappled with the question of how best to use their time. For them, leisure wasn't just time off; it was an opportunity to devote yourself to art or philosophy. It was also when you stopped searching for new knowledge, and immersed yourself in what you already knew, becoming receptive and reflective rather than inquisitive. Through this inwardly focused contemplation, you could engage more deeply with the world.

Sounds like the classical philosophers had the right idea. So what happened between then and now?

Our medieval ancestors would have had plenty of time to think – while doing manual work in the daytime, on long dark nights at home or during the many hours they spent simply walking from place to place. But the Industrial Revolution changed all that. Work moved from the home to the factory, becoming noisier and more crowded in the process. Then, as manufacturing processes were automated and accelerated, the supply of goods outstripped our demand for them. In simple terms, there was too much stuff, and not enough money and people to buy it.

One solution would have been more leisure. Give people back the time that machines had saved, and they would be free to work less, earn less and buy less. On this theme, John Maynard Keynes predicted in 1930 that economic growth would cut the working week to fifteen hours within a century.

But the suits in the boardroom didn't want that. They wanted *more* of everything, not less. They didn't want us sitting around all day, feeling content in ourselves, enjoying Greek-style leisure. They wanted us mindlessly toiling from nine to five, making more stuff, generating profits for them and disposable income for ourselves, which we could spend on more and yet more stuff. The new discipline of marketing sprang up, eager to cultivate new needs and desires that could only be met by buying products.

Meanwhile, management thinkers like Frederick Winslow Taylor exhorted managers to seek ever-increasing efficiency. A company was nothing but a big machine with human components, and it had to run like clockwork. Writing in 1911, Taylor predicted, 'Up to now, the personality has come first; in the future, the organization and the system will come first.'[82] How right he was.

If that way of thinking had stayed on the factory floor, it wouldn't have been so bad. But the cult of efficiency gradually seeped into every aspect of our lives. We took the values and attitudes of the workplace and applied them to everything else we did.

Now, so far from being content with less, we're all about *more, faster* and *better*. We're constantly trying to save time, do more and acquire more stuff, without ever asking ourselves why, or what would happen if we didn't. We're so obsessed with means that we forget about ends. As a result, we feel constantly hassled and overworked – even though we actually have far more free time than our parents or grandparents ever enjoyed.[83]

Digital technology has turned the 'more, faster, better' philosophy up to eleven. We're bombarded by notifications, inundated by information and awash with entertainment options. Everything's available, all the time. Our inboxes have become infinite to-do lists that anyone can add to, and our smartphones allow us to do everything from learning a language to shopping for food. The result is that while our lives are excitingly packed with activity, they can also feel out of control. In response, we turn to 'personal productivity' hacks like Inbox Zero to try and squeeze more out of our time. But the faster we shovel, the quicker the stuff piles up.[84]

The problem is that while the world around us has got faster and more intense, our brains have stayed pretty much the same. Even though we might talk about 'processing' things, or our mental 'bandwidth', our minds are not really like computers at all. While machines can perform their calculations in milliseconds, we still need time to think things through.

Anthropologist Thomas Hylland Eriksen draws a distinction between 'fast time' and 'slow time'.[85] Some tasks, like laundry, are fast-time activities, which means they can be accelerated with no ill effects. However, other things, like planning a holiday or writing a book, can't be sped up in the same way, because they depend on deep thought. And thinking is a slow-time activity.

I think we know all this, deep down. But it's still easy to internalise 'more, faster, better' values until they seem like our own character traits. I've certainly done this, under the guise of what I tell myself is a Protestant work ethic. I feel that I should always be productive, or doing something useful, and that 'doing nothing' is a waste of time. *Don't just sit there*, scolds my inner Puritan. *Make yourself useful!*

There's an altruistic, social angle to it too. My busywork usually benefits someone else one way or another. If I clean the bathroom or mow the lawn, I'm helping my family. If I edit an article for a client, I'm helping them get published. In contrast, 'just thinking' can feel selfish.

Thinking may not be visible, or have any visible effects, but it's still real. And it's very far from being a waste of time. It's how we make big plans and decisions, or have new ideas, or come to important realisations. The thoughts we have in the present improve the quality of the actions we'll take in the future. And in the long run, that might unlock far more value – for others and ourselves – than merely 'keeping busy'.

What's more, 'just thinking' might not be quite as arduous as we imagine. In one study, people found it hard to gauge the value of contemplation in advance, and would generally gravitate towards some other activity if they could. But when they were encouraged to let their minds wander, they actually enjoyed it far more than they thought – surprisingly, just as much as another group who were allowed to use their phones. Even when they were stuck on their own in a deserted conference room, or a darkened cupboard, nothing could dent their enjoyment of a good long think.[86]

## sharpening the saw

> The fight is won or lost far away from witnesses—behind the lines, in the gym, and out there on the road, long before I dance under those lights.
>
> MUHAMMAD ALI[87]

If you want to get better at something, solitude is the ideal place to do it. You can hone your ability in private until you're ready to reveal it to the world. And the best way to learn and ultimately perfect a skill is *deliberate practice*. That means not just mindlessly repeating a task, but consciously seeking out the aspects you need to improve:

> When you practice deliberately, you identify the tasks or knowledge that are just out of your reach, strive to upgrade your performance, monitor your progress, and revise accordingly.
>
> SUSAN CAIN[88]

Deliberate practice is best done alone because it depends on intense concentration, self-motivation and self-direction. If you're studying in a group, you have to study what everyone else does, and trudge along with the slowest among them. But when you're alone, you can work on the things that most interest or challenge you, and move at your own pace in the directions you choose.

## in the flow

> We just concentrate on the activity which we do in each moment. When you bow, you should just bow; when you sit, you should just sit; when you eat, you should just eat.
>
> SHUNRYŪ SUZUKI[89]

In solitude, you can give tasks and activities the attention they deserve. The Japanese Zen phrase *ichigyo-zammai* means to focus all your attention on a single task. It's sometimes called *the practice of one thing at a time.* Whatever you're doing, you concentrate on the sights, sounds and feelings of actually doing it in the here-and-how. You don't think about finishing the task, or what you'll gain from it, or what others will think about it. You just do it, for its own sake.

Give it a try the next time you're doing the dishes or waiting for a bus. It's a *lot* harder than it sounds. Our thoughts are always trying to escape to somewhere else – but *Ichigyo-zammai* turns that impulse back on itself, allowing us to escape *into* our experience. Instead of casting around for something more interesting 'out there', we discover the fascination that's already under our nose.

Closely related to *ichigyo-zammai* is the idea of a flow state, which was originally proposed by psychologists Mihaly Csikszentmihalyi and Jeanne Nakamura. When you enter flow, distractions melt away and you become completely absorbed in what you're doing, almost becoming one with it. Everything becomes clear: you have total awareness of the activity, your actions and their effects.

> There's this focus that, once it becomes intense, leads to a sense of ecstasy, a sense of clarity: you know exactly what you want to do from one moment to the other; you get immediate feedback.
>
> MIHALY CSIKSZENTMIHALYI[90]

Flow doesn't usually arise from relaxation, but from taking on the most physically and mentally challenging activities. It's what high-performing athletes experience when they get into 'the zone' and feel that they can't put a foot wrong.

For the rest of us, almost any physical activity can be a gateway to mindfulness. The practical work occupies your hands and the rational side of your mind, allowing the more contemplative side to wander. The overall effect is powerfully calming, and can help you dispel stress from other parts of your life.

That's how British diver Tom Daley uses knitting. He took it up just before the 2020 Olympics in Tokyo, and fans could clearly see him purling away as he waited his turn to dive. 'I find it to be a great form of mindfulness and a way of escaping the competition for a while,' he said.[91] He even called knitting his 'secret weapon'.[92]

As Tom's knitting shows, you don't have to be in total seclusion to achieve mindful task focus. You can be alone with your work, yet still in company – a form of abstracted solitude. Or, if you are left

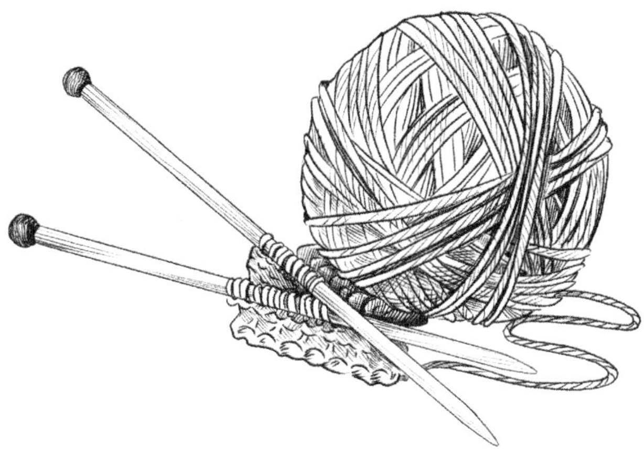

alone, you might find your thoughts wandering to something more expansive, like Virginia Woolf's Mrs Ramsay:

> She could be by herself, by herself… All the being and doing, expansive, glittering, vocal, evaporated; and one shrunk, with a sense of solemnity, to being oneself, a wedge-shaped core of darkness, something invisible to others. Although she continued to knit, and sat upright, it was thus that she felt herself; and this self having shed its attachments was free for the strangest adventures. When life sank down for a moment, the range of experience seemed limitless.[93]

## make it on your own

> The world is the product of the designer's dream. We should be careful what we carry in our heads – it is the future.
>
> Peter Gabriel[94]

Sometimes, creativity is collective. As a group, The Beatles were bound together by both collaboration and competition, each one compensating for the quirks and excesses of the others and helping the group to achieve more than its individual members ever could. Their later solo work, while still excellent, shows them indulging too much in their own idiosyncrasies – free of their bandmates' influence, but missing it too.

For other creative people, collaboration is always a compromise. The limitations of working with other people aren't constructive, but merely constraints. In their solitude, they have developed a vision of what they want their work to be, or what it *must* be, and they also need to be alone to realise it. Their art is a trophy of their solitude, unearthed by mining in the soul.

> Without time and space unburdened from external input and social strain, we'd be unable to fully inhabit our interior life, which is the raw material of all art.
>
> Maria Popova[95]

Elizabeth Cobb studied the life stories of over 300 creative geniuses. She discovered that creative energy can often be traced back to some sort of epiphany, often related to nature, that the artist experienced while spending time alone in childhood. This experience illuminates their own unique sensibility and their place in the world, creating a lifelong landmark. Later on, artists 'return in memory… to renew the power and impulse to create at its very source'.[96] They reach within themselves to make something in the real world that expresses the ideal world within them. When life falls short of expectations, art makes up the difference.

Creative solitude takes the benefits we've already seen, multiplies them and directs them towards a creative end. Freedom becomes the freedom to try new things, and to keep working on the creation until it's right. Time to think allows the creator to reflect deeply until they become one with their work and discern the right way to develop it. Inner strength becomes creative confidence. Last but not least, creative work can be a way to heal, as past hurt is overcome through art, or used as its raw material.

In solitude, the work has the time and space it needs to grow. As the solitary artist works on their creation, it lives inside their mind, gradually becoming itself. Here's how it worked for Ludwig van Beethoven:

> I carry my thoughts about with me for a long time, sometimes a very long time, before I set them down... since I am conscious of what I want, the basic idea never leaves me. It rises, grows upward, and I hear and see the picture as a whole take shape and stand forth before me as though cast in a single piece, so that all that is left is the work of writing it down.[97]

The process is like growing a garden in the mind. Rather than bending the universe to the creator's will, it's all about waiting, watching and nurturing. Solo creators need to 'trust the process', as the modern saying goes. If you don't have human collaborators to talk to, you need to keep holding a dialogue with yourself, and with the work, until the right way forward becomes clear.

Science can be creative too. Einstein arrived at his special theory of relativity by imagining how the universe would look if he was travelling at the speed of light. The nineteenth-century German chemist August Kekulé had a vivid daydream of an ouroboros – a snake eating its own tail – that helped him discover benzene rings, which served as the foundation of many subsequent inventions.[98]

What will you create in your solitude? It doesn't have to be a great symphony or ground-breaking discovery. It could be a short story, a garden, a model, a home movie, a poem, a wicker basket, a dish. But whatever you create, it will be something that could only

come from you; a way to turn your unique solitary sensibility into something real in the world that others can share.

As introverts, we want recognition for our work, but we don't necessarily want to put ourselves in the spotlight. Instead, we want the *things we create* to go out into the world and speak on our behalf. That's why you'll probably want to work on your creation on your own before you choose to share it with anyone else. Then, when the time is right, you open the cage and let your creation fly.

FIVE

# THE IDEA OF SOLITUDE

Thoughts on solitude
through the ages.

# is solitude good?

> Solitude rehabilitates the soul, corrects morals, renews affections, erases blemishes, purges faults, [and] reconciles God and man.
>
> PETRARCH

All philosophers, and all religions, are concerned with what it means to be good. What makes a good person? How do we live a good life?

Solitude has been as hotly debated as any other aspect of life. Some thinkers have prized it as a 'palace of learning' where the lone thinker could retreat to pursue enlightenment and truth. For some, solitude was a way to hear the voice of God. However, some have seen solitude as solipsistic, self-indulgent, degenerate or even debilitating – and sure to bring misery one way or another.[99]

The questions echo down the ages. Do we find truth in ourselves, or in others? Is it good and right to be alone, or are we missing out on what life is all about? More profoundly, what *is* a self? And is that self ultimately isolated and alone, or inextricably bound to others?

In this chapter, we'll take a quick tour around some of the cultural and philosophical ideas about solitude from centuries past.

# be like water

> Virtue does not remain as an abandoned orphan;
> it must of necessity have neighbours.
>
> CONFUCIUS

In the sixth century BCE, two venerable schools of philosophical thought emerged in China: Confucianism and Taoism. Both argued that people needed to discover inner peace and self-confidence. But they differed sharply on whether solitude should be involved.

As his quote above suggests, Confucius believed that our character can only be measured by our social behaviour. The basic virtue is *jen*, or expressing our humanity by helping those around us. A person who remains in solitude is all potential and no progress.

Lao-Tzu, a student of Confucius, held a very different view. His famous work, the *Tao te Ching*, teaches that wisdom comes not through ineffective action, but through effective *in*action, known as *wu wei*. Instead of being impulsive and aggressive, like a storm, we should be gentle and slow-growing, like vegetation. And the very highest virtue in Taoism is to be like water: humble and commonplace, yet also powerful and vital to life. Water is flowing and yielding, but it can also wear away the rock.

For Lao-Tzu, all these things could only be found through solitude – and a long-lasting solitude at that. To develop freely, we must break away from the malign influence of the civilised world and aspire to independence, poverty and self-knowledge:

> At the centre of your being
> you have the answer;
> you know who you are
> and you know what you want.
>
> LAO-TZU

## a word with yourself

Solitude was a hot topic in ancient Greece. Socrates' perspective was all about society and conversation. He argued that even when we're alone, we talk to ourselves, in a sort of internal dialogue. Cicero called this *secum loqui*, or 'speaking with oneself'.[100]

The Stoic philosopher Epictetus argued that we should be able to solve all our problems through self-dialogue:

> For as Zeus converses with himself, acquiesces in himself, and contemplates his own administration, and is employed in thoughts worthy of himself; so should we too be able to talk with ourselves, and not to need the conversation of others, nor suffer ennui; to attend to the divine administration; to consider our relation to other beings; how we have formerly been affected by events, how we are affected now; what are the things that still press upon us; how these too may be cured, how removed; if anything wants completing, to complete it according to reason.

Plato saw solitude as more of a mixed blessing. 'Haughtiness lives under the same roof with solitude,' he warned. Pursue it too intently and you might start taking yourself a bit too seriously. Far better to restrict yourself to short bursts of time alone, then bring yourself back down to earth with a healthy dose of company.

Plato's words embody an attitude that many modern introverts will know all too well: the idea that solitude is a pedestal that you put yourself on. Just by being alone, you mark yourself out as special. But of course, we might seek solitude for the exact opposite reason: feeling that we're unprepared, or simply unable to see anybody else. Rather than feeling too good, we might not feel good *enough*.

For Aristotle, the aim of a good life was *eudaimonia*. The word is often translated as 'happiness', but it also has a sense of 'wellbeing' and 'flourishing'. Eudaimonia is about fulfilling your potential by living in a virtuous way – 'living your best life', as we might say today. However, since living virtuously means helping others, happiness is inherently social. You can't really be a good person on your own, since there's no-one around for you to be good *to*.

Epicurus took a slightly different view. He valued pleasure above all else – but it wasn't quite as simple as just doing whatever you want. Epicureans distinguished between *moving* pleasures, which we get from satisfying basic needs like hunger, and *static* pleasures, which are more cerebral, and therefore superior.

However, even static pleasures were seen as something to be shared. A life of tranquillity was best achieved by walking round a beautiful garden in pleasant conversation with friends. In fact, friends were one of the most important things in life, because they shared our best-loved pleasures. 'To eat and drink without a friend,' said Epicurus, 'is to devour like the lion and the wolf.'

## gods and beasts

The myths of Greece reflect the same range of views as its philosophers. On one hand, the Greek gods are a pretty gregarious bunch, spending much of their time scheming for power or chasing lovers. And when a god has to be punished, they are usually sent to suffer alone – like Prometheus chained to the mountain, or Sisyphus forever rolling his stone up a hill. But on the other hand, warriors like Theseus (who slayed the Minotaur) followed the generic story arc of the 'hero's journey': one who ventures out alone, vanquishes evil and returns. And Hercules completed his twelve labours pretty much single-handed.

Maybe solitude just hits different when you're immortal. Aristotle said, 'Whoever is delighted in solitude is either a wild beast or a god.' Only godlike beings have the power to be alone in an enlightened way, and since their only worthy companion is themselves, solitude makes sense. However, since no mortal can claim to be a god, solitary humans are left with the beast option: swayed by base instincts, snuffling for truffles in the mud. Solitude may be good for the highest or the lowest, but not for the rest of us who are somewhere in between.

This idea persisted right through the medieval period and the Renaissance. To our ancestors, solitude was a special state of being that not everyone had a right to: [101]

> For the god-like few – philosophers, saints, geniuses – solitude brought the noble joys of speculative wisdom, religious inspiration, and artistic creativity; for the common herd it spelled vice and debility.
>
> Barbara Taylor[102]

Because solitude was associated with religious devotion, it came to be seen as something powerful and mysterious; something to be both respected and feared. To frighten their congregations into obedience, sermon writers invited them to imagine themselves alone in 'lonelinesses' – places like deserts, the grave or even hell. Safety lay in numbers, so to be on your own was to be in danger. Best not stray too far from the flock.[103]

## solitude in the sands

Hermits were religious devotees who spent most or all of their lives in seclusion from others, often in an isolated place. By giving up on their lives in the temporal world, they hoped to build a new life in the spiritual realm.

> They did not talk, not because they hated conversation, but because they wanted to listen intently to the voice of God in silence; they did not dislike eating, but were feeding on the Word of God so that they did not have room for earthly food or time to bother with it; they did not avoid company because it bored them, but, as one of them said, 'I cannot be with you and with God.'
>
> BENEDICTA WARD[104]

Many Bible figures sought solitude in the wilderness. Elijah made two trips there, and Abraham gave up his fertile land in Jordan to live in the desert. David, Moses and John the Baptist all spent long periods in the wilderness, and Jesus spent forty days and nights there, withstanding the temptations of the devil.[105] Thus, the wilderness isn't just a place, but a state of mind:

> The wilderness is a locale for intense experiences… There is a psychology as well as a geography of wilderness, a theology gained in the wilderness.
>
> HOLMES ROSTON[106]

Seeking the same sort of experience for themselves, the Desert Fathers (and Mothers) of early Christianity headed off into in the sands of Egypt, beginning the traditions of Christian monasticism. The first and foremost of them was St Anthony. At the age of twenty, he was struck by Jesus' advice in Matthew 19: 'If you want to be perfect, go, sell your possessions and give to the poor, and you will have treasure in heaven. Then come, follow me.' Anthony duly gave away his goods and headed into the Egyptian desert alone. While there, he's said to have endured supernatural temptations including demonic assaults and visions of women, centaurs and silver coins. Apart from a few years spent teaching his disciples, Anthony would spend the rest of his life in solitude and prayer.

Anthony's hermeticism, while impressive, pales in comparison with that of Simeon Stylites. Born the son of a shepherd around 390 CE, he developed a zeal for Christianity in his teens. Finding that monastery life was not for him, he moved to a mountain outpost, but found himself besieged by pilgrims. When he discovered a pillar among some ruins, he decided to build a platform on the top and live there – which he did for the next thirty-seven years. Pilgrims and sightseers could climb a ladder to speak with him during visiting hours, while local boys kept him supplied with bread and goat's milk. Simeon's death inspired a tradition of *stylites* (Greek for 'pillar-dwellers') that endured for a thousand years.

Hermetic life was extreme and challenging – but normal society was distracting and corrupt. Anchorites solved this conundrum by withdrawing socially, but not physically. By taking a vow of 'stability of place', they committed themselves to living in a single enclosed location for the rest of their lives, where they would spend most of their time in prayer and contemplation. Anchorite cells – known as *anchorholds* or *reclusories* – were often small rooms attached to churches, many of which survive in England.[107] Through small windows, the anchorite received whatever they needed from outsiders. In return, they acted as religious counsellors, acquiring a reputation for great wisdom.

As the anchorite entered their cell for the first and last time, a bishop would carry out a consecration similar to the funeral rite, signifying their 'death' and new life as a kind of living saint. No wonder anchorites inspired such awe and fascination.

Hermits enjoyed a strange renaissance during the eighteenth and nineteenth centuries. Wealthy English landowners, hoping to give their estates an ascetic touch, built hermitages, follies, grottoes or rockeries on their estates and appointed so-called 'garden hermits' to live in them. Some were little more than living garden gnomes who only had to maintain a mystic silence, but others were required to provide entertainment and even dispense advice. In return, they received a modest stipend in addition to bed and board in the hermitage. However, recruitment could be a challenge: in the eighteenth century, Charles Hamilton offered £700 (well over £100,000 today) to any man who could live for seven years in the hermitage of Painshill, Surrey, without speaking, shaving or cutting his hair. After a while, a single prospective hermit came forward – but he lasted only three weeks before fleeing to the pub.[108]

So far, we've been focusing on Christianity, but there are hermits in other religions too. China has a long tradition of revering hermit-sages who follow the 'way of the white clouds' – an isolated life lived on mountain slopes.

Taoist hermits have lived in the Zhongnan mountains, in Shaanxi province, since the Qin dynasty (221–206 BCE). Some retreated from society to avoid working for a corrupt government – but they ended up being offered high-ranking government posts anyway, as emperors pleaded for their hermetic wisdom.

The lonely life of the hermit stands in sharp contrast to the collectivism of mainstream Chinese culture, and the Cultural Revolution of the 1960s and 70s saw the Taoist hermits come under attack. However, the lifestyle survived, and is now enjoying a resurgence: today, there are 600 hermits living the white-cloud life among the Zhongnan peaks. Jaded city dwellers come out to learn the ways of the Tao and discover a quieter way of life. 'In the past, real hermits went somewhere quiet to muse about the world,' says Zhang Shiquan, a former salesman who made the trip. 'Now, many people come here just because they're sick of it.'[109]

Master Hou, a hermit who lives in an unheated, mud-brick hut and lives mainly on cabbage, has never been happier. 'Here is where you can find inner joy,' he says. 'Now I'm happy to be alone.'[110]

## the emerging self

> No man is an island,
> entire of itself;
> every man is a piece of the continent,
> a part of the main;
> if a clod be washed away by the sea,
> Europe is the less…
>
> JOHN DONNE[111]

In medieval times, people would have held a firm conviction that they were part of a family, church, village or nation, and less sense of themselves as individual beings. John Donne's lines above express the idea that everyone has a part to play in a greater whole – and no-one can truly stand alone.

This emphasis on the bonds between people held sway until the late sixteenth century, when the focus began to shift towards the individual and their inner life. As people's sense of themselves changed, so did their ideas about solitude. What had previously been the preserve of hermits became something that anyone could experience for themselves.

> From the 1660s to the 1820s, an English-speaking person might use 'solitude' to mean leisure (*otium* in classical Latin), country life, religious devotion, philosophical contemplation, self-love, covertness, introspection, daydreaming, a melancholy disposition.
>
> BARBARA TAYLOR[112]

By the end of the seventeenth century, the word 'self' took on its modern meaning and words like 'self-sufficient', 'self-knowledge', 'self-examination' and 'self-conscious' began to enter the language. Around the same time, 'individual' lost its sense of 'indivisible' and began to mean something more atomic and fragmented. People had been parts of a whole, but now they were whole in themselves.[113]

Since then, the concept of the self has been gradually developed and refined, generating a range of theories. In modern psychology, the self is defined through the distinction between 'I', the one who knows, and 'me', the one who is known. We gain self-awareness by turning our outward gaze back on ourselves to reflect on the question, *What am I like?*

Our self is formed through a combination of life events, the culture we live in, our role models (good and bad) and the choices we make. Over time, we gradually 'become ourselves' as these factors combine and perhaps conflict. Life experience also helps to make us who we are – although our sense of self is separate from our memories; we're more than the sum of everything that has happened to us.[114]

The theory of the 'looking glass self' suggests that we visualise how we appear to other people, or how they might judge us, and then respond to what we imagine. However, our self-concept isn't purely defined by what other people think. For example, we might think of ourselves as essentially warm and friendly, yet still come across as uptight if we're feeling shy. On the other hand, we might have many worthy or lovable traits that we're not aware of, even though they're crystal clear to everyone else.

Related to the looking glass is social comparison, when we judge our work, status, character or achievements against other people's. While we can't control the outcome of the comparison, we *can* choose who to compare ourselves with. So while there may always be someone richer than we are, for example, we can still choose to compare ourselves with those less fortunate – and usually feel better as a result.

In terms of solitude, we can learn about ourselves through introspection, when we focus inwards on our own emotions, thoughts and beliefs. Introspection can reveal why we might be thinking certain things, or feeling a certain way. However, at a more basic level, it can reveal *what* we're thinking or feeling in the first place, which we aren't necessarily aware of. For example, studies have found that people sometimes buy things in shops without really knowing why, and only formulate their 'reasons' later on.[115]

It's surprisingly easy to skim along the surface of life without ever peering beneath it. Caught up in the busyness of life, we can end up 'moving forward' and 'getting things done' without ever considering the self behind it all. Solitary reflection is a way to get back in touch with our own reasons for doing what we do – and consider whether they still hold true.

## a male luxury?

> The wild man is alone at will, and so is the man for whom civilization has been kind. But there are the multitudes to whom civilization has given little… to them solitude is a right foregone or a luxury unattained… Their share in the enormous solitude which is the common… possession of all mankind has lapsed, unclaimed.
>
> ALICE MEYNELL[116]

As the idea of the self developed, solitude became more socially acceptable. However, not all selves were created equal. Even if people had the motive for solitude, they may have still lacked the means or the opportunity to achieve it. Women, in particular, were frequently tied down by the obligations of housework and childcare, leaving them very little time to themselves – as many still are today. That's one reason why so much historical writing on solitude is by men: only they had had the means and time to enjoy it.

What's more, many male writers' 'solitude' was really *withdrawal*: time away from their male peers. For example, Michel de Montaigne wasn't really alone when he wrote 'On Solitude':

> Now since we are undertaking to live, without companions, by ourselves, let us make our happiness depend on ourselves; let us loose ourselves from the bonds which tie us to others; let us gain power over ourselves to live really and truly alone – and of doing so in contentment.[117]

This makes it sound like Montaigne was all set to follow St Anthony into the desert for a twenty-year stretch. But as a landed gentleman, he actually went into 'retreat' on his estate. What he called 'living without companions' we would probably call 'being at home' or 'spending time with family'.

Similarly, when Jean-Jacques Rousseau moved to Paris in 1770, he resolved to be 'alone for the rest of my life... Since it is only in myself that I find consolation, hope and peace of mind, my only remaining duty is towards myself and this is all I desire'. In fact, he was living with his faithful companion, Thérèse.[118] For these men, solitude was an intellectual fancy rather than a physical trial – a spiritual quest on which they could embark safe in the knowledge that women would still be around to look after them.

The more material wealth men had, the more elaborately they could indulge their solitude. William Bentinck-Scott, Fifth Duke of Portland, employed up to fifteen thousand builders at his Welbeck Abbey estate in Nottinghamshire to build him a ballroom, a series of libraries and a glass-roofed conservatory – all underground, and all painted pink – even though he never entertained a single guest. The Duke also built a mile-long tunnel to the nearest village, big enough for a carriage, so he wouldn't have to meet anyone *en route*. Along similar lines, the distinguished philosopher Henry Cavendish, who demonstrated the composition of water, had a second staircase built so he could avoid his own servants.[119]

Those women who could spend time alone often faced ridicule, condemnation and even fear. One of these was philosopher and writer Margaret Cavendish (no relation to Henry), who declared herself an 'addict' of contemplative solitude. Showing her detractors more sympathy than they showed her, she even wrote a play where a male character exclaimed:

> 'Tis a sin against Nature for women to be Incloystred, Retired or restrained... [T]hose women which restrain themselves from the company and use of men, are damned.[120]

The meaning is pretty clear: women have a duty to sacrifice their own solitude so they can keep men company, look after their homes and raise their children. For centuries, female solitude was seen as unnatural and dangerous, and any woman who insisted on spending time alone was suspected of being up to no good – if not in league with the devil. It's no coincidence that wicked witches in folklore are usually depicted as older, childless women living on their own in the woods, far from civilised society.

It would be nice if such ideas were a thing of the past. But unfortunately, they've just morphed into a new form. Women who choose solitude may not be accused of witchcraft these days, but they still face plenty of resistance that men rarely have to deal with. Perhaps the most powerful force is a nagging sense of guilt that they 'should' be caring for others rather than enjoying themselves. In men, solitude is a sign of independence, intellect or mystique. But a woman on her own has somehow abandoned her post or even betrayed her entire sex:

> The solitary woman must constantly combat the idea that she is not living 'as she should,' that she is not a true woman, a good woman, because she is not caring for others.
>
> EILEEN MANION[121]

If being a woman means always putting other people first, then solitude is always out of reach. Or at least, it can't be enjoyed until all the caring has been done – if that day ever comes.

Another weapon against female solitude is the idea of loneliness. We often hear about the 'epidemic of loneliness', framing it as a social 'disease'. For some people, such as the housebound elderly, loneliness is indeed a torment, and one we should compassionately address. But for many others, their aloneness is not an illness that needs to be cured, but a healthy, life-enhancing state of freely chosen solitude. Caricatures like 'crazy cat lady' equate living alone with madness, while derogatory labels like 'old maid', 'spinster' and 'on the shelf' portray solitude as a failure to attract a partner and raise a family – in contrast to 'eternal bachelors'. In this context, to be 'lonely' or even just 'alone' is not just a neutral status, but a personal failing that should be corrected, or a gap that should be filled.[122]

Words are powerful because they embody value judgements. If we accept someone else's words for our experience, we also accept their ideas and opinions about it, regardless of whether they are helpful or even true.

> Men have the power of naming, a great and sublime power. This power of naming enables men to define experience, to articulate boundaries and values, to designate to each thing its realm and qualities, to determine what can and cannot be expressed to control perception itself.
>
> ANDREA DWORKIN[123]

Everyone should be free to name their own experience – particularly solitude, which is, by definition, nobody else's business.

If women do choose to have children, they may be dismayed to find that traditional family culture seems purposely designed to grant solitude to men, while denying it to women. When children are very young, going out to work can be an escape to solitude – a welcome opportunity to gaze out of a train window or sit quietly at a desk rather than contend with a wailing infant. Caring for a baby can be far more demanding than any office task, yet the dismissive phrase 'staying at home' makes it sound like a six-month vacation.

Even when Dad does finally make it home, he's often granted a solitary sanctuary in the form of a 'man cave' or garden shed. But Mum has no equivalent leisure zone to which she can retreat when family life gets too much. Male solitude is indulged as something homely and eccentric, while women's is interdicted simply because there's no domestic space where it can happen, and no language to enshrine it as part of family life.

Why is the idea of a woman spending time alone so threatening? Maybe because a woman on her own has the time and space to think for herself, question what others want for her and decide exactly what she does and doesn't want to do. If Mum gets a chance to break out on her own, what might she do? What new horizon might she explore? *What if she never comes back?*

Solitude also confers the freedom of creative expression: to reflect on your own truth and capture it in art. As Virginia Woolf said, 'A woman must have money and a room of her own if she is to write fiction.' But while the room may be bought with the money, it's more than a possession, or even a physical location. It's also a mental space: a quiet fortress where no-one can barge in and ask what's for tea, or where their socks are. Fiction writer or not, every woman deserves a room like this just so she can be herself.

When the ideas of feminist thinkers steadily gained ground in the 1960s and 70s, solitude was one of the privileges that they wanted to reclaim. A woman on her own was free of the obligation to be 'feminine' – that is, to conform to other people's ideas of what a woman should be. That could mean the opportunity to read and think, or just to disregard the pressure to look or act a certain way. Writing in 1984, Susan Brownmiller described the unending quest to become 'feminine' as 'bafflingly inconsistent at the same time [as]... minutely demanding... Femininity always demands more'.[124] Solitude, in contrast, is a chance to make a positive choice for *less* – and to have it be enough.

Today, a new generation of authors are encouraging women to own their solitude. In *Alonement*, Francesa Specter recounts her journey from fearing loneliness to actively embracing time alone, following the breakup of a relationship she had expected to be lifelong. She proposes the term 'alonement' for quality time spent alone, by choice, and argues that being alone is not just good for introverts who crave it, but also for extroverts who may fear it – or, at least, not see the point of it:

> The way I define it, alonement is quality time spent alone; it is to value and respect the time you spend with yourself. It means to be alone and absolutely own it… I see it as embodying a necessary change in the way we acknowledge and value alone time.[125]

Alonement is a state where you can get to know yourself, build inner strength and cultivate self-love – which, in turn, allows you to have better and more balanced relationships. But in Specter's view, it's more than that: a vital step in building a society that allows everyone, women in particular, to be who they choose.

## the haters

> As sickness is the greatest misery, so the greatest misery of sickness is solitude… Solitude is a torment which is not threatened in hell itself.
>
> John Donne[126]

You'd think that quietly heading off for some alone time would be something nobody could really complain about. But over the years, solitude has had its fair share of critics. Some argued that solitude could only benefit certain people, or was only right in certain circumstances. Others felt there was nothing good about it at all.

Attitudes towards solitude reflected wider currents in thought. From the later Renaissance onwards, solitude gradually lost its religious overtones, making it fair game for criticism. Modernists even began to deride Christian scholars as obscure pedants, sequestered in their ivory towers and poring over some irrelevant metaphysical point. The philosopher Francis Bacon accused them of spinning 'laborious webs of learning… admirable for the fineness of thread and work, but of no substance or profit.' [127]

Solitude came to be seen as a cause of sickness, both physical and psychological. In his *Anatomy of Melancholy*, Robert Burton laid the blame for melancholy, the 'disease of learning', firmly at solitude's door. Solitary scholars were afflicted by 'fear, sorrow, suspicion… [and] weariness of life'.[128] Cut adrift from society, they would soon fall prey to 'phantastical meditations' that would 'overcome, distract and detain them'. This concern that loners will somehow 'lose touch with reality' is still with us. But frankly, looking at reality on the news, why *wouldn't* you want to lose touch with it?

One of the most vociferous Renaissance takedowns of solitude was by diarist, courtier and government officer John Evelyn. Having painted a deeply unflattering picture of the solitary as greedy layabout or 'a *Contemplator* like a *Ghost* in a *Church-yard*', he lets fly with this pronouncement:

> The *result* of all is, *Solitude* produces *ignorance*, renders us *barbarous*, feeds *revenge*, disposes to *envy*, creates *Witches*, dispeoples the *World*, renders it a *desart* and would soon *dissolve* it…[129]

During the Enlightenment, attitudes towards solitude hardened still further. Some began to question the Christian idea that only solitude revealed the authentic self, or that you had to retreat from society to discover it. Company and good conversation were seen as healthy, refreshing and vigorous, while solitude was a state of stagnation, madness and moral decay. Dr Johnson was particularly vociferous on the theme:

> Solitude is dangerous to reason, without being favourable to virtue... Remember that the solitary mind is certainly luxurious, probably superstitious, and possibly mad: the mind stagnates for want of employment, grows morbid, and is extinguished like a candle in foul air.[130]

In the same vein, Adam Smith argued that solitude would drive us to emotional extremes:

> In solitude, we are apt to feel too strongly whatever relates to ourselves: we are apt to over-rate the good offices we may have done, and the injuries we may have suffered: we are apt to be too much elated by our own good, and too much dejected by our own bad fortune.[131]

Philosopher David Hume said solitude was 'the greatest punishment we can suffer'[132] and one of the 'monkish virtues' that would 'stupify the understanding and harden the heart, obscure the fancy and sour the temper'.[133]

Even those who appreciated solitude had words of caution. For example, Jean-Jacques Rousseau felt that solitude wasn't something you could just *do*. You couldn't just wander off into the woods and wait for poetic sentiments to strike – you needed the right knowledge and personality, or it could all go horribly wrong:

> It is necessary that the heart should be at peace, that no passion should arise to disturb this calm; it requires not only a disposition adapted to it on the part of the person who is to experience this felicity, but a concurrence of surrounding objects; neither an absolute repose, or too much agitation, but a uniform and moderate disposition, not subject to sudden gusts of passion, or utter despondency.[134]

Even today, people sometimes share this sense that solitude is something you shouldn't mess with unless you know exactly what you're doing. As Khalil Gibran puts it, 'The strong grows in solitude where the weak withers away.'

## on the lonely shore

> Then stirs the feeling infinite, so felt
> In solitude, where we are least alone.
>
> LORD BYRON[135]

The writers we now call the Romantics were a diverse bunch, and Romanticism as a belief system is difficult to pin down. However, what united most Romantic thinkers was a belief in the importance of art, beauty and insight. While the Enlightenment had prized reason, Romanticism enthroned emotion in its place.

> 'Beauty is truth, truth beauty,' — that is all
> Ye know on earth, and all ye need to know.
>
> John Keats[136]

While human art might express some part of this truth, nature revealed it directly. And such a revelation was best experienced alone. Emotions that arose in solitude were authentic because they flowed from nature – not from the cold machinations of reason or the manipulative contrivance of the social world.[137]

Jean-Jacques Rousseau, a recluse and self-described 'bear', saw society as a corrupting influence:

> *Amour-propre* [self-love], the principle of all wickedness... thrives in society, which caused it to be born and where one is forced to compare oneself at each instant. It languishes and dies for want of nourishment in solitude. Whoever suffices to himself does not want to harm anyone at all.[138]

Rousseau believed that the remedy lay in 'self-collection' through solitude and returning to a state of nature. Instead of being a place of purgation and punishment, as the desert had been for hermits, nature was seen as a place where you could rediscover your authentic self, and perhaps get closer to God too.

The mood of Romantic solitude was wistful, but it was far from the raging 'black melancholy' that had tormented Robert Burton two centuries before. Instead, it was the milder 'white melancholy': a state of quiet, calm solitude ideal for wistful philosophical musing.

> There is a charm in Solitude that cheers
> A feeling that the world knows nothing of
> A green delight the wounded mind endears
> After the hustling world is broken off...
>
> JOHN CLARE[139]

Solitude was seen as encouraging a quiet, watchful mindset that was ready to receive the truth. Here, William Wordsworth urges a friend to close their book and open their mind:

> Enough of Science and of Art;
> Close up those barren leaves;
> Come forth, and bring with you a heart
> That watches and receives.[140]

Romantics were drawn to big spaces: rolling hillsides, long valleys, far-reaching beaches and the open sea. In these empty places, nature seems to embody a solitude of its own through its sheer presence, its wordlessness, its overpowering here-and-now-ness. As Philip Larkin would later put it, it is 'unfenced existence, facing the sun, untalkative, out of reach.'[141] Standing here, we feel fully alive and centred in ourselves – yet we also let go of ourselves at the same time.

> There is a pleasure in the pathless woods,
> There is a rapture on the lonely shore,
> There is society, where none intrudes
> By the deep sea, and music in its roar:
> I love not Man the less, but Nature more...
>
> LORD BYRON[142]

For Wordsworth, being in nature meant communing with some ineffable force that lies behind or beyond everyday existence:

> And I have felt
> A presence that disturbs me with the joy
> Of elevated thoughts; a sense sublime
> Of something far more deeply interfused,
> Whose dwelling is the light of setting suns,
> And the round ocean and the living air,
> And the blue sky, and in the mind of man:
> A motion and a spirit, that impels
> All thinking things, all objects of all thought,
> And rolls through all things.[143]

## a world all to yourself

> I never found the companion that was so companionable as solitude.
>
> HENRY DAVID THOREAU[144]

While the Romantics were swooning about on hillsides, across the Atlantic the American settlers were contending with a very different landscape – and it was no place to be alone. Here, the wilderness was properly wild, presenting a clear and present danger to the frontiersman. Sticking together was the only way to survive.

The children of the pioneers, who no longer had to fight so hard to tame the land, were in a better position to appreciate it. They willingly ventured out into the deserts and forests alone, seeking to savour their grandeur, discover their own humanity and loosen the bonds of the civilisation that their forbears had worked so hard to build. Their movement was known as *transcendentalism*.

The transcendentalists gave European Romantic ideas about solitude a new twist. Like the Romantics, they believed in the unity of creation and the power of insight and emotion over logic. They also felt that the society of their time was far too conformist, turning people, in Thoreau's words, into 'slavedrivers of themselves'. As the movement matured, these ideas became more political, and transcendentalists turned to opposing the treatment of Native Americans and the expansion of slavery.[145]

Ralph Waldo Emerson argued that each person should follow their own voice and find their own 'original relation to the universe'. Such a link could only be discovered by suspending reason and fully opening up to nature and the divine:

> Standing on the bare ground, – my head bathed by the blithe air, and uplifted into infinite space, – all mean egotism vanishes. I become a transparent eye-ball; I am nothing; I see all; the currents of the Universal Being circulate through me; I am part or particle of God... In the wilderness, I find something more dear and connate than in streets or villages.[146]

Henry David Thoreau explored similar themes in *Walden,* his extended reflection on simple living in natural surroundings that includes an entire chapter dedicated to solitude:

> My nearest neighbor is a mile distant, and no house is visible from any place but the hill-tops within half a mile of my own. I have my horizon bounded by woods all to myself; and a little world all to myself.

For Thoreau, nature itself is a kind of company – and a beneficial one, too. The rain watering his crops, the fluttering leaves and the sounds of frogs and birds all soothe him, offering reassurance that nature is enfolding and enveloping him, protecting him from harm.

> While I enjoy the friendship of the seasons I trust that nothing can make life a burden to me... I have never felt lonesome, or in the least oppressed by a sense of solitude... I was suddenly sensible of such sweet and beneficent society in Nature, in the very pattering of the drops, and in every sound and sight around my house, an infinite and unaccountable friendliness all at once like an atmosphere sustaining me, as made the fancied advantages of human neighborhood insignificant, and I have never thought of them since.

When people ask if he gets lonely out there in the woods, Thoreau muses that solitude is not a place or a circumstance, but a state of mind:

> What sort of space is that which separates a man from his fellows and makes him solitary? I have found that no exertion of the legs can bring two minds much nearer to one another. What do we want most to dwell near to? Not to many men surely... but to the perennial source of our life...

Being close to others in body does not necessarily mean being close together in mind, says Thoreau. If we want to know what's really going on, we should head out to a cabin in the woods – alone.

# alone in the dark?

For Sigmund Freud, mental health depended on understanding our relationships with other people. Only once we have resolved issues and repressed memories from our childhood can we hope to forge intimate bonds with partners, family and friends. Forming relationships is seen as emotionally mature, while opting out of them is considered pathological. The sure sign of happiness and health is a fulfilling sex life, while all neurosis has its roots in a failure to move through the stages of sexual development. In other words, one way or another, happiness lies in others.

Freud saw the root of anxiety as separation: the child's fear of being alone and helpless in the absence of a parent or guardian. Solitude was a state of insecurity and danger.

> While I was in the next room, I heard a child who was afraid of the dark call out: 'Do speak to me, Auntie! I'm frightened!' 'Why, what good would that do? You can't see me.' To this the child replied: 'If someone speaks, it gets lighter.'[147]

Freud regarded the withdrawal from society in adult life as a defensive reaction, often to losing a loved one. To avoid the suffering of lost love, people withdraw into their work, the enjoyment of art or simply intoxication with drink or drugs:

> Against the suffering which may come upon one from human relationships the readiest safeguard is voluntary isolation, keeping oneself aloof from other people.[148]

However, writing in the 1980s, psychologist Anthony Storr questioned whether solitude was always so defensive and dysfunctional. He pointed out that the capacity to be alone is also a form of emotional maturity, and that solitude is a chosen experience with value of its own:

> It seems to me that what goes on in the human being when he is by himself is as important as what happens in his interactions with other people.[149]

Many people live happy, fulfilled lives, and achieve great things, while having relatively few close ties and spending much of their time alone. Storr cites literary luminaries such as Anthony Trollope, Enid Blyton, Rudyard Kipling, Edward Lear and Saki (H.H. Munro). Instead of putting time and energy into relationships with others, these famous writers poured it into their work. They succeeded not *despite* their solitude, but *because* of it. Had they been madly gregarious, they might not have achieved so much.

## self and other

Philosophers throughout the ages have pondered on the nature of the self. Are we self-contained individuals, or part of a whole?

For René Descartes, truth lay solely in the self. After years spent pondering, 'shut up alone in a stove-heated room', he arrived at his most famous dictum, *cogito ergo sum* – 'I think, therefore I am.'[150] In other words, our own thoughts are the only thing that is certain, and the self is the basic unit of existence. Unsurprisingly, Descartes had a 'too many cooks' attitude towards his own work:

> There is very often less perfection in works… carried out by the hands of various masters, than in those on which one individual alone has worked.[151]

Descartes' intrepid journey into himself made him something of a pin-up among the intelligentsia: an emblem of the solitary scholar on a lonely quest for truth. But Georg Hegel rejected Descartes' view. He argued that self-consciousness could only be constituted through patterns of mutual recognition – that is, seeing ourselves as others see us. D.H. Lawrence agreed:

> Everything, even individuality itself, depends on relationship… the light shines only when the circuit is completed. My individualism is really an illusion. I am part of the great whole, and I can never escape.[152]

In this view, we can never be truly or perfectly alone, however strongly we may feel that we are. Our solitude is only ever a temporary hiatus from our real being, which is social. It may even be a kind of delusion: a story we tell to place ourselves at the centre of our own universe.

In a similar way, Buddhist thought teaches that everything is interdependent. Even though things may seem individual, they can only exist because of other things. A loaf of bread looks like a self-contained object, but it can only exist when there is flour, water and yeast; the flour can only exist when there is wheat; the wheat can only exist when there is sunlight, earth and a seed; and so on. Author and mountaineer John Muir echoed this idea when he said, 'When we try to pick out anything by itself, we find it hitched to everything else in the universe.'[153]

However, another strand of thinking holds that we are all, ultimately, alone. We come into the world alone and we leave it the same way. Author Octavio Paz sees the self as a kind of prison:

> Solitude is the profoundest fact of the human condition. Man is the only being who knows he is alone, and the only one who seeks out another… when

> he is aware of himself, he is aware of his lack of another – that is, of his solitude.[154]

That sounds pretty bleak – but there is a potential silver lining. If solitude really is the primary, fundamental state that lies under everything else we do, then being alone might also grant us access to some universal truth:

> Only when the soul is alone can the magic of the universe flow through it. It needs the silence for the murmur of the long centuries to grow audible, and for the mystery of the cosmic procession to make itself felt.
> John Cowper Powys[155]

Transcendentalist Ralph Waldo Emerson took a more robust view of the same idea. For him, self-containment was something to celebrate – and to live by. In his famous essay 'Self-Reliance', he argues that each person should follow their inner calling no matter what, defying the expectations of society, science and even religion:

> Society everywhere is in conspiracy against the manhood of every one of its members. The only right is what is after my constitution; the only wrong what is against it.[156]

Self-reliance has long been a core tenet of conservative thinking. The individual has a duty to take care of themselves, rather than a right to demand assistance from the state. Emerson's ideas were echoed by Margaret Thatcher's infamous pronouncement that 'there's no such thing as society'.[157] At the extreme, the individual can become a free-floating economic agent with no allegiances to anyone and no bonds other than ownership. 'I create nothing!' exults Gordon Gekko in *Wall Street*. 'I *own*.'

Karl Marx, unsurprisingly, took a very different view. In his philosophy, humans are inherently social beings. Human nature is not to be found in the characteristics of individuals, but in the totality of social relations between them. Hence, for the progressive, it's all about togetherness. Capitalism seeks to divide and conquer; the answer lies in solidarity and mutual support.

So which view is correct? Are we lone stars in the void, or cells in an organism? As ever, the truth is somewhere in between.[158]

We're certainly *separate* from others, in the sense of being individual beings. But our lived experience is very far from lonely isolation. For starters, we begin our existence in literal symbiosis with another being: our mother. Most of us grow up in a family, learn and play with friends, live with a partner or work alongside colleagues. Recluses aside, even the most solitary introverts have at least *some* deep relationships with other people. Sometimes, we may struggle to believe in our bonds with other people – but the stories of our lives show very clearly that those bonds are real.

What's more, we can spend a great deal of time alone without breaking those bonds. The bleak notion that we are 'always alone' is completely different from a positive choice to be alone *for a while.*

In the same way, we may *feel* very lonely from time to time. At those low points, we might well subscribe to the despondent view that every human is an island in an endless sea, or a prisoner in their own mind. But metaphors, however vivid, don't necessarily tell the truth. However alone we may feel, others are always there.

## a fount of healing

> Solitude is for me a fount of healing which makes my life worth living. Talking is often torment for me, and I need many days of silence to recover from the futility

> of words… What you think of as a few days of spiritual communion would be unendurable for me with anyone, even my closest friends. The rest is silence!
>
> CARL JUNG[159]

Jung was one of the first to set out the distinction between extroverts and introverts – showing, for the first time, why people's psychological makeup might make them prefer company or solitude. His definition hinged on the distinction between the inner and outer worlds. Extroverts are outwardly focused, preferring to engage with the external world of objects, sensory perception and action. Introverts, meanwhile, are more thoughtful and insightful.

After centuries of philosophers pontificating on the value of solitude as a monolithic 'thing', it's a relief to finally meet someone who acknowledges human difference. Solitude is not some abstract philosophical principle, but a lived experience that takes different forms and holds different meanings for everyone.

As the quote above suggests, Jung was a big fan of solitude, seeing it as an essential part of the psychotherapeutic process:

> The highest and most decisive experience of all… is to be alone with his own self… The patient must be alone if he is to find out what it is that supports him when he can no longer support himself. Only this experience can give him an indestructible foundation.[160]

After enough time on our own, we realise that we alone are responsible for our own lives. There's no 'magical other' riding to our rescue, no Santa coming down the chimney to gift us a new life. And when we finally understand that, we can start to do for ourselves what others have so far been unable, or unwilling, to do.[161] On the other hand, if we spend all our time in company, we never face up to these basic truths.

Jung also argued that solitude led to 'the animation of the psychic atmosphere'. He meant that when we're alone, our unconscious can come to life, releasing creative energies that would otherwise have been unknown. However familiar our selves may seem to us, they still hold the promise of something truly new.

SIX

# COMPANY AND ITS OPPOSITE

On being with others
and with ourselves.

# the right measure

> Solitude and company may be allowed to take their turns: the one creates in us the love of mankind, the other that of ourselves; solitude relieves us when we are sick of company, and conversation when we are weary of being alone, so that the one cures the other.
>
> SENECA THE YOUNGER

To introverts like us, it can seem that extroverts just can't get enough when it comes to company. First, they have a 'more the merrier' mindset, with a blithe disregard for either the quality or the quantity of a social occasion. While the introvert host is still wringing their hands over who knows whom, and why Edna might not get on so well with Eddie, the extrovert is already on WhatsApp telling Edna, Eddie and everyone else to come round and hang out. They'll even happily yank people that they hardly know – *sometimes even complete strangers!* – into a gathering, while introverts look on aghast.

Second, extroverts can spend an astonishing proportion of their time with other people – meeting up more often, and remaining in company for longer too. They can even chain-smoke social occasions, going directly from one to the next with no apparent ill effects. How do they *do* that? How have they not melted into a grease spot on the floor?

I guess when you love company, you want a lot of it. But even the most outgoing people do have their limits. One study found that social time, like monetary earnings, exhibits what economists call *diminishing marginal utility*. In other words, both cash and company may bring you joy – but once you get beyond a certain threshold, getting more of either one won't make you any happier.[162]

The only question is where the limit falls for you. As introverts, we have to balance the same equation, but our tolerance for company is *way* smaller. We have much lower thresholds for how many people we can see, how often we can see them and how long we can stay – and we feel much worse when we go past these limits.

However, that doesn't mean we have no interest in company at all. We enjoy both company and solitude – but only in the right measure. That's what makes the difference between an introvert on one hand and a recluse, a loner or a misanthrope on the other.

If you find yourself suffering social overload, it might occur to you that you could be a lot nicer to all these people if you didn't have to be around them. Even more ironically, you might reflect that you feel closest to people, and have your warmest feelings about them, when they're not actually there. It's the classic introvert dilemma: having problems with situations that involve other people, but *not* with the people themselves.

The philosopher Francis Bacon said, 'The worst solitude is to be destitute of sincere friendship.' Sometimes, we may have very close friends who we only see every now and then. That may be due to circumstance, but it can also be by choice, in which case we may feel rather guilty. But the thing is, introverts are happy in the knowledge that good friends will be there when we need them, and we don't need to have it proven to us every day. As Epicurus said, 'It is not so much our friends' help that helps us, as the confident knowledge that they will.'

The only downside of rare meetings is that when you're finally together, the expectations are so high that reality can't rise to the occasion. You can feel that you *should* be having an amazing time, or maybe have to get to know the other person all over again before the conversation can flow. I prefer it when meetups have a casual, easy quality, as if this was something we did every day. If you're young, enjoy it while you can – in my experience, it gets more difficult with the passing years.

## a frame around the self

> I owe my solitude to other people.
>
> Alan Watts

We saw in chapter two how good it can be to have an unbounded, uninterrupted stretch of time all to yourself. But sometimes, you need a little bit of company to truly appreciate your solitude, in the same way a frame sets off a painting.

This framing can happen in time or in space. An example of temporal framing is when you get an unexpected visit during a long period alone, and that makes you appreciate your solitude even more when you return to it. Or you know that you only have one evening at home to yourself, and that makes it even more important to enjoy it. Spatial framing is when you're aware of other people nearby, and that makes you even more aware of being alone in a certain physical space. For example, you might hear someone speaking in the street outside, or practising a musical instrument in the flat upstairs, and their presence at one remove throws your aloneness into sharper relief.

For framing to have the desired effect, you have to be secure in your solitude. As May Sarton put it, you want your solitude to be 'animated but not broken'.[163] While it can be reassuring to know that other people are around, you also want the reassurance that they won't intrude, and that your solitude won't be brought to an end against your will.

## selfish solitude

> *All solitude is selfish.* No one now
> Believes the hermit with his gown and dish
> Talking to God (who's gone too); the big wish
> Is to have people nice to you, which means
> Doing it back somehow.
> *Virtue is social.*
>
> PHILIP LARKIN[164]

Is solitude selfish? Is it really self-centred to want time alone?

It can sometimes feel that way, because in a sense we're withholding ourselves from other people. We often think of time as a resource or currency, and talk about 'giving' our time to others or 'spending' it on things we want to do. We might also feel that we 'owe' our time to somebody, or to the occasion they've arranged. As Larkin's words above suggest, if virtue is a transaction in the social sphere, we have to spend in order to receive.

So, if we decide that we prefer to be alone, we must be saving up our time to splurge on ourselves. Or, perhaps, just hoarding it for its own sake – perversely choosing solitude even though we have 'nothing better to do'. And even if we don't believe these things ourselves, we might still worry that other people do.

In reality, time is more than a number or a quantity, and choosing what to do with it isn't a zero-sum game, like dividing up a pie or allocating a budget. Just because we 'gain' some time for ourselves, that doesn't mean that anybody else has 'lost' anything. Unlike money, time has *quality* as well as quantity, and by spending time alone, we can improve the time we spend with others – for them and for us. As Thoreau put it, 'Just so sacred and rich as my life is to myself, so it will be to another.'

We introverts aren't self-obsessed egomaniacs, oblivious to the needs of those around us. We care very deeply about the loved ones in our lives. It's just that we need our alone time in order to offer that care in the right way. The care we give to others *depends on* our own self-care – which, for us, means spending time alone.

I have a partner, a daughter and a dog. I love them all dearly, and I'd never want to live without them. But I still need a lot of time on my own – or rather, I need a *certain amount* of time on my own, which other people might judge to be 'a lot'. Indeed, without my solitude, I can't relate to my family the way I want to. I can't show the love I feel, because it gets buried under a pile of tetchiness. Solitude is the seasoning that gives my personality a tolerable taste.

Now, you may feel that your threshold for social time is distressingly low. Or, like me, you may feel dismayed that it seems to be falling ever lower as you age. I certainly don't want to alienate or offend anyone with my wish to be alone – but to add a layer of guilt on top just makes things worse. Surely it's better to own the feeling than try to repress or deny it?

Having said that, it's certainly possible to take self-care too far. For example, some studies suggest that the pursuit of individual happiness can actually make us lonely, because it leads us to neglect interpersonal connections.[165] That's why our happiness usually involves caring for someone else, one way or another. We can only be happy when they are.

Taking a broader view, if we're hoping to see a change in society, pursuing our own solitude can sometimes feel selfish. There's so much work to be done out there in the world, and we're just hiding away in our shells, metaphorically fiddling while Rome burns.

However, there's more than one way to make a difference. Yes, you could get out there in your community and volunteer at a food bank, say, or foster a child. But society needs its thinkers and writers as well as its doers. You could throw yourself into worthy good deeds, but if you really dislike doing them, you probably won't help society that much. Introverts often make their most useful contributions quietly, in the background, rather than through grand gestures. It's not selfish to want to be your best self.

## apanthropy

*L'enfer, c'est les autres.*

JEAN-PAUL SARTRE[166]

The word 'misanthropy' refers to a hatred or contempt for people or human nature. To the misanthrope, people always turn out to have flaws like stupidity, selfishness, immorality or just plain ugliness. Why hope for something better when you'll only wind up being let down?

However, introversion is not misanthropy. Introverts don't hate everybody. Instead, what we feel is *apanthropy*: an aversion to human *company* – or, to frame it in a more positive way, a love of solitude. While misanthropy is a prejudice, apanthropy is merely a preference. It's a taste for being alone; a penchant for privacy.

Unlike the misanthrope, who frankly sounds a bit unhinged, the apanthrope isn't happy to watch the world burn on the grounds that humans are irredeemably evil. They just need a quiet hour alone to read a book or watch a film.

If you're an introvert, I'm sure this feels entirely natural and obvious to you. We don't hate people, just situations. Liking solitude doesn't mean you dislike other people – just that you don't want the *experience* of being with them at this moment. *I like you, I just don't want to spend this time with you.* However ridiculous or unbelievable extroverts might find it, that is how the introvert feels.

## the opposite of loneliness

When lockdown began, we heard a lot from fretful extroverts about how hard they would find it to be isolated and alone.

Of course, those emotions were real, as were the mental health problems that they sometimes led on to. And I certainly don't mean to make light of them. But what I find interesting is that when someone says they feel lonely, or they want some company, we don't question it. It's seen as completely natural; a basic human need. However, we rarely hear the flip side: someone who really wants to be alone, but is unable to.

For introverts, the need for solitude is always there, just below the surface. It's like psychological gravity, pulling us away from the crowd and into the quiet. We sense the promise of solitude all the time, like a room we could enter, a lake we could dive into or a path we could take into a secluded garden. But we never put that feeling into words, precisely because we *are* introverts. We don't speak out because we're not outspoken. All too often, we keep quiet about the very thing we need the most, and how much we need it.

Part of the problem is the gap in the language. If only there was a word for the yearning for solitude, some socially accepted way of asking for it, maybe things would be easier. The word to describe someone who needs *more* company is 'lonely'. But what's the word for someone who needs *less*?

I originally thought it should be an imposing German compound – something like *Einsamkeitdurst* ('solitude-thirst') or *Stillehunger* ('silence-hunger'). But as it turns out, sharper minds than mine have already solved this problem. In 2021, psychologist Rob Coplan and his colleagues set out to explore the links between motivations for solitude, time spent alone and wellbeing.[167] They developed the Solitude and Aloneliness Scale, which participants in their study used to rate their own agreement with statements like these:

> It would be nice if I could spend more time alone each day.
> I wish I could just be by myself more often.

If you felt a pang of recognition reading those words, you may be experiencing *aloneliness*. That's the term that the researchers coined for the negative feelings that come from the sense that you're not spending enough time alone. (The 'a-' prefix means 'not', so 'alonely' literally means 'not lonely'.)

However, feeling alonely is more than a wistful yearning or an idle thought. If your need to be alone is continually thwarted by the demands of day-to-day life, you gradually become more and more irritable, overwhelmed or drained. Eventually, this 'negative degenerative cycle' can lead to stress and even depression.[168]

The answer to aloneliness is to deliberately plan or schedule some time alone, rather than just waiting or hoping for it to happen. Crucially, the science shows that this isn't some sort of self-indulgence, but a vital part of self-care. However, it's not just a question of clocking up a few hours on your own, like recharging a battery. The *quality* of the solitude matters too – that is, what you actually *do* when you're alone.

For example, the same research team found that adolescents who spent their alone-time doing something purposeful and motivated – like reading or going outdoors – were less likely to feel alonely than those who frittered it away on their phones.[169] So don't just count the hours – make the hours count.

## oversocial

While we're on the subject of words, let's talk about another antonym that would really help introverts.

We have a word for people who aren't social enough: *unsociable.* 'Come to the party. You'll enjoy it! Why are you being so *unsociable*?'

'Unsociable' defines the introvert by what they're against. It denounces us as social refuseniks, obstinately holding out against everything that's good and right. But we should have another word for people who are too social. Something like… *oversocial.*

OK, maybe we *are* unsociable – at least sometimes. But extroverts are against something too: our solitude. They're being oversocial, forcing company on those who don't desire it. And armed with our new word, we will open the eyes of the world to our plight.

## shyness

> I never wish to offend, but I am so foolishly shy, that I often seem negligent, when I am only kept back by my natural awkwardness… Shyness is only the effect of a sense of inferiority in some way or other. If I could persuade myself that my manners were perfectly easy and graceful, I should not be shy.
>
> Jane Austen[170]

When I was growing up, if I felt uncomfortable in a social situation, or didn't want to meet new people, adults would say 'He's just a bit shy.' So that was how I came to understand myself.

A neutral label is no big deal. But shyness was seen as a problem to be got over, or a childish habit to be grown out of. At best, it was a quirk rather than a viable character trait. And it definitely wasn't a strength.

Fast-forward forty years and I've just published my book *The Freelance Introvert*. Readers tell me that they recognise themselves on every page; one even calls the book 'life-changing'. That surprises me, because I'm only sharing my own experience and some mainstream psychological ideas. But I've forgotten that these days, I'm fully in touch with my introversion. I know what an introvert is, and I've known for many years that I am one, so my own emotions and reactions are predictable and known.

It's easy to take language for granted, but having the right words to describe yourself is no small thing. As Fred Rogers put it, 'Anything that is mentionable can be more manageable.' Once you can put a name to your experience, you can understand it, learn about it and explain it to others.

Like all introverts, I learned over the years how to deal with daunting social situations. I can meet new people without blushing and I've even done some (rather stilted) public speaking. My coping strategies are probably the same ones that every introvert uses: support from sympathetic others, psychological 'hacks' to bootstrap myself into brittle confidence and sheer, bloody-minded grit.

The symptoms of shyness range from a general social unease to physical awkwardness around handshakes or hugs. In conversation, you may have a blank mind that can't think of the right words or a dry mouth that blurts out the wrong ones. Shy people particularly dislike large groups, and will often attempt to prise a lone interlocutor away from the flock so they can initiate a simpler bilateral interaction.

If social life is a performance, shy actors are those who miss their cues, forget their lines or fumble with props. As Joe Moran puts it in *Shrinking Violets*, 'Shy people unsettle others because they unsettle the tacit conventions of social life.'[171] By bringing the play to a grinding halt, the shy person exposes the off-stage machinery that the audience should never see, while throwing their fellow actors off their stride.

Those who are utterly at ease in company often misunderstand shyness. To them, it can come across as aloofness or even arrogance. In an age where everyone shares everything all the time, giving nothing away can seem like a way of grabbing attention by ostentatiously deflecting it, or arousing curiosity by cultivating mystery. As Richard Ayoade says, 'Shyness can be interpreted as a kind of aggression.' Shyness can also seem lazy, in the sense that the shy person is sitting back and forcing others to make all the running.

Another misapprehension is that shyness is a sign of emotional detachment or a buttoned-up 'English reserve'. But if anything, it comes from an *excess* of feeling rather than a deficit. The awkwardness comes from an overwhelming desire to be liked, accepted or socially adept. If we truly didn't care about others' reactions, we could happily disregard them. But we *do* care – and too much. Far from ignoring social cues, shy people observe them obsessively, desperately seeking some insight that they can use to fix their own behaviour.

As Joe Moran explains, shyness is perfectly natural, and many animals exhibit something very close to it. When looking for food, for example, some creatures are intrepid hunters and foragers, happy to expose themselves to danger, while others are more cautious and hang back:

> In the study of animal personality this became known as the 'shy–bold continuum'. At one end of the continuum animals are aggressive, adventurous and risk-taking; at the other they are fearful, unadventurous and risk-averse.

Humans, too, may exhibit the shy–bold continuum – and that's comforting, because sometimes shyness can seem like an illness for which the only cure is solitude. But it's more than that. Just as solitude is more than the absence of people, so shyness is more than a lack of social poise. It's how you express your introverted personality in company. It's a way of relating at a distance, or combining presence with absence. Shyness is solitude doing its best to dance.

## wallflowers

When I first heard this expression, I pictured a flower that was literally *on the wall* – an insipid 1970s wallpaper, or a faded print in a battered frame. That imagery seemed apt for someone who lingers on the margins, unseen, uninvolved and most likely unwanted.

However, when I got my own garden, I realised that wallflowers are an actual thing. They are most definitely wanted, and in terms of the plant population, they are definitely no shrinking violets. In fact, they're feisty little blooms the colour of a sunset, with an intoxicating peppery scent. Since they laugh at dry conditions, they readily seed themselves into inhospitable, sun-baked nooks like the gaps in stone walls, where they flourish. Taking up practically no space and needing little water, the wallflower is happy to share its colour but demands nothing in return.

Actually, being a human wallflower isn't so bad either. As long as you're not feeling shy or awkward, it can be nice to stay on the margins – quiet, reflective, observant. When you're not speaking, you can listen more closely, observe more keenly and understand more deeply. You can 'think all you speak, but speak not all you think'. In Stephen Chbosky's novel *The Perks of Being a Wallflower*, introvert teenager Charlie is told, 'You see things. You keep quiet about them. And you understand.'[172]

In *The Dictionary of Obscure Sorrows*, John Koenig coins his own term for the feeling of wanting to observe without participating:

> *Slipfast* (adj.): longing to disappear completely; to melt into a crowd and become invisible, so you can take in the world without having to take part in it—free to wander through conversations without ever leaving footprints, free to dive deep into things without worrying about making a splash.[173]

If sociability is a transaction, there's a sense that you should have something to show for the time and effort you put in. This sort of balance-sheet reckoning is made fully explicit in speed-dating or business networking, but it's also reflected in metaphors of social life, with their subtext of acquisition and productivity: *gaining* friends, *building* relationships, *making* a good impression. As a wallflower, you renounce this social materialism in favour of a radical, Zen-like acceptance of whatever the garden offers and whatever the weather brings. By reconciling yourself to less, you end up with more.

## what the heart wants

> The Heart wants what it wants—or else it does not care.
>
> EMILY DICKINSON

The biggest advantage that extroverts enjoy is being able to say what they want, and having it acknowledged and accepted. While the desire for company is seen as something inherently positive and healthy, the need to be alone, no matter how deeply felt or sincerely expressed, is rarely fully understood or appreciated. Solitude isn't regarded as something natural and wholesome that everybody can and should enjoy. Spend too much time alone, and you'll turn into a loner, a freak or a weirdo. Solitude is the cloak that deviants use to hide their oddness.

What's more, if you choose solitude, you run the risk of being seen as aloof or standoffish. If you feel hassled in company, and show it, you could be labelled as grumpy or misanthropic. Others might interpret your actions as a commentary on theirs, in which case they might decide you're judgemental, arrogant or over-critical. Or, if they think you're only seeking attention, you could be dismissed as narcissistic, manipulative or vain.

Some people are convinced that introverts must be 'putting it on'. For an example, see this interview with introvert musical genius Frank Ocean:

> Interviewer: Why don't I know much about you, Frank? Is that on purpose?
>
> Ocean: I don't know… I think that's just my personality.
>
> Interviewer: Are you going for the 'man of mystery' thing?
>
> Ocean: I'm not even going for it. It's just kinda… how it is.[174]

Since extroverts are happy to talk about themselves, they find it hard to understand how someone else would *not* enjoy it. Or, like the interviewer above, they go one step further, and decide that introverts must be using some fiendish reverse-psychology tactic. In their eyes, introversion is an affectation, or even a provocation.

It really isn't. For introverts, solitude isn't just a want; it's a *need* – and it's certainly not a pretence, a ruse or a ploy. Far from putting our introversion on, we often wish we could turn it off. There have been many times when I've wished I could just deactivate my personality for a while, like silencing the notifications on my phone. But that's not the way it works.

People find it hard to believe that solitude truly makes us happy, and many eminent thinkers back them up. Over recent years, 'happiness science' has investigated what brings people happiness, and what we can do to feel happier in our lives. It all began from the finding that greater prosperity doesn't necessarily lead to greater happiness. So if money doesn't make us happy, what does?

For many happiness writers, a big part of the answer is 'other people'. For example, 'happiness tsar' Richard Layard states:

> **Humans are deeply social beings.** Most people prefer to be in company most of the time. Friendship and marriage make people happier… In fact to a large extent our social ties define our personal identity and give meaning to our life.[175]

On a similar theme, Martin Seligman, the positive psychology guru, argues that 'when we are happy, we are less self-focused, we like others more, and we want to share our good fortune even with strangers'.[176]

Fair enough. They can have their view, and we can have ours. But once boffins identify 'happiness factors' and work out how to measure them, it's a short step to telling people how to be happy. If we're feeling down, we just need to do the 'right' things, which will duly 'make' us happy. Becoming happier is a responsible act of self-improvement, like taking up jogging or drinking less – not just something we *can* do, but something we *should*. Happiness is not just a mood, but a moral imperative – what Sarah Ahmed calls the 'happiness duty'.[177] And since happiness is inherently social, we have to be happy with others, and *for* others too; our smile must always face outwards.

But what if our ideas of happiness aren't all the same? Or if we find that the things that should make us happy simply… don't?

The concept of happiness embodies the values of whoever invokes it. Historically, the assertion that certain people were 'happy' was used to erase their lived experience or silence their voice. For example, the image of the 'happy housewife' kept women tied to the home, while slave owners promoted the idea of the 'happy slave' to suggest that enslaved people had no wish to be free. The cliché of 'domestic bliss' elevates the traditional nuclear family over any other sort of happy home that people might have, or want.

Sometimes, when people decide that someone else is 'happy', what they really mean is that that person, in their view, is in their proper place or living the right way:

> There is no possibility of measuring the happiness of others, and it is always easy to describe as happy the situation in which one wishes to place them.
>
> Simone de Beauvoir[178]

On the other hand, deciding that someone must be *un*happy can be a convenient pretext for offering them some unsolicited life advice, or making an intervention to 'help' them change.

Although introverts or solitary people may feel a bit alonely or hassled from time to time, we're never actually *forced* to spend time with others. We can choose what we want. However, there might still be some social cost to our choices. Because we live in such an extrovert world, we might find ourselves at odds with received ideas about what 'should' make us happy, and we might end up feeling bad if we take those ideas to heart ourselves.

For example, we might feel vaguely guilty for finding happiness in solitude rather than company, or anxious that our choices might be bringing other people down. We might feel puzzled as to why ostensibly 'happy' social occasions, like parties, don't actually make us feel that good. Or we might find ourselves drawn to things that others see as downbeat or depressing, finding in them a quieter, deeper sort of happiness that superficially 'happy' stuff just can't provide. We might also find that others worry that we must be 'sad', when in fact all we need is a bit of time alone.

In the end, your happiness can never be claimed or proclaimed by another; it can only come from yourself. The heart wants what it wants, and the only person who decides when you're happy is you.

## when you just don't want to go

One of the toughest situations you face as an introvert is the social invitation that you just don't want to take up.

You probably like the person who's offering you the invitation, so you'll be anxious not to offend them. And it's not that you don't like the people who'll be present at the occasion, either. But when you get them all together, they become something far bigger, and more daunting, than the sum of their parts. And that's why, when you're totally honest with yourself, *you just don't want to go.*

Of course, there are always plenty of reasons why you *should* go. People might make these arguments out loud, or they might imply them, or you might second-guess that they're secretly thinking them. You might even hear them inside your head, perhaps in the voice of a friend or relative from the past. But wherever they come from, they're always there: a greatest hits of reasons to get involved.

The first, most common argument is that people just want you to be there. And on the face of it, it seems like a compliment. 'Come along!' they say. 'It'd be great to see you!'

Would it, though, really? Would it actually be so great to have a sullen introvert around who really doesn't want to be there?

Admittedly, this position could seem a bit melodramatic. 'I choose not to go, in order to spare others the anguish of my crabbed and cantankerous company. In so doing, I nobly sacrifice myself to the greater good.' But in a quieter way, it often rings true. If you're really not going to enjoy yourself, or you think you might bring people down, why go?

Next up is the 'fun' argument. You should go, because you'll probably have a nice time. And in fact, this is sometimes true – but that doesn't take away your right to feel unsure right now. You're allowed to feel how you feel.

For me, this argument has gradually lost its power over time. When I was young, any party or trip to the pub was a dark, sparkling jewel of possibility. Just think, literally *anything* could happen! But as the years flew by, I stopped yearning to see new people and places, and began craving the familiar and reliable instead. If this hasn't happened to you yet, take it from me: it will.

The next argument is a sort of managerial, resource-utilisation perspective. All this company is going to be available, and if you don't go, it will go to waste. Maybe someone will be there you don't see very often. Or maybe this is the only chance for everyone to get together for six months or more. Are you going to let the opportunity slide?

Well, yes you are. Because *you just don't want to go*.

Closely related is a sort of Protestant leisure ethic. The idea is that anything requiring exertion must be virtuous somehow, and it's expressed in phrases like 'I suppose I should make the effort.' But why should pleasure be hard work?

Then there's the moral argument. You *should* go, simply because it's good to be sociable. In tandem with this, your reluctance or discomfort may be minimised – for example, through a baseless assertion that 'it won't be *that* bad' or even an old-fashioned exhortation to 'pull yourself together'. This is pure emotional blackmail, and it can be really hard to take.

Resisting casts you as a sulky child. 'I don't *care* how naughty I'm being,' you pout. 'I'm still not going.' And you stamp your little foot, fold your arms and turn away.

However, there's a more reasoned, adult response too. As children, we have to live by our parents' values – but when we grow up, we develop our own rules to live by. And 'should' only has the power that you give it. For you, there's nothing wrong with staying away; it's just the choice you're making in this moment. Others may have their own 'should', but it doesn't have to be yours.

Besides, why does the moral compass always point towards company? Why do we feel we 'should' spend time with others, but never that we 'should' spend time alone? Why is it always right to socialise, but never right to withdraw?

Imagine telling someone else that they could do with spending a little time alone. 'You know what? I think some solitary self-reflection would do you the world of good.' You'd need to know them pretty well to avoid giving offence. But why should that be? As we've seen, time alone can be the best medicine for a host of ills. If we can prescribe it to ourselves, why not to others too?

Finally, we come to the last resort: straight-out character assassination. This is a personal judgement – or just an insult – based on your refusal to attend. It's not open to everybody, but close friends and family might well use it. For example, since I'm a middle-aged dad, it's easy to characterise me as a 'grumpy old man' whenever I don't want to go to something.

You may or may not be a dad, but if you're an introvert, I'm betting that you've probably experienced a reaction along these lines. You like to be alone, and you'd prefer to be alone on this occasion. But others see someone who's being arrogant, aloof, moody, difficult, selfish, stubborn, self-absorbed… take your pick. Since they won't take your answer at face value, your natural reaction becomes an active choice – and an evil one at that. You're not just choosing to stay home; you're also choosing to be horrible. Why are you doing that? Just what the hell is *wrong* with you?

Maybe you *are* a grumpy old man, a stubborn teenager, a drama queen or a mardy old cow. But such a status neither alters nor rebuts your position. You still *just don't want to go*.

Remember: all you're ever doing is saying what you want. Nobody can really blame you for that – and if they do, that's on them. It might even be helpful to gently point this out. 'I'm not sulking or being stubborn,' you could say. 'I'm just saying what I want.' Maybe if you keep saying it, it will eventually sink in.

The larger and more expectation-laden the occasion, the sweeter the thought of opting out of it. The mere idea of non-attendance ignites a giddy, wide-eyed euphoria. *I could just not go!*

I think this feeling deserves its own name. If extroverts are compelled to socialise by the fear of missing out, or FOMO, then introverts are tempted to stay away by JOMO: the joy of missing out. JOMO is when you know all the reasons why you *should* go, but still choose to ignore them. And I think you should always allow yourself the luxury of JOMO, even if it's only for a moment, and you know that, in the end, you will in fact go. Savour the delicious thought of what you could do if there were no consequences, no morning after, no need to face anyone ever again. Then come back down to earth and do what has to be done.

Besides, we almost certainly overestimate the impact of our decisions. If we don't go, people may be a bit pissed off, but they'll get over it:

> We assume other people are more fragile than we are; that a single disappointment will break them. We also overestimate the space each of us takes up in the imaginations of others, even among our close friends and family. People have lives. They're just as self-obsessed as we are.
>
> EMMA BROCKES[179]

Anyway. I can't tell you whether you should say yes to that invitation. But I will say this. Your time, your presence and your attention are yours and yours alone. They're precious, you don't owe them to anyone, and if you share them, it should be your choice. You belong to you.

# one for sorrow

I'm sure you recognised where the title of this book came from. It's an alternative take on the ancient rhyme about magpies:

> One for sorrow, two for joy
> Three for a girl and four for a boy
> Five for silver, six for gold
> Seven for a secret, never to be told.

The idea is that the number of magpies you see indicates your fortune, reflecting the ancient superstition about them being birds of ill omen.

Magpies form couples and stay together year after year, but they only forage together in fine weather. This gave rise to the belief that a single magpie meant bad weather on the way. In Scotland, a magpie near a window is even said to foretell death.

Poor single magpies. I've always felt a bit sorry for them, seeing what bad press they get. For millions of years, they went about their avian business completely undisturbed. Then, all of a sudden, medieval peasants were pointing at them and shrieking about death

and bad weather. That must be a downer when you're just about to tuck into a nice juicy vole.

We sometimes look to 'social' animals, like bees making honey, for proof that social interaction is essential for survival. But bees buzzing around the hive aren't really socialising; they're collaborating. What's more, bees spend a fair amount of time on their own. You've probably had more encounters with solitary bees, bumbling randomly through your living-room window, than you have with entire swarms. Lone bees are simply out on a nectar quest on behalf of their fellow bees.

In other words, behaviours that we anthropomorphise as 'friendly' or 'sociable' may be merely practical. Company is a preference rather than a need – and many living things are meant to spend time alone.[180] An animal, including a human one, may be perfectly happy on its own.

Maybe if people reflected on the animals behind their metaphors, they'd have a better sense of how introverts feel. If you're prickly, like a hedgehog, it's only because you want to protect yourself. If you're grouchy, like a bear, it's only because you have to hibernate from time to time. If you're retreating inside your shell, like a snail, it's only because there's danger out there. Solitude is just what the introvert species needs to live in the world.

SEVEN

# THE MIND ALONE

What goes on in your head
when you're alone?

# first steps

You could think of solitude as something that 'just happens' when no-one else is there. One step on from that, you could think of it as something you actively choose and seek out. But then you could go further still, by considering solitude as a skill that can be learned and improved.

Paradoxically, we first learn to be alone in the company of those who are closest to us. Think about a newborn baby. In her first few months, she's completely dependent on her main carer. As the months go by, she gradually builds up her confidence, both physical and psychological, and starts to learn more about the outside world.

Between the ages of three and six months, the baby wants her carer to be there all the time, and she'll probably cry when they leave the room, even for a few moments. This is known as *separation anxiety*. The baby has learned how dependent she is on those around her, so she feels anxious when they go away.

After a while, though, she realises that people leave, but then they come back. She learns to be with people other than her carers, or even on her own, for a little while. Over the years that follow, she learns how to sustain herself through longer and longer periods on her own, by using comforting thoughts of those who can't be there. So-called *transitional objects*, like teddy bears, help to comfort her.

Psychologist Donald W. Winnicott saw the ability to be alone as a sign of healthy emotional development. Focusing on the early months of life, he proposed the idea of *primary aloneness*. Just after a baby is born, she experiences an *aloneness of predependence* – completely dependent on her carer but unaware of her situation. During her first year of life, her *noncommunicating self* appears, and she gradually becomes aware of herself as separate from her carer. Finally, she learns her first words and begins to communicate about the world around her.

Unlike Hegel in chapter five, then, Winnicott believes that there *is* an essential self that exists before and beyond language, never to be seen or touched by anyone else:

> Although healthy persons communicate and enjoy communicating, the other fact is equally true, that each individual is an isolate, permanently non-communicating, permanently unknown, in fact, unfound.[181]

Winnicott also drew a distinction between the *true self* and the *false self*. The true self is rooted in the newborn's simple experience of being alive and inhabiting a body. From this, she develops her sense of reality, and a feeling that life is worth living. As long as this feeling is reflected and nurtured with what Winnicott called 'good enough parenting' – not perfect, but fit for purpose – the true self will continue to develop and grow. The false self, meanwhile, arises from the need to comply with other people's wishes:

> Other people's expectations can become of overriding importance, overlaying or contradicting the original sense of self, the one connected to the very roots of one's being.[182]

The false self grows into a façade through which a person creates and maintains false relationships, stifling the spontaneity of the true self. There's a parallel with Erving Goffman's idea of performance from chapter three: the mask we put on for the sake of being sociable and polite. However, the false self is also a kind of armour. It forms a shell around the true self, protecting it from being exploited or destroyed. By learning to be 'false', we keep our inner selves true.

## in your room

> The strongest person in the world is the person who isn't scared to be alone.
>
> 'ALICE HARMON' IN *THE QUEEN'S GAMBIT*[183]

Adolescents repeat a similar process to the one they went through as babies – but on a grander scale, and with higher stakes. As a baby, the teenager learned to be alone for a few minutes and relate to his immediate environment. Now, as a young adult, he has to create himself as an individual by forming new relationships and finding a place in the world. Reflecting in his solitude, he breaks free of what others want for him, and considers what he might want for himself.

> Through desire the child discovers his solitude, and through solitude his desire.
>
> ADAM PHILLIPS[184]

Research shows that adolescents need solitude to build their adult identities. By spending time alone, they can work on their *individuation* – that is, understanding exactly how they're different from other people.[185] All those hours up in your room reading and playing guitar aren't wasted time; they reveal who you really are.

Solitude is where teenagers do their 'psychological homework'. They develop the skill of introspection – the ability to take other people's perspectives, weigh up abstract concepts, analyse their own behaviour and consider future scenarios. They also learn to reconcile the two sides of their 'divided self' – the face they put on in public and the 'real me' inside their head. Solitude offers a welcome respite from the youthful self-consciousness that can sometimes feel overwhelming.[186] Researchers have found that young people who choose to spend a lot of time alone experience more self-expression, creative expression and spiritual renewal.[187]

As introverts, we never grow out of needing that bedroom sanctuary. Growing up as an introvert also means accepting yourself as someone who loves and needs solitude. That state of aloneness, which is such a comfort when you're growing up, is something you'll want to return to for the rest of your life. Your solitude isn't an angry, defiant gesture, like storming off to your bedroom, but a rational, measured choice to be alone.

## learning to be alone

> The greatest thing in the world is to know how to be for yourself.
>
> Michel de Montaigne

Are there solitude skills that we need to learn as adults? Could solitude even be taught, like other life skills? Psychologist Virginia Thomas of the University of Santa Cruz thinks so:

> Some psychologists consider solitude a basic human need just as important as relationships… Many of us could benefit from learning how to have a better

> experience of solitude, whether we enter into it by choice or not. The problem is that we often don't know how.

Based on her research, Thomas discovered eight traits of people who get the most from solitude, grouped under three themes.[188]

The first theme is *self-connection*. People who enjoy solitude find great satisfaction in solitary pursuits, and rarely get bored. They are willing to self-reflect, and protect themselves through *integrative emotion regulation*: exploring their feelings with a sense of curiosity rather than judgement.

The second theme is *protecting time*. Before you can benefit from solitude, you need to find the time to be alone. Sometimes, you might have to negotiate with friends or family, or explain to them why solitude is so beneficial to you. Then, once you're actually alone, you need to make sure you use your solitude in a mindful way, on something you find fulfilling.

The third and final theme is *finding balance*. You need to listen to your solitude signals: the physical and mental signs of overload that tell you it's time to withdraw. However, you also need to know when to exit solitude. If you start feeling genuinely lonely, or your boredom isn't leading to creativity (see 'boredom' below), it may be time to rejoin the world.

## empty hours

> It is not when he is working in the office but when he is lying idly on the sand that his soul utters, 'Life is beautiful.'
>
> LIN YUTANG [189]

The poet Philip Larkin wrote of remorse at 'time torn off unused', as if the hours were blank leaves in a notebook that we should have filled with writing.[190] But one of the pleasures of solitude is allowing the time to pass without using every second of it. Maybe you want to spend time without being judged, either by others or by yourself. Maybe there's nothing you want to gain, optimise or improve. Maybe everything is already in its right place.

Life is more than a mathematical equation of time used versus benefit gained. If an hour of 'doing nothing' is actually an hour of mindful presence, emotional reflection or focused thought, that might ultimately bring you more benefit than an hour of frantic activity. For example, once your mind is free to wander, it might stumble across some wonderful new ideas:

> A writer could get more ideas for his articles or novels in this posture [lying in bed] than he could by sitting doggedly before his desk morning and afternoon. For there, free from telephone calls and well-meaning visitors and the common trivialities of everyday life, he sees life through a glass or beaded screen, as it were, and a halo of poetic fancy is cast around the world of realities and informs it with a magic beauty.
>
> LIN YUTANG[191]

In her book *I Didn't Do the Thing Today*, Madeleine Dore argues that we should let go of our 'productivity guilt' once and for all. Like the idea of 'more, faster and better' from chapter two, productivity guilt convinces us that we can and should fill each and every day with useful activity. But we are more than just cogs in a machine.

> …each of us is entangled in a culture that measures our value through productivity—how much we do, how well we do it, whom we do it for… When we

> conflate productivity with worthiness, what we do is never enough.[192]

Whatever self-help books might try to tell us, we can't optimise every aspect of our lives. Sometimes we won't finish our to-do list – or even start it. Instead of going into a spiral of self-reproach, we have to accept that we have good days and bad days, and that this variance is part of the natural rhythm of life. And the 'unproductive' times in our lives are not monuments to failure, but spaces that we can fill with other, better things: enjoyment, kindness or self-care.

## boredom

> Boredom is the dream bird that hatches the egg of experience. A rustling in the leaves drives him away.
>
> WALTER BENJAMIN[193]

When was the last time you allowed yourself to be bored?

To be bored is to accept the present moment for what it is, even if it doesn't have that much interest or excitement to offer us. But even though we can only ever live in the present, we do all we can to avoid confronting the reality of the here-and-now. We think about things we'd rather be doing, or people we'd rather be with. We long for things we want, and worry about things we don't. Our bodies are here, but our minds are wandering elsewhere.

For Søren Kierkegaard, this compulsive somewhere-else-ness was the root of all human unhappiness:

> The unhappy person is one who has his ideal, the content of his life, the fullness of his consciousness, the essence of his being, in some manner outside of himself.

> The unhappy man is always absent from himself, never present to himself.[194]

And Blaise Pascal made the same point more bluntly:

> All of humanity's problems stem from man's inability to sit quietly in a room alone.

If you want to be happy, you have to do it in the here-and-now. Otherwise, what you're feeling is not happiness, but nostalgia or anticipation. And to be happy here and now, you have to accept that your current reality might be less exciting than fantasy.

However, boredom is more than just an absence of interest. It's the blank page of the mind: a deserted station at which a new train of thought might arrive. Even though boredom is a negative feeling, it also has an 'approach orientation', because we're engaged in a positive search for interest. When nothing much is going on, we start looking for something new, and that can stimulate creativity. Simple relaxation doesn't have the same effect.[195]

Epictetus, the stoic philosopher, pointed out that we all have the innate capacity to create our way out of boredom:

> Why do we make ourselves worse than children? What do they do when they are left alone? They take up shells and dust; they build houses, then pull them down; then build something else; and thus never want amusement. Suppose you were all to sail away; am I to sit and cry because I am left alone and solitary? Am I so unprovided with shells and dust?[196]

So if boredom is so productive, why do we recoil from it? Probably because it can feel like an ending, an absence or a loss – at least when it first appears. Boredom is the leftovers of life: the stuff that we're stuck with when all the 'interesting' things have run out. In that moment, we have no choice but to look at ourselves – and we don't always like what we see.

We certainly have plenty of distractions to save us from ourselves these days. But are we really any different from previous generations? Almost 100 years ago, Bertrand Russell wrote:

> We are less bored than our ancestors were, but we are more afraid of boredom. We have come to know, or rather to believe, that boredom is not part of the natural lot of man, but can be avoided by a sufficiently vigorous pursuit of excitement. [197]

Probably every generation feels that younger people are spoilt for distractions. I grew up in the 1970s, so I remember watching Open University programmes because there was nothing else on TV, or reading my favourite books time and again. But was I *really* bored, or am I imposing the perspective of the present on the past?

And besides, although those times supposedly held no interest, *I still remember them*. They've become minor formative experiences. They helped that bored child grow up into the rounded, and incredibly boring, adult of today.

Now I look at toddlers in the pram, already plugged into their parents' phones, and I wonder if they will ever know an empty minute in their waking lives. But maybe they, too, will grow up to wax nostalgic about the years before they had a chip implanted in their brains that they can never switch off.

It would be easy for me to dwell on the pictures or stories I made and lament the uncreativity of the modern mind. But each generation has their own way of being bored. Somehow, culture survives, as the young remake it in their own image – because there is *nothing* quite as boring as something your parents like. When you're bored to tears with the old world, it's time to make your own.

# dreaming with open eyes

> I personally love being alone. It's when I'm the funniest, the sexiest, the most powerful. It's when I'm a Grammy-winning country artist and a competitive hip-hop dancer. It's when I'm a fairly paid, totally empowered and consenting stripper. It's when I am a witch.
>
> LENA DUNHAM[198]

Daydreams are a solitude within solitude: an impregnable mind-castle that no-one can breach. Even if we *wanted* to let someone into our daydreams, all we could ever offer them is a pale description of what goes on there. Daydreams are the one place where we can be perfectly, truly ourselves:

> Even in our best lives, our daydreams allow us to retain secret lives that no one else can access or touch. They are the ultimate privacy: the thing that remains secret even inside our closest intimacies… The things we imagine doing are more private than any of the things we've done.
>
> LESLIE JAMISON[199]

What's more, daydreams are a form of solitude that we can enjoy in company. On the train, in the office, even at the bar… there's always time for a daydream. And no matter how loud or sociable your surroundings, your dreamworld remains inviolate. Even as someone else is looking you right in the eyes, you can be gazing at some far horizon in your mind.

But why do we daydream? Are our daydreams just a mental movie for our own entertainment? Or are they something more? Psychologist Jerome Singer thought so.[200] He argued that daydreaming is *adaptive* – in other words, it helps us understand life events, manage emotions and solve problems. For example, through daydreams, we can try things out, switch things round or imagine how other people would react if we did this, or said that.

Singer proposed three main 'styles' of daydreaming. Positive-constructive daydreaming is about wishful thinking, playful fantasy or practical plans. This is where daydreaming overlaps with creativity and problem-solving. It's like the pretend-play we did as children, but in our minds rather than the sandpit.

On the flip side, there is guilty-dysphoric daydreaming, which is anxious and obsessive, and often dwells on failure. It's like when you picture your plane crashing, or colleagues falling about laughing at your work presentation. Sometimes, this is genuinely distressing – but it can also be weirdly indulgent, as you savour the sense of danger while knowing you're actually quite safe.

Finally, some daydreaming is simply poor attentional control, where the dreamer flits between their internal and external worlds without being fully present in either.

Singer was unusual in seeing daydreaming in a positive light. Many other researchers consider it more as a fault to be corrected, as reflected in the modern term 'mind-wandering'. But that view neglects the beauty and fascination of daydreaming: a waking, daylight dream that we ourselves direct. It also presupposes that all the value is to be found in conscious, deliberate, rational thought – when in fact, many of the best and most creative ideas are found off the beaten track, or when we let our minds off the leash for a while.

You can place your daydreams on a sliding scale of realism. Some are utterly impossible fantasies, like having dinner with Shakespeare, turning into an eagle or travelling a thousand years into the future. Others are scenarios that are admittedly unlikely, but still *theoretically* possible. Here, you take an object, event or person in the real world as a starting point for your own flight of fancy. (Sex and romance often feature, as you know.)

Sometimes, these fantasies provide us with an emotional and moral simplicity that real life can't match. Love and lust are uncomplicated and guilt-free. Monsters are evil and deserve their fate. Perilous situations are neatly resolved. And we ourselves act with courage and purpose, knowing we're certain to succeed.

In James Thurber's famous short story 'The Secret Life of Walter Mitty', the eponymous hero pictures himself as a navy commander, a brilliant surgeon and a criminal on trial. Even as Mitty's mundane life threatens to suffocate him – 'things close in,' as he mutters darkly – his imagination offers a reliable way out.[201]

On a more prosaic level, there are 'productivity porn' daydreams: fantasising about all the useful things you'd do if only you had infinite time and energy. And one step down from that, there are daydreams that are downright mundane, like thinking about what you'll cook for dinner.

Of course, we don't have to be alone in our daydreams. We can rope other people into them, making them do and say whatever we want. Here's Tina Belcher of *Bob's Burgers* enjoying a daydream featuring Jimmy Junior, her teenage crush from school, in which she writes, directs and acts in the drama all at the same time:

Jimmy Jr: You're the baddest girl in detention, Tina.
Tina: Tell me about it… stud.
Jimmy Jr: *(Giggles)* I'm a stud!
Zeke: I'm an idiot!
Tina: I know, Zeke. Don't talk any more. Tammy, spill that [drink]. Jimmy Junior, mop that up with your pants.
Jimmy Jr: *(Taking off his trousers)* OK.[202]

In Tina's 'erotic friend fiction', Jimmy, Zeke and Tammy – plus some teen zombies – are little more than mental meat puppets, there to do her bidding. But people can also figure in our daydreams as romanticised ideals, becoming whatever we want them to be – or, if we know them well enough, what *they* want to be.

Sometimes, daydreams can be a sign of problems. Something's missing from our life, and the daydream provides it. Working backwards from that, we could ask ourselves: if this daydream is the cure, what's the symptom? What do I feel in the daydream that I don't feel in real life? These therapeutic daydreams can show us a way out of a situation we don't like – or, at least, give us a brief respite from it. If nothing else, they tell us that things *could* be different: we can at least imagine a different future, even if we don't yet know how to bring it about.

However, some daydreams can also be a sign that everything is fine. They make 'real life' more vivid, not less so. And they're appealing not because they could be real, but precisely because they're *not*. They represent alternative realities that are not necessarily better, just different. When you look across at other paths, you feel reassured that you chose the right one. You come back to your real life and think *Yes, this is what I want.*

You can also reconnect with parts of yourself that have got buried or forgotten. In the daydream, you think, *This was important to me*, or *I used to love this*. And then, on awaking, you realise that it still is, or you still do. And perhaps what has been, can be again.

## madeleine moments

> Let us live for the beauty of our own reality.
>
> Charles Lamb

There are two very different flavours of nostalgia. The first is collective, and it happens when we retell stories of the past with others who were there. These tales grow in the telling, gradually becoming a shared mythology.

The other kind of nostalgia lives in our own individual memories – and here, the picture is even hazier. Events are misremembered, mingled and even made up to form a palimpsest of precarious facts and inadvertent fictions, all jumbled together in a tea-chest marked 'memories'. Your past, which *was* an objective reality once upon a time, is now an ever-changing work of imagination that is utterly unique to you.

> Past events exist, after all, only in memory, which is a form of imagination. The event is real *now*, but once it's *then*, its continuing reality is entirely up to us, dependent on our energy and honesty. If we let it drop from memory, only imagination can restore the least glimmer of it.
>
> URSULA LE GUIN[203]

Your memory is a diary that you wrote back then, and continue to rewrite now, on every page at once. And it's a book that no one else can ever read, because whatever description you share with someone else will be reconstructed from *their* sensory experiences, not yours. And even if you could somehow teleport the memory from your mind to theirs, it would still never have the same significance that it does for you. So you enjoy your innermost memories in solitude because there's simply no other way to do so. Even in our hyper-social age, some things cannot be shared.

Solo activities can be gateways to nostalgia. For instance, cooking certain dishes can evoke a time, place or person in a way that nothing else quite can. To cook this memory-food is to enact a ritual that brings the past alive in the present; to eat it is a sensual communion with the gone-before. As Laurie Colwin puts it, 'No one who cooks, cooks alone.'[204]

Perhaps the most powerful anchors for nostalgia, though, are sensory experiences. The smell of cut grass, the feel of velvet, the sound of a crackly radio – you never know when some everyday happening will suddenly leap out at you and release an unstoppable rush of recollection. This is sometimes known as an *involuntary autobiographical memory* or 'mind pop'.

Marcel Proust was famously transported back to his childhood by the taste of a madeleine cake dunked in tea:

> No sooner had the warm liquid, and the crumbs with it, touched my palate than a shudder ran through my whole body, and I stopped, intent upon the extraordinary changes that were taking place. An exquisite pleasure had invaded my senses, but individual, detached, with no suggestion of its origin. And at once the vicissitudes of life had become indifferent to me, its disasters innocuous, its brevity

> illusory – this new sensation having had on me the effect which love has of filling me with a precious essence; or rather this essence was not in me, it was myself.[205]

The madeleine transports Proust both into and out of himself. He is simultaneously lifted out of his 'weary, mechanical' present self to a suddenly remembered past, and at the same time restored to his 'essence': his sense of who he really is.

Our own madeleines, whatever they may be, are paths along which we can return to ourselves. But as Proust explains, those paths cannot be found and followed by choice – only by chance:

> It is a labour in vain to attempt to recapture [our past]: all the efforts of our intellect must prove futile. The past is hidden somewhere outside the realm, beyond the reach of intellect, in some material object… which we do not suspect.

These humble objects are always there, patiently waiting in your attic or garage to remind you of a memory you didn't even know you had. Then, when you rediscover them, a forgotten event or person comes to mind like they've never been away.

Sometimes, the object is a single star in a constellation of things: the doll evokes the toybox evokes the attic evokes the house evokes the grandmother. And like the lines that form the constellations, these links are only visible if you know they're there; to everyone else, the doll is just a doll, with no connection to anything.

Although I'm not a fan myself, I do understand why people of my generation want to get back into vinyl. It's because 'the records we liked can lead us back to the lives we once led and the people we once were,' as music writer David Hepworth puts it.[206] An LP is a compact time machine, instantly evoking the time and place you bought it, how you listened to it and what (or who) you thought about as you did.

As more and more aspects of our lives are digitised, these tangible anchors to our past recede and dissolve. Digital photos, ebooks and streaming music put our memories in our pocket, but they're physically rootless. We can search them at the tap of a screen, but we'll never come across them while looking for something else in our parents' loft. We'll never open an ebook and unexpectedly encounter the smell of our grandparents' living room, or be surprised when a ticket for a gig we went to 20 years before drops out of its pages.

Since digital media are so immaterial, the audience's emotions might be infused into the devices used to consume them instead. Younger listeners might want to hang on to their phones, earbuds and smart speakers, so they don't miss out on their evocative power 30 years from now. I know I'd be blown away if I was reunited with the Sony Walkman that accompanied me on my early-morning milk round in the 1980s. The things we own end up owning us.

EIGHT

# DIGITAL SOLITUDE IS IMPOSSIBLE

Why you can't be on your own and on your phone.

# what's the problem?

> We fill our days with ongoing connection, denying ourselves time to think and dream.
>
> SHERRY TURKLE[207]

Our experience of solitude has always been shaped by technology. The printing press, the telephone, the TV and even the postal service all changed what it meant to be alone. So on the face of it, using digital technology or social media while alone is just another form of networked solitude. We're physically alone, but psychologically connected to others, just as we would be if we wrote a letter or watched a film in solitude. But I would argue that modern, digitally connected solitude is different by nature from other, earlier forms.

Rather than helping us achieve our own purposes, the digital world overrides them or exploits them for its own ends. It uses novelty, intrigue and spectacle to aggressively hijack our attention in ways that other experiences – like reading or listening to music – just don't. It promises quick, frictionless human connection that exerts a powerful emotional pull, yet leaves us unfulfilled. It flatters us that we're the centre of the world, and that everything out there is somehow for, or about, ourselves. In reality, though, it's run by powerful corporations who make fat profits from all our clicking, sharing and browsing, and use their formidable intelligence to keep us online, engaged and – let's be honest – addicted.

All this makes it harder to choose, sustain and enjoy solitude when digital technology is involved. If we stay connected to the digital world during solitude, we can end up degrading the very things that make solitude worth having: a calm mood, a reflective mindset and a deeper awareness of ourselves and the world.

## get off your phone

The invention of the smartphone changed solitude for ever.

No doubt, cultural artefacts like books and records can be beautiful things, but they're still static and inert. Your phone is something else entirely: a fluid and infinitely flattering mirror to the self. Eagerly unlocking at your merest touch or glance, it presents you with a constellation of your chosen apps. By allowing you to curate the content (and people) you prefer, it puts you at the centre of your own digital world, guaranteeing that there will always be someone or something that speaks to you.

However, it goes even deeper than that. Several studies have found that the boundary between the 'human self' and the smartphone is becoming blurred, and we see our phones as part of our 'extended selves'.[208] The more our happy memories are linked to our phones – through photos, messages and so on – the stronger this feeling gets. That's why allowing someone else to touch your phone, or even just look at it, feels so weird and invasive. It's also why spending time without your phone can make you feel tense and strung out, like you've left a part of yourself behind and you need to get it back.

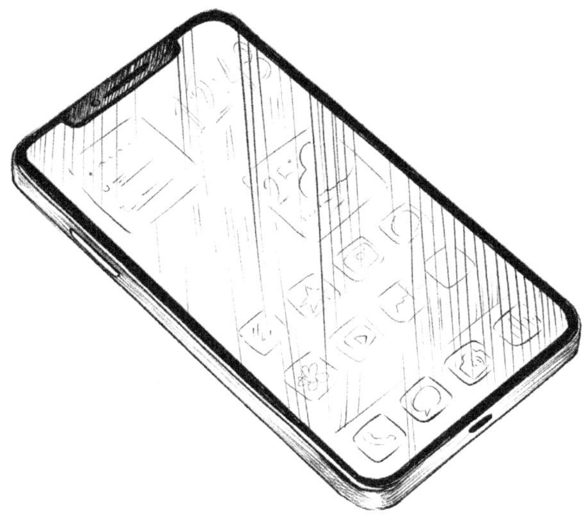

Phones are a physical possession, a part of yourself and a window on your world, all at the same time. That's what makes them so different from all the other objects in your life. Phones have a unique hold over us, and they arouse strong emotions – not always positive.

> …the mobile [phone] mixes up presence and absence, me/not-me, subject and object; and it seems to mix these things up in *us*. Such mixing can provoke anxieties.[209]

Technology becomes a problem when the user becomes the used. So have we reached that point with our phones? Well, the numbers don't lie. In one survey, Americans were found to check their phones around fifty-two times a day,[210] while eighty-nine percent say they interrupted their last social interaction to look at their phone.[211]

The Smartphone Addiction Scale (SAS), developed by a team of Korean academics,[212] looks at factors like being unable to control your phone use, taking your phone to the toilet, feeling stressed when there's no Wi-Fi or being told to 'get off your phone'. While phone addicts are using their devices, they feel calm, excited, cosy, confident, or liberated. On the other hand, they can never really feel good when they're without them, and may begin to suffer from nomophobia – the fear of being without a phone. Sound familiar?

## always somewhere else

> And yet our dear self is so wearisome to us that we can scarcely support its conversation for an hour together.
>
> ABRAHAM COWLEY[213]

As we saw in chapter four, one of the main benefits of solitude is the chance to be with ourselves in the here-and-now. But the digital world actively encourages the exact opposite. Whenever we want to escape ourselves, or an empty moment, our phones are there, eager to whisk us away. If we don't want to spend any time with our 'dear selves', we don't have to. And if we don't like one avenue of distraction, another one is always close at hand.

Although we talk about phone addiction, what really attracts us is not the technology itself, but the human connection that it promises. Social media gives us the feeling of sharing something with someone else – a joke, interest, idea, taste, judgement, emotion or experience. That makes us feel validated and valued; in internet-speak, we feel *seen*. The moment may be brief, the connection weak, the relationship shallow or even fake – but it still gives us that little shot of emotion we're looking for. So we keep going back.

> We desire to be seen and acknowledged. To exercise meaningful degrees of agency and judgment. In short, to belong and to matter. Social media trades on these

> desires, exploits them, deforms them, and never truly satisfies them, which explains a good deal of the madness.
>
> L.M. Sacasas[214]

Humans are social animals, which is why this promise of connection has such a powerful hold. But it has its dark side too. The digital world places itself between us and the world, mediating our lived experience for its own ends. It pulls our attention outwards, away from ourselves and the here-and-now. Social media is constantly telling us – or taunting us – that something better is happening somewhere else, and we're missing out. Lured by that promise, we subordinate our own experience to someone else's.

> The tragedy is that the stroll, the camping trip, and the face-to-face chat are now themselves suffused with digital ephemera. *Here* is under constant bombardment from *elsewhere*.
>
> Nicholas Carr[215]

Thanks to social media, we see our lives through a sharing lens. Everything we do, think or see is a potential post. All day long, we're thinking *Could I share this? Should I? Would people like it?* We might even feel pressure to do something that's *worthy* of being shared, or worry that what we're doing isn't shareworthy enough. If we're not using our phones with our hands, we're using them in our minds.

We might also feel that because we *can* make ourselves available at all times, we should do so. The pressure might come from other people or ourselves – but either way, it's emotionally exhausting:

> In solitude, we don't reject the world, but have the space to think our own thoughts. But if your phone is always with you, seeking solitude can look suspiciously like hiding.
>
> SHERRY TURKLE[216]

In the digital world, numbers are everything. We measure our worth in metrics that masquerade as aspects of human life, but actually reflect technological functions and statistics: likes, followers, connections, notifications. The more we share and engage, the higher the numbers climb and the more digital rewards we receive.

All this counting encourages us to compare ourselves with others and internalise their judgements. At the time when teenagers should be doing their 'psychological homework' (chapter seven) and becoming young adults, they're looking outwards, comparing themselves to their peers or, worse, an unattainable ideal of beauty, corroding their body image.[217] In chapter three, we saw how being 'on stage' all the time is unbearable; a phone plus social media plus peer pressure makes it practically unavoidable.

None of this has happened by accident. Big Tech is deeply suspicious of solitude. Social media platforms do not want us out on a windy hillside somewhere, thinking thoughts that are never tweeted or taking photos that are never shared, because that private experience is not open to analysis and monetisation. There are no likes for self-knowledge, no stars for self-reflection, no comments on leaving your phone at home.

> Society is growing ever more skeptical of the value of solitude, ever more suspicious of even the briefest of withdrawals into inactivity and apparent purposelessness… We see it in the general desire to make all experience interactive and transactional.
>
> NICHOLAS CARR[218]

The medium is the message, and the message from our phones is crystal clear: online life is exciting, dynamic and social, while offline life is dull, lonely and staid. Why would you leave your phone at home, or switch it off? Why limit the great stuff you can enjoy? Why cut yourself off from the world?

In the digital world, everything is on our terms. We can choose when and how we engage, and who with. But as Sherry Turkle explains, nothing comes for free:

> When offered something that can make things easier, we forget our human purposes… In our excitement about how great a technology makes us feel or how amazing it is that a technology can do *x* or *y*… we forget the more important question: What is the *human value* of *x* and *y*?[219]

So if we allow the digital world to invade our time alone, are we gaining human value, or giving it up? And if we have gained something of value, what might we have sacrificed in return?

# pay attention

Our attention is the origin of everything we do and achieve. To understand a situation, solve a problem or learn to do a task, we must first focus our attention on it. Sustained attention is what allows us to follow through and reach our goals – but when our attention is scattered, our energy is dissipated and wasted. And crucially, attention is a choice: we *decide* what we'll pay attention *to*. That's what makes the difference between just looking and actually seeing, or between vaguely listening and truly hearing.

We can think of attention as a possession as well as a power. We can't pay attention to everything all the time, because there are only so many minutes in a day, and so many neurons in our brains. That's why the phrase 'paying attention' is so appropriate. Our attention is like a fund of cognitive 'currency', and if we spend it on one thing, we can't spend it on another. Moreover, when we 'consume' content online, it's also consuming something of ours: our attention.

This leads naturally to the idea of the *attention economy*, popularised in the late 1990s by Michael Goldhaber:

> We are drowning in information, yet constantly increasing our generation of it. So a key question arises: Is there something else that flows through cyberspace, something that is scarce and desirable? There is… It's called attention. And the economy of attention—not information—is the natural economy of cyberspace.[220]

Twenty-five years on, Goldhaber's prescient vision has become all too real. Whenever we go online, we find ourselves amid a frantic battle for our attention, constantly at risk of tumbling down a rabbit-hole of distraction. One minute we're reading the headlines, the next we're watching a random cat video. Content that we had no knowledge of, let alone interest in, until about ten seconds ago, is suddenly at the very centre of our attention. Every site and app does everything it can to capture our attention and turn it into profit.

> They're coming for every second of your life... No matter how nice they try to be, they're trying to get more engagement from you... Every single free moment you have is a moment you could be looking at your phone.
>
> Bo Burnham[221]

It's an unequal struggle, to say the least. In Hank Green's words, 'The most sophisticated software in existence is tasked with figuring out how to keep you from leaving a website.'[222]

Social media promises connection on demand: it's like a sausage machine where we put in our own words and feelings, turn the handle and a bit of attention pops out. But when our attention is mediated by digital technology, that technology is attending to *us* at the same time, through its algorithms and analytics. That is not being 'seen' by another person, but merely analysed by a machine. When we let Big Tech into our solitude, we give corporations a free pass to inspect, dissect and redirect our attention.

> Solitude has become a resource. Like all resources, it can be harvested and hoarded, taken up by powerful forces without permission or inquiry, and then transformed into private wealth, until the fields of empty space we once took for granted first dwindle, then disappear.
>
> Michael Harris[223]

# arguing about nothing

Having said all that, there's no doubt that social media can expand your horizons. Using Twitter for a decade or so has shown me countless other lives, experiences and viewpoints that I'd never have encountered otherwise. It's made me more thoughtful, more tolerant and more broad-minded – or so I like to think.

However, the downside to diverse opinions is the divisions between them. Twitter, in particular, seems to actively encourage conflict by amplifying the extremes. There are only two views on any issue, and we must choose a side and defend it to the last. Everyone on our side is good, right and well-intentioned, while the other lot are irredeemably stupid or evil and act only in bad faith.

Pretty soon, the original issue fades into the background, as we obsess over the reactions to it, and our own reactions to those reactions, and how other people might judge our reactions, or our failure to react. We become preoccupied with policing language, evaluating others' emotions or vetting the membership of our own communities. Actively encouraged by Twitter's 'quote-tweet' function, we spiral into a meta-discourse of tweets about tweets.

When this happens, we neglect the people behind the content. We forget – perhaps even *choose* to forget – that we're talking to living, breathing people, with feelings and failings of their own.

> When I am on Twitter, I find myself hating everything and everyone – especially myself – wasting their lives arguing about nothing. I lose my ability to empathise, to see humanity beyond the avatars. Never am I more disconnected than when I am plugged in.
>
> MOYA LOTHIAN-MCLEAN[224]

These days, instead of plunging into the fray, I try to remind myself that there are a range of opinions on *every* issue, and that I'm unlikely to influence anybody's outlook with an angry online retort. Having found that social media enhances a good mood but worsens a bad one, I take my own irritation and despondency as a sign that I shouldn't be online at all. Otherwise, I start treating social media like a digital casino: scrolling on endlessly like I'm spinning a roulette wheel or a slot machine, hoping for some nebulous jackpot, when what I really need to do is cash in my chips and walk away.

## how to switch off

Knowing all this is one thing, but successfully saying no to it is another. You may already agree with a lot of what I'm saying, but still find it almost impossible to stay offline for even a short time. Becoming a gatekeeper of your own mind is no small thing.

As I said in chapter one, this isn't a self-help book. But having dwelt on the problem at such length, I feel I should offer a solution of some sort. So here goes.

Firstly, I suggest reflecting honestly on how the digital experience actually is for you. Next time you reach for your phone, ask yourself some useful questions. Why do you need to check your socials right now? What will happen if you don't? What are you hoping to find?

When you're online, stop for a moment and notice how you're feeling. Are you happy and carefree, or fretful and obsessed? Are you calm and centred, or tense and strung out? Then ask yourself how you *want* to feel, and how you could bring that about.

Another question you could ask is *cui bono* – who benefits? Facebook doesn't care how you feel. It just wants you online every day doing your job, which is to post content that will engage other people and put some padding around the adverts. As poker players say, 'If you look round the table and you don't know who the sucker is, it's you.'

When we think of attention as cognitive 'cash', that helps us reflect on where we 'spend' it. However, it can also bind us to a financial perspective where *everything* is a transaction. There are aspects of life that can't be calculated, quantified and compared: intimacies like family, friendship and love, and joyful solitary experiences like meditation, nature, music or art. When we think about these things, the question is not where to 'invest' our attention for the best possible 'return', but our deeper sense of *what is good.* What is unique, irreplaceable or unrepeatable about this moment? What is its essential human value? And what's the best way for us to honour and nurture that value?

One way to deepen your appreciation is to imagine that you're doing something for the last time. We're usually aware when we do things for the first time, but the last time can pass by unnoticed. When we're living through it, we think it's just another time, with plenty more to come in the future. Only later do we realise that the last time has already been and gone.

The idea of attention as a resource can also lock us into a mindset of scarcity and not-enough-ness. When you're convinced that your attention is somehow insufficient for the life you lead, you inevitably feel like you're spinning too many plates. Instead, you could try thinking that *you already have all the attention you need.*[225] Then, instead of fretting about malign forces 'stealing' your attention, you can contemplate what you should really be attending to, and why.

As well as treating others as they would like to be treated, we can extend the same mindfulness to objects and ideas. How would the view prefer to be seen? How would the book like to be read? How would the record choose to be heard? 'Everything waits to be noticed,' as Art Garfunkel sang.[226] Will we respond?

The digital world may be new(ish), but the issues it raises have always been with us. In a letter to his friend Lollius Maximus, the

Roman poet Horace invites him to consider 'how you can get through your life in a peaceable, tranquil way'. Urging Lollius to rise above 'hope and fear about trivial things', he asks:

> Where does virtue come from; is it from books?
> Or is it a gift from Nature that cannot be learned?
> What is the way to become a friend to yourself?
> What brings tranquillity?
> What makes you carefree?[227]

Horace raises the ultimate question of our lives: *what do you want?* And our answer depends on where and how we direct our attention.

Going further, instead of thinking of attention as something we *have*, maybe we should reframe it as something we *do*. It's not a resource we own and allocate, but a process we follow: *attending* as opposed to attention. We should develop our attending skills so we can better attend to the world, other people and ourselves.

While attention is an abstract concept, attending is a mental and physical act. We attend with our minds, but also with our bodies and senses. For example, attending to the digital world might involve holding your phone, touching its screen, looking at text and video and listening to speech and music. To understand how your ways of attending affect you, notice how your body feels when you're online. Are you relaxed? Are you frowning or smiling? Are you holding your breath, tensing your shoulders, grinding your teeth? In Horace's words, is your experience bringing tranquillity and making you carefree? Or is it more like the opposite of that?

By reaching for our phones over and over again, we turn digital habits into physical ones. Once these routines are encoded into muscle memory, we follow them with almost no conscious effort. For example, when writing gets tough – as it always does – my reflex is to bolt to Twitter, where I can merrily dissipate the very energies that should be going into my work. I'm hardly aware of thinking, *now I will check Twitter*; it just seems to happen. As we repeat 'distraction routines' like this, we unwittingly train our attention to run on certain tracks, and leave others unexplored. By unthinkingly giving in to our short-term desires, we betray our long-term wants. To prevent that, we need to attend to what is going on for us, break into the routine and choose what we really want instead.

You don't have to throw your phone away or do a week-long 'digital detox'. You can just decide not to go online *for now*. 'For now' can be as long as you want, or as long as you can make it today.

Back in the day, I was a twenty-a-day smoker. Cigarettes were a reward for wins, a consolation for losses, an enhancement to the good times and a comfort during the bad – and a companion in solitude. Nowadays, instead of lighting up, I reach for my phone.

I eventually kicked the tobacco habit with a book that explained how grand gestures and determined resolutions don't work, because they merely accentuate the deprivation. Smoking will always be there, and ex-smokers will always have *some* desire to smoke; that fire can never be stubbed out. So instead of 'giving up', you have to keep making a conscious, positive choice for what you want *instead* of smoking, from moment to moment.[228]

Finally, while it's good to cultivate self-responsibility, it shouldn't curdle into self-blame. You are not wrong or broken just because you use your phone a lot, and your 'inattention' is not a disease that needs to be cured. It's just that you might want to make some different choices in certain situations. What's more, you don't have to become a hermit; you can still spend time in the digital world in the right measure, as long as you willingly choose it and genuinely enjoy it. When you're on your phone, be on your phone – but when you're on your own, be on your own.

NINE

# SOLITUDE STORIES

On solitary heroes and the times they spent alone.

**Major spoilers follow.**

# cast away

Robinson Crusoe is the original solitary hero. The character was based on several real-life shipwrecked sailors, and so vividly described by Daniel Defoe that many readers thought he was real – not least because the book credited Crusoe himself as the author:

> The Life and Strange Surprizing Adventures of Robinson Crusoe, of York, Mariner: Who lived Eight and Twenty Years, all alone in an un-inhabited Island on the Coast of America, near the Mouth of the Great River of Oroonoque; Having been cast on Shore by Shipwreck, wherein all the Men perished but himself. With An Account how he was at last as strangely deliver'd by Pyrates. Written by Himself.

We might expect someone who spends so long by themselves to lose their grip on sanity, but Crusoe proves surprisingly resilient and resourceful, building himself a shelter, cultivating crops and domesticating wild goats. He sees his island as a 'little Kingdom' and himself as the king – an attitude that prompted James Joyce to describe him as 'the true prototype of the British colonist'.[229]

Only rarely does Crusoe's loneliness show through, as when he witnesses a nearby shipwreck with no survivors:

> O that there had been but one or two, nay, or but one soul saved out of this ship… that I might but have had one companion, one fellow-creature, to have spoken to me and to have conversed with![230]

Most of the time, though, he maintains that he has been happier in his 'Solitary Condition' than in 'any other Particular state in the world'. That's partly because he's so industrious – a trait that reflected his creator's own commercial ambitions. He also has God for company, just as a solitary hermit would. However, a Protestant author like Defoe would have been loath to endorse Catholic monasticism, and just one year after *Crusoe* was published, he was penning a furious essay decrying solitude as 'a very mean thing' and a 'breach of Christian duties', putting himself firmly in line with mainstream opinion at the time.[231]

*Crusoe* gave rise to so many imitators that a new term was coined to describe them: Robinsonades. Many dealt with isolation, self-reflection, new beginnings, social commentary and encounters with local inhabitants of one sort or another. *The Swiss Family Robinson*, *Lord of the Flies* and *Lost in Space* are all examples.

In *Cast Away* (2000), Tom Hanks plays Chuck Noland, a Federal Express employee marooned for four years on a desert island when a delivery plane crashes in the Pacific. He keeps himself alive with several useful items recovered from parcels and makes an imaginary friend in Wilson, a volleyball on which he paints a rudimentary face. On returning to society, Noland finds that he has been declared dead, while his girlfriend has married and now has a child. These events leave him feeling more alone than he was on his island and, in the film's final shot, standing at a metaphorical crossroads.

Victor Sage's 1984 short story 'Crusoe' imagines a castaway who is just as physically resourceful as Defoe's, but far less mentally robust, leaving him susceptible to all manner of paranoid imaginings and flights of fancy. Finding a mysterious footprint on the beach (just as the original Crusoe does), he is pitched into a spiral of fantastical supposition:

> Perhaps it wasn't a footprint at all, but a piece of erosion. A minuscule version of the Grand Canyon. It just happened, by one of those coincidences of which nature is such a brimming repository, to look like a human foot. In fact, it was a configuration of the elements. The meeting point for hundreds of years of wind and sand...[232]

Sage's story considers one of the most exciting, yet scary questions raised by solitude: if your mind was truly free, with nothing and no-one to rein it in, where would it wander? If you ventured deep into your own imagination – deeper than everyday life could ever allow you to go – what would you find? And if no-one is there to witness your madness, are you truly insane, or just the undisputed ruler of a one-person universe?

J.G. Ballard coined the term 'inverted Crusoeism' to refer to those who, instead of becoming castaways against their will, gladly maroon *themselves*. For Ballard, becoming a castaway is not necessarily a torment, but a healing and empowering process through which people can discover deeper meaning.[233] Throughout history, islands have been seen as places of 'penance, purification, rebirth, pilgrimage and miraculous happenings' – like Prospero's 'bare island'[234] in *The Tempest*, where he learns magic to protect himself and control others.

For the Ballardian castaway, the island is a refuge from the forces of globalisation – a force that connects us, but also alienates us. It's a place far beyond society, where the normal order of civilisation can be suspended or overthrown. It even offers an escape from free will and the obligation to make decisions, since the 'rhythms of tides, wind, and storms decide what you will and will not do'.[235] On the island, natural time replaces human time; natural order supersedes human order. And the 'island' doesn't even have to be in the sea; in Ballard's *Concrete Island*, the hero is stranded in an urban interzone of derelict land delineated by intersecting motorways.[236]

Inverted Crusoes choose to be cast away because it gives them a chance to remake and rediscover themselves. Like the original Crusoe, they learn about their own inner strengths and resources. Unlike him, however, they don't try to change their 'islands', but allow themselves to be changed. The buried treasure they unearth is their own forgotten self.

# solitary journeys

Crusoe aside, solitude rarely gets a good press in books and films. It's often portrayed as a place where characters get stuck: a symptom of a problem they need to overcome, a trait they need to change or a situation from which they need to move on. Once they make the required change, they also leave their solitude behind; on the other hand, if they don't change, they remain alone.

Travis Bickle (Robert de Niro), the anti-hero of *Taxi Driver* (1976), lives alone as he grapples with a past trauma – military service in Vietnam – that we never see. Disgusted and infuriated by what he regards as the decadence of society, he goes through life like a powder keg ready to explode. He clumsily attempts to form relationships with those around him, but can only speak freely to his own reflection when he's alone in his apartment: 'You talkin' to me? Well, I don't see anybody else!'

A gentler Travis is Harry Dean Stanton's Travis Henderson in Wim Wenders' *Paris, Texas* (1984). After mysteriously disappearing for four years, he stumbles out of the Texan desert in a fugue state and starts trying to piece his scattered life back together. Staring mutely out of a back porch across the expanse of sand, Travis turns his solitude into a character in itself, bringing his protracted aloneness into the midst of a human drama.

As *Taxi Driver* vividly showed, a car interior can be an effective dramatic setting for a solo character, allowing them to travel through all sort of situations while still remaining apart and alone. In Steven Spielberg's *Duel* (1970), David Mann (Dennis Weaver) is driving through California when he finds himself terrorised, for no apparent reason, by an almost unseen truck driver relentlessly pursuing his car and using his vehicle as a weapon. The absence of dialogue makes David's plight even more compelling than if he was travelling with someone else.

In *Locke* (2017), Ivan Locke (Tom Hardy) is driving to see a colleague before she gives birth to his child following a one-night stand. In the course of one hectic night, Locke – the only character to appear on screen – makes a total of 36 phone calls to his wife, children and colleagues, juggling his chaotic personal life while remotely supervising the construction of a concrete foundation and nursing a heavy cold. As film critic David Thomson commented, 'No film I've seen in recent years is more eloquent on where we are now, and on how alone we feel.'[237]

Staying with the theme of transport, *The Station Agent* (2003) is a study of quiet, chosen solitude and how it can lead into friendship. Finbar (Peter Dinklage) keeps himself to himself partly because he wants to, and partly because of his short stature, which those around him often find curious or peculiar. A lover of railroads, he is delighted when he inherits an abandoned rural train depot, and happily moves out to the country to live there in solitude. However, he's soon befriended – largely against his will – by the talkative Joe, and ultimately finds love with Emily, a reclusive artist. Everyone in this film struggles with uncertain feelings that resist being put into words; as Elvis Mitchell of the *New York Times* observed, 'quiet… occupies the same space as a character'.[238]

*Lost in Translation* (2003) depicts two people combining their solitudes to form a brief connection. Charlotte (Scarlett Johansson) is a young woman accompanying her photographer husband on a work trip to Tokyo, while Bob Harris (Bill Murray) is a fading movie star in the midst of a mid-life crisis who has travelled to the city to shoot a lucrative whisky advert.

As its title suggests, the film deals with themes of dislocation and alienation. 'It's about things being disconnected and looking for moments of connection,' says director Sofia Coppola.[239] Both Bob and Charlotte contend with jet lag, the disorientation of being in an unfamiliar culture and the insulating effect of their high-rise hotel. Both feel distant from their respective partners, prompting them to reach out to connect with each other. However, *Lost in Translation* also shows that while romance grows from empathy and communication, there's a deep fascination in the sides of each other we *don't* understand: not the literal 'meaning' we express, but all the other things that resist translation from one person to another. We are always saying more than other people hear, and we are always missing a lot of what they say. But the extra meaning we express is not really 'lost'; rather, it remains our own.[240]

Other characters begin their stories in solitude and wind up pretty much where they started. Boo Radley, from Harper Lee's *To Kill a Mockingbird,* is so rarely seen outside his house that the local kids have spun a myth of a monster with pop-eyes, yellow teeth and bloodstained hands who 'dined on raw squirrels'. It's up to their neighbour, Miss Maudie, to gently point out that Boo is, in fact, a human being who just happens to prefer being alone:

> 'Arthur Radley just stays in the house, that's all... Wouldn't you stay in the house if you didn't want to come out?'

The children Scout and Jem become obsessed with Boo, attempting to understand him by 'trying on his skin', as Atticus Finch puts it. Towards the end of the novel, when Boo has saved the children from being murdered, he whispers his one and only line: 'Will you take me home?' In Boo's time, the most likely reason for his solitude – autism[241] – was even less understood than it is today. We can only hope he was happy on his own.

Few characters make the journey from company to solitude, ultimately finding fulfilment on their own. One exception is Robert Munsch's *The Paper Bag Princess,* which turns the damsel-in-distress trope on its head. Princess Elizabeth is all set to marry Prince Ronald when a dragon incinerates her castle and carries him off. Wearing a paper bag (since her clothes have all been burnt), she travels to the dragon's cave and rescues Ronald. However, he ungratefully mocks her dirty hair and paper-bag-no-shoes look, so she decides not to marry him after all.

In George Orwell's *Nineteen Eighty-four*, sociability has become a tool of oppression, while solitude is effectively criminalised:

> In principle a Party member had no spare time, and was never alone except in bed. It was assumed that when he was not working, eating, or sleeping he would be taking part in some kind of communal recreations; to do anything that suggested a taste for solitude, even to go for a walk by yourself, was always slightly dangerous.[242]

The heart of the novel is Winston Smith's affair with Julia, but just as important is his relationship with the room he rents above Mr Charrington's shop. Here he can snatch some moments of solitude away from the unblinking gaze of the telescreen (a two-way television that allows broadcasters to observe the audience). His later 'solitary' confinement in the Ministry of Love is monitored by a telescreen around the clock. (Having done my anti-tech rant in the previous chapter, I'll leave you to draw the smartphone analogies.)

The description 'Orwellian' usually denotes mass surveillance, truth-bending propaganda and the policing of words and thoughts. But for me, the thought of twenty-four-seven company is even more chilling. Which is worse: a lonely exile on your own, or a world where you can never be alone when you want to? Orwell, an introvert himself, clearly felt it was the latter.

Horace Fyfe's 1952 sci-fi short 'Manners of an Age', written three years after Orwell's novel, imagines a future scenario that is almost the exact opposite. Most of humanity has deserted the Earth for other planets, leaving a few holdouts living alone in luxurious dwellings spread many miles apart, where they're tended to by obsequious robots.

> 'Much better than things were in the old days,' he told himself as he crossed the lawn to his sprawling white mansion. 'Must have been awful before the population declined. Imagine having people all around you, having to listen to them, see them, and argue to make them do what you wanted!'[243]

Imagine indeed. Fyfe correctly anticipated that technology would atomise society and make us lazy, self-regarding and spoilt, and accurately envisaged video calling too. However, not all of his predictions were so prescient. While the hero's robots can handle all his household chores, they're also despatched to find him information from the 'automatic scanners of the city library'. Living in the future as we do, we actually find ourselves drowning in information delivered right to our armchairs, yet *still* cleaning the bathroom by hand. Fix your priorities, scientists!

## scary solitudes

Solitude is rarely a good sign in horror. Leaving your friends to check out that weird noise in the basement? The cellar door will soon be slamming behind you, and the light will go out too. Conducting scientific research at a remote outpost in Antarctica? Something will be scratching at the door soon after sundown. Exploring a spooky house as a group? You'll soon be splitting up for no discernible reason, then getting picked off one by one. And if you're looking at your reflection in a bathroom cabinet, pushing its door closed is almost certain to reveal a villain standing just behind.

What if you weren't just alone for a while, but the last person left on earth? In *I Am Legend* (2007), Will Smith plays virologist Robert Neville, the only human immune to a man-made virus that was originally created to cure cancer but ends up turning everyone into crazed mutants. He withstands his solitary torment by talking to his dog, Sam, and some mannequins from a shop window. The original novel by Richard Matheson, published in 1954, was the source text for pretty much every 'zombie apocalypse' tale that came after.

One of the most striking examples was *28 Days Later* (2002), where Jim (Cillian Murphy) wakes from a coma to find himself naked in a deserted hospital with a head wound, an impressive beard and no memories of the previous twenty-eight days. Venturing out, he finds himself in an eerily deserted London, where he's soon being pursued by zombies who do not shamble, as is traditional, but sprint.

People being *completely* alone rarely makes for compelling cinema; there's only so much plot you can get out of a single character. But the fiction writer can place you right inside a character's head, so you feel the full weight of their isolation. In 'The Pit and the Pendulum', Edgar Allan Poe's nameless narrator is flung into a pitch-dark cell by Spanish inquisitors, where he has to contend with – and choose between – a range of horrific and surprisingly elaborate torments, from a bottomless pit to a slowly descending pendulum fitted with a lethal blade. Every word of Poe's story is focused on ratcheting up the terror and suspense, until it's abruptly resolved in a happy ending that's fairly implausible, yet still gratefully received by the harrowed reader.

Stephen King's short story 'Survivor Type' gives the Crusoe formula a grisly twist by imagining a disgraced surgeon who's improbably marooned on an island with surgical tools, a stash of heroin and practically nothing to eat.[244] When he breaks his ankle signalling to an aeroplane, he has to amputate his foot – and then realises that his only hope of survival is to eat it. Thereafter, the story pursues the disturbing question of how long a person could survive by literally eating themselves. The idea was so grossly compelling that King could think of nothing else for days – nor sell the finished story to a magazine for several years. Even he admitted that it 'goes a little bit too far, even for me'.[245]

King continued with the unsettling foot amputations in his 1987 novel *Misery*. Novelist Paul Sheldrake is held in solitary confinement by a deranged fan, Annie Wilkes, who forces him to write works featuring his fictional heroine Misery Chastain. When Paul tries to escape, Annie hacks off his foot with an axe. King admitted that Annie symbolised both his restrictive typecasting as a horror writer and his dependence on cocaine.[246] So rather than a claustrophobic two-hander, *Misery* was a solitary self-portrait of someone who was fed up of being with himself.

*Let the Right One In* (2008) is a brooding horror film where everyone seems to be alone. Lonely, bullied teenager Oskar spends his time collecting newspaper clippings about murders and hanging around the park. There he meets the pale and enigmatic Eli, who says she's 'twelve, more or less'. Things take a macabre turn when a loner – a crazy cat *man*, in a twist on the formula – witnesses a bloody assault. Oskar is left wondering why Eli seems to have no parents or carers, and never comes out by day. And what does she mean when she insists that she's 'not a girl'?

## looking for space

> To sail on a dream in the sun-fretted darkness
> To soar through the starlight, unfrightened, alone…
>
> DIANE DUANE (AFTER JOHN DENVER)[247]

In space, no-one can hear you scream.[248] But on the upside, they can't interrupt your reading to ask you whether you think they should take an umbrella. On balance, space seems like the perfect place to be alone.

Intense space battles, photon torpedoes and green-skinned aliens certainly have their place. But there's also room for quiet, contemplative deep-space stories, like Stanley Kubrick's *2001: A Space Odyssey* (1968), where gracefully rotating spacecraft take centre-stage in place of dialogue, and Dave Bowman (Keir Dullea) takes what can only be described as a space trip. In Duncan Jones' *Moon* (2009), Sam Bell (Sam Rockwell) spends three years alone on a lunar mining station, finding himself in more ways than one, while Ridley Scott's *The Martian* (2015) shows Dr Mark Watney (Matt Damon) keeping himself alive for 543 Mars-days as he awaits rescue, musing 'I'm the first person to be alone on an entire planet'.[249] And in John Carpenter's parody *Dark Star* (1974) Talby (Andreijah Pahich) spends every spare hour alone in an observation dome atop the spaceship *Dark Star*, gazing out at the inky depths like a serene spaceborne stoner:

> Doolittle: Must get lonely being up here so much…
>
> Talby: I can watch things up here, Doolittle. I love to watch things, just stare at the planets and meteors and asteroids…[250]

Even in big-budget epics like *Star Wars*, people find space to be alone. Boba Fett, 'the most notorious and dreaded bounty hunter in the galaxy',[251] tracks his prey alone in his spaceship *Slave I*. It must have been this compact, one-seater craft that I had in mind when I drifted off to sleep, aged nine, by picturing myself wandering through the stars alone. (*Slave I* is 'elephant-head-shaped', but my own imaginary ship resembled a crab, in honour of my star sign.)

Former Jedi Obi-Wan Kenobi lives like a proper hermit in the deserts of Tatooine, from where he can watch over Luke Skywalker. Luke himself, meanwhile, becomes more and more solitary as the series of films unfolds. Beginning life as a farm boy working for his uncle, he leaves home to battle the Empire before making a lone pilgrimage to the swamps of Dagobah to learn the ways of the Force from Yoda (who lives there alone, standing guard against some ancient evil).[252]

Tormented by his own perceived failure, Luke later goes full hermit when he travels to Ahch-To, 'the most unfindable world in the galaxy', to make his home on a rocky outcrop amid an endless sea. Clearly, this is a guy who *really* needs his space. But in a way, it's the only natural endpoint for a character who always seemed different from everyone around him, and who meets his final challenge with a *tour de force* of together-yet-apartness.

Luke's arc is echoed by that of Rey (Daisy Ridley), who first appears as an orphan and seems to become even more alone as she walks the path to becoming the last Jedi – despite her friendship with former stormtrooper Finn (John Boyega) and twisted romance with Kylo Ren (Adam Driver).

The more affable Han Solo was part of a double act (a Han duo, perhaps) with Chewbacca. But his surname, as well as his character, still mark him out as a gun-toting cowboy-renegade who's out on his own and out for himself. The most solitary character in *Star Wars*, though, must be Darth Vader. Having forsaken friends and family, and inspiring only fear in his comrades, his only real confidant is his Sith counterpart, the evil Emperor. One of the most chilling shots in *The Empire Strikes Back* (1980) is Admiral Piett's brief glimpse of Vader's bare, lacerated head as he sits in his *Qabbrat*, or meditation chamber – a sort of spherical, jet-black isolation tank. Since this was the only place where he could survive without his suit, the chamber was solitude made manifest: a place where Vader could, quite literally, be 'just himself'.

# into the labyrinth

> Solitude – the very condition of our lives – appears to us as a test and a purgation, at the conclusion of which our anguish and instability will vanish. At the exit from the labyrinth of solitude we will find reunion (which is repose and happiness), and plenitude, and harmony with the world.
>
> OCTAVIO PAZ[253]

Do kids still solve mazes in puzzle books? I feel like I spent half my childhood pushing my pencil point through printed passageways – pausing thoughtfully at each junction, running into dead ends, retracing my 'steps' and finally finding the exit.

Since only one person could really draw that path, puzzle mazes were an inherently solo activity. It wasn't like a crossword, where you could call on someone else and divide the mental labour. You were in there on your own. And if you closed the book and gave up, you had a strange feeling of leaving yourself behind, stranded for ever at the point your pencil left the page.

Solving a maze for fun is one thing; spending your whole life in one is quite another. The original maze-dweller was the Minotaur of Greek mythology: a creature with the head and tail of a bull and the body of a man, born to King Minos' wife Pasiphaë. He was imprisoned in the Labyrinth of Crete, where he sustained himself by eating the fourteen unlucky Athenian teenagers who were sent in every seven years. This grisly meal plan was brought to an abrupt end when the Minotaur was slain by Theseus, who then found his way back out of the labyrinth with the thread given to him by Minos' daughter Ariadne.

Like so many mythical monsters, the Minotaur doesn't get a lot of dialogue, so we can only speculate how he felt about all this.

Argentinian writer Jorge Luis Borges put that right by reimagining the tale from the viewpoint of the Minotaur himself, in his gemlike short story 'The House of Asterion'. In Borges' telling, the Minotaur is perfectly free to leave his palace (as he calls it) – just as others are free to visit:

> It is true that I never leave my house, but it is also true that its doors (whose numbers are infinite) are open day and night to men and to animals as well. Anyone may enter. He will find here no female pomp nor gallant court formality, but he will find quiet and solitude. And he will find a house like no other on the face of the earth.[254]

Borges portrays a figure who is proud and haughty – as befits the son of a queen – yet also playful, running through the passageways as he eagerly awaits his 'redeemer'. Since this turns out to be Theseus, he may have been happier in his solitude after all.

## solitary survivors

> I am the sea, and nobody owns me.
>
> Pippi Longstocking[255]

Few children's characters are quite as unconventional as Astrid Lindgren's Pippi Longstocking – or, to give her full English name, Pippilotta Delicatessa Windowshade Mackrelmint Efraimsdotter Longstocking. She has bright red pigtails, a freckled nose 'the shape of a very small potato', a blue dress patched with red, shoes 'twice as long as her feet' and a pet monkey named Mr Nilsson.

What makes Pippi most radical, though, is her fierce independence. Having spent the first nine years of her life at sea and then lost both her parents, she now supports herself with a suitcase of gold coins and lives alone in Villekulla Cottage, which stands in an overgrown Swedish orchard:

> She had neither mother nor father, which was really rather nice, for in this way there was no one to tell her to go to bed just when she was having the most fun, and no one to make her take cod-liver-oil when she felt like eating peppermints.[256]

What's more, she's strong enough to lift a whole horse above her head if she wants to – 'and there were times when she did want to'. She even challenges a circus strongman to a wrestle, and beats him:

> 'But you could *never* do it,' said Annika. 'Why, that's the strongest man in the world!'
> 'Man, yes,' said Pippi. 'But I'm the strongest *girl* in the world, don't forget.'[257]

The inevitable description for Pippi is *feisty*. She's bold, she's adventurous and she doesn't particularly care what anyone thinks. However, she's also something of a compulsive liar, fairly destructive and arguably an attention-seeking *schlemiel* – always messing up, then apologising.[258]

Maybe we should cut Pippi some slack, particularly when we consider the past life of her creator. Astrid Lindgren became pregnant at 17 from an affair with her 50-year-old boss, but he offered her no help – and neither did her mother. Left alone to endure a traumatic pregnancy, then forced to abandon her baby son, she had no choice but to make it on her own.

Happily reunited with her son a few years later, Lindgren began telling him a tale of children who were sent away by grownups and 'went to a new land to live all on their own'. Behind her outlandishness, 'Pippi Longstocking *is* Astrid Lindgren. She is Astrid's child self.'[259] Pippi's radical solitude and superhuman strength reflect the inner fortitude and self-reliance that her creator had to find so she could survive and tell Pippi's own story.

When Pippi grew up, what would she be like? Stieg Larsson's answer was Lisbeth Salander, the main character in the Millennium series of novels that begins with *The Girl with the Dragon Tattoo*.[260] (The door to Lisbeth's flat bears the alias 'V. Kulla', an allusion to Pippi's home Villekulla.) A survivor of childhood trauma, Lisbeth is a gifted computer hacker who uses her skills to resolve a series of crimes and conspiracies, dishing out some satisfying retribution to male abusers and misogynists along the way. She's also fiercely protective of her solitude:

> Normally seven minutes of another person's company was enough to give her a headache, so she set things up to live as a recluse. She was perfectly content as long as people left her in peace.[261]

In Greek mythology, Circe was a minor goddess born to Helios, the sun god, and the nymph Perse. Circe used her formidable knowledge of plants and herbs to become a sorceress, with the power to transform enemies into animals (usually pigs).

In Madeline Miller's fictionalised account of Circe's story, she is exiled to the island of Aeaea as punishment for turning the beautiful nymph Scylla into a monster. Arriving there, she settles into a homely, bucolic existence that's very different from the pampering she was accustomed to at the palace of Helios, as well as a solitude she finds both unfamiliar and unsettling:

> But no, that was part of my exile. To be utterly alone. What worse punishment could there be, my family thought, than to be deprived of their divine presence?[262]

For the Greek gods, punishment usually entailed some sort of solitude. Prometheus was chained to a rock on a mountain for ever, his only companion an eagle tearing at his liver; on the whole, he probably would have preferred to be on his own. Sisyphus, meanwhile, was condemned by Zeus to roll a boulder up a hill in the underworld over and over again for eternity – utterly alone. Some have interpreted the myth as a metaphor for a life made meaningless by repetitive drudgery, but Albert Camus saw Sisyphus as a hero of the absurd, who finds a sort of comfort in his battle against a meaningless universe. 'The struggle itself toward the heights is enough to fill a man's heart,' he says. 'One must imagine Sisyphus happy.'[263]

Over time, Circe's punishment becomes a pleasure too. She grows to love both her solitude and the many opportunities for self-discovery it opens up. With no gods looking over her shoulder, deriding her for living like a mortal, she discovers the joys of a self-sufficient life on the island, free of oversight or judgement:

> At night I went home to my house. I did not mind its shadows anymore, for they meant my father's gaze was gone from the sky and the hours were my own. I did not mind the emptiness either. For a thousand years I had tried to fill the gap between myself and my family; filling the rooms of my house was easy by comparison.

Soon, she's developing her abilities in the magic of transformation, which she uses for self-protection – and revenge.

Charlotte Brontë's Jane Eyre is another solitary survivor. 'I am no bird; and no net ensnares me,' she says. 'I am a free human being with an independent will.'[264] Moreover, she has no fear of solitude, but thrives on it, and certainly prefers the good company of herself to the poor company of others:

> I can live alone, if self-respect and circumstances require me so to do. I need not sell my soul to buy bliss. I have an inward treasure born with me, which can keep me alive if all extraneous delights should be withheld, or offered only at a price I cannot afford to give.

Throughout the novel, Jane struggles to form emotional bonds, but only because she refuses to compromise. Although she ultimately marries, choosing an emotional home with Edward Rochester rather than with herself, she does so on her own terms, on an equal footing with her husband and with a clear conscience.

Brontë's triumph is to use first-person narrative to put us right inside Jane's private thoughts, where she weighs up her difficulties and dilemmas. Even when Jane is alone, we're there with her, listening in on her thoughts. Radical for its time, this writing technique earned Brontë the distinction of 'first historian of the private consciousness'.[265]

Not every character comes out of solitude so well. The counterpart to Jane's happy ending is the mentally disturbed Mrs Rochester, who is locked away on the third floor of Edward's house until her dramatic suicide near the end of the story. In their book *The Madwoman in the Attic*, named for Mrs Rochester, Sandra Gilbert and Susan Gubar explain how (predominantly male) writers of Brontë's era wrote women who were either perfect angels or rebellious devils, with nothing in between.

Even today, there are still plenty of female characters who live at the meeting point of solitude, madness and witchcraft. In *The Simpsons*, there is Crazy Cat Lady (real name Eleanor Abernathy), who lives in a dilapidated house outside Springfield and screams gibberish – or flings cats – at anyone who comes near. She once studied both medicine and law, but succumbed to burnout and alcoholism; if there's a moral in there, it's a dubious one.

*Donnie Darko* (2001) presented a deeper take on the same theme with Roberta Sparrow, known to local kids as 'Grandma Death', a wild-haired recluse who shuffles out to check her empty mailbox several times a day. As we discover, she's actually the author of a book called *The Philosophy of Time Travel*, and it's strongly implied that she's a time traveller, just like Donnie himself.

Time travel, as a plot device, allows writers to create characters who are solitary twice over: separated from their loved ones in time, and isolated by the fact that nobody believes where they're from. Aptly titled time-travel chiller *Dark* (2017) flings its ensemble of characters back and forth across the decades, twisting the story into a contorted pretzel of causation where everybody is someone else's parent and/or murderer. Splitting single characters into differently aged versions of themselves leads to some head-spinning moments of high drama, as when callow youngster Jonas confronts the wizened Adam, the mastermind of all these temporal tribulations. 'Don't you see it already?' asks Adam, pityingly. 'I am you!'[266]

## just an illusion

> Have you ever had a dream, Neo, that you were so sure was real? What if you were unable to wake from that dream? How would you know the difference between the dream world and the real world?
>
> 'MORPHEUS' IN *THE MATRIX* (1999)[267]

What if the entire world was an illusion, and only you knew? You would be more alone in the phantasmagorical crowd than you could ever be on your own. In fact, solitude would be your only escape; the only real experience left.

In Robert A. Heinlein's story 'They', the hero is convinced that he is one of the few 'real' entities in existence, while his fellow real beings are conspiring to manipulate earthly reality to deceive him:

> He came wearily back to his original point: Since the world could not be as crazy as it appeared to be, it might necessarily have been arranged to appear crazy in order to deceive him as to the truth. Why had they done it to him? And what was the truth behind the sham?[268]

At this point, we wonder whether we might be reading an account of mental illness, but then comes the kicker: *the hero is absolutely right*. Although he can never prove it, he is indeed the subject of an elaborate deception maintained by the all-powerful Glaroon and his subordinates:

> 'It is necessary to adjourn this sequence. I am no longer able to influence his decision.'
>
> They had expected it, nevertheless they stirred with dismay.
>
> The Glaroon addressed the First for Manipulation.
>
> 'Prepare to graft the selected memory track at once.'

Makes you think, doesn't it? Perhaps *you* are the only conscious being in the cosmos, and everything and everyone around you has been intelligently crafted to perpetuate an illusion of 'reality' – right down to this book, with its carefully judged description of the very situation you are in, and this self-referential comment as the final cruel taunt.

*The Truman Show* (1998) takes the same premise and updates it for the age of reality TV. Truman Burbank (Jim Carrey) is the unwitting star of a long-running TV show devised by the cynical

Christof (Ed Harris). Seahaven Island, where Truman has lived his entire life, is nothing more than an elaborate set populated by actors where hidden cameras observe his every word and action and beam them around the world to millions of avid fans.

As the movie unfolds, Truman gradually twigs what is going on, ultimately battling through the obstacles placed in his way to open a door to the outside world. Whatever awaits him may be less forgiving – but at least he'll have chosen it himself.

> He feels trapped into a familial and social world to which he tries to conform while being unable to entirely identify with it… Eventually, Truman gains sufficient awareness of his condition to 'leave home'—developing a more mature and authentic identity as an adult, leaving his child-self behind and becoming a *True*-man.[269]

The concept of the film is so compelling that some people develop the delusion – known as Truman Syndrome – that they really are living in reality shows, or are being constantly observed.

*The Matrix*, released the following year, goes one better by considering what happens after the hero breaks out of their cage. Finding his regular life as Thomas Anderson unfulfilling, computer hacker Neo (Keanu Reeves) sits at home night after night, searching online for the mysterious Morpheus, who eventually reveals to Neo that his entire life has been lived inside a simulation.

Like *Truman*, *The Matrix* has a powerful appeal for those who feel alone, alienated or misunderstood, or are tormented by a nagging sense – 'like a splinter in your mind', as Morpheus puts it – that the world around them is somehow *not quite right*.

Neo and his comrades refuse to live in a world of conformity. They need to find, or build, a reality where they can choose not only how to be, but *who* to be (hence their self-chosen aliases). No wonder the story has been interpreted as an analogy for emergence and transformation of pretty much every kind, from turning Republican to coming out as transgender.

In *Groundhog Day* (1993), Phil Connors (Bill Murray) is alone in both a place *and* a time. He's condemned by some unknown power to relive a single day of his life over and over again – and to be the only one aware of what's happening. Release is only granted once he learns to see the good in the humdrum town of Punxsutawney and the people around him. *Russian Doll* (2019) gives the same idea a bleak twist: Nadia Vulvokov (Natasha Lyonne) must repeatedly relive (or rather, re-die) the night of her own death until she finds the one other person in the same situation.

In video games, dying – or 'losing a life' – is merely a temporary setback, an occupational hazard and a chance to learn. Modern action-adventure games cast the player as an all-powerful, immortal demigod in a world of pliant half-beings who are only there to be killed, reveal information or yield resources. *Free Guy* (2021) explores a scenario when one of these non-player characters (NPCs) starts thinking for themselves. Guy (Ryan Reynolds) soon throws off his regulation outfit ('blue shirt guy' no more!) and starts buffing his stats to the level of a human player. He also does his best to enlighten his fellow NPCs to their plight, since no-one is lonelier than the one-eyed man in the kingdom of the blind. But while Truman found an exit door off Seahaven Island, Guy bumps up against an invisible wall on the shoreline of Free City; he's too human to live in a game-world, but too digital to cross over into ours.

Guy learns to see reality by putting on sunglasses, which are only worn by human players and reveal the hidden mechanics of the game-world. This echoes *They Live* (1988), when Roddy Piper's unnamed protagonist discovers a pair of sunglasses that reveal skull-faced aliens walking unnoticed among the human race, and the subliminal messages they're pumping out to keep us all in line. Like Guy, he struggles to convince his friend to just *put on the glasses* and

see what is staring him in the face – an argument that degenerates into a ridiculously protracted street brawl. But if you've ever tried to convince a doubter of your own worldview, you know exactly how that feels: there are none so blind as those who will not see.

## inside man

> We all know that art is not truth. Art is a lie that makes us realise truth – at least, the truth that is given us to understand. The artist must know how to convince others of the truthfulness of his lies.
>
> Pablo Picasso[270]

It's strange now to recall the height of the pandemic. Lockdown was so disorienting at the time, yet the memory of it is melting way like a dream. That time was so utterly different from normality that it's hard to know where in your mental filing cabinet to place it.

The art borne from lockdown, however, remains vivid and sharp. Confined to their homes, creative people made isolation the mother of invention. And one of the most inventive works was *Bo Burnham: Inside* (2021), a TV special in which the American comedian performs songs and sketches, all alone, in a single room.

The critical reaction to *Inside* was ecstatic. Pretty much everyone agreed that Burnham had captured the unique flavour of networked solitude during lockdown – isolated at home, yet hyper-online all the while. As in all his comedy, Burnham missed no opportunity to get metatextual or self-referential – like the reaction vid about a reaction vid about one of his own songs, or the Twitch livestream of himself crying. The plaintive acoustic ditty 'That Funny Feeling' eloquently captured how the internet reduces everything to mere content by presenting the trivial and the overwhelming side by side.

What really made *Inside*, though, was its emotional weight. The tone ranged from mischievous and manic through to ominous and then on to tormented, as Burnham mined his isolation for both laughs and tears. Even before lockdown, he'd been suffering from anxiety, and had not performed live for five years due to stage-fright – but *Inside* presents an even steeper decline. As the film progresses, the material becomes gradually darker and more unsettling, while Burnham himself becomes progressively shaggier and more Crusoe-like as his isolation deepens. Reaching the nadir, he sobs 'I'm… not OK' to a dark and silent room, his face in shadow. Seeing moments like that, many viewers felt genuine concern for his mental health, and some felt inspired to seek help for their own problems too.

After a while, though, sceptical voices began to question exactly what they were watching. They pointed out that Burnham did not, in fact, live alone in a single room eating nothing but cereal. He lived with his film-director girlfriend and dog in a beautiful house, of which the room seen in *Inside* was just one part.

So did *Inside* really document Burnham's lived experience of lockdown, or was he playing a version of himself, 'inspired by real events'? And, if *Inside* was partly fictionalised, should Burnham really be play-acting at isolation when people out there were genuinely confined in spaces a lot smaller and grimmer than his gadget-stuffed man-cave – often with people they were desperate to escape?[271]

The reaction from most of Burnham's fans to these revelations was pretty much a shrug – and in the grand scheme of things, a comedian pretending to live alone is not that big a deal. Particularly when that little lie enabled him to tell a big truth.

The measure of a poet of solitude isn't how many 'proper' hours of alone-time they've managed to rack up, but whether they can say something resonant about the experience. And Burnham's room, whatever it was in reality, was a true representation of our minds on lockdown. Even for those of us who weren't metatextual millennials, his obsessive self-analysis, bordering on self-annihilation, captured the feeling of tumbling down a mental rabbit-hole – going 'inside' in every sense. It was a message from his solitude to our own. And even if it wasn't strictly true, it still *rang* true; it had the feeling of truth. Even if the situations were artificial, the emotions were real.

## maverick cops

Every police force, it seems, has one. The renegade who breaks the rules but gets results. The gifted detective who can read a murder suspect like a book, but is blind to their own faults. The single-minded obsessive whose only lasting relationship is with 'the job'. In other words, the maverick cop.

Harry Callahan, played by Clint Eastwood in *Dirty Harry* (1971) and four sequels, was the template for many mavericks who came after. Scornful of police procedure, Harry regularly strays into violence and intimidation to apprehend villains. Technically, he works with a partner – but over the course of the films, most of them end up getting shot or leaving the force, leaving Harry out on his own once more. Sullen and unshaven, he clashes with his superiors over every case and is constantly being reprimanded, suspended and demoted – yet somehow never fired. He lives alone, ignores his neighbours and seems to subsist on coffee and junk food, though that doesn't stop him from maintaining peak physical condition and enviable combat skills.

Like many Eastwood characters, Harry is a man out of place and time, caught between society's values and his own. He's a rugged frontiersman teleported into twentieth-century society. Back in the Old West, he could have blown away those varmints in a high-noon shoot-out – but that won't fly on the streets of San Francisco.[272]

Harry's closest relationship is with the killer Scorpio – his alter ego, his mirror image and the only adversary worthy of his grudging respect. A similar dynamic plays out in Michael Mann's *Heat* (1991) between detective Vincent Hanna (Al Pacino) and his prey, arch-criminal Neil McCauley (Robert de Niro). Hanna is on his third marriage, as a result of working round the clock to 'take down crews'. When the two come face-to-face over coffee, McCauley shares his personal creed: 'Don't let yourself get attached to anything you are not willing to walk out on in thirty seconds flat.' Nevertheless, he describes himself as 'alone, but not lonely'. Both men are isolated by having no equal apart from each other, and the film ends with them clasping hands on an isolated airstrip as McCauley, shot by Hanna in pursuit, slowly slips away.

Sarah Lund, played by Sofie Gråbøl in the Danish TV series *The Killing* (*Forbrydelsen*) (2011), brought a new depth and complexity to the trope of the maverick cop. With her scraped-back hair, watchful gaze and grave demeanour, Lund moves through the drama like some animal predator, homing in on what she needs to know and brusquely dismissing the misapprehensions of her colleagues. Although a skilled interrogator and perceptive psychologist, she often fails to pick up social cues, and has a perennially awkward relationship with her grown-up son Max; some viewers concluded that she must be on the autistic spectrum.[273] 'She has a strong connection to what feels right,' Gråbøl notes, 'Yet there was something very lonely about her.'

> Lund isn't married to the job, because that would imply that they are separate. She *is* her job, and she must follow her case even as it costs her everything… She can spot the tiniest detail, read the most impenetrable crime scene, pick the truth from the lies in an interview room. Yet she can also nearly kill her father-in-law because she simply doesn't hear that he is allergic to nuts when she's been told to bring a cake.
>
> NATALIE HAYNES[274]

The surname 'Lund' means 'grove', and Lund the person is so still, so centred, that she seems to be almost a place in her own right: a world within the world into which she herself has retreated. At the same time, her sketchy domestic habits (a dinner of a single fried egg, eaten standing up in the kitchen) and frumpy dress sense (that legendary black-and-white Faroe sweater) made her profoundly relatable. For many, Lund was the ultimate comfort watch during lockdown: a best friend who you knew was unbearable, yet couldn't take your eyes off and never wanted to leave.[275]

## lone rangers

The High Plains at sunset. As a gentle breeze ruffles the prairie grass, a lone rider slowly mounts the ridge, then pauses, standing motionless, a black silhouette against the burning sky. A stranger just drifted into town – and that spells trouble for the outlaws who've been terrorising the townsfolk and humiliating the hapless sheriff.

Thus began many a classic Western. It seemed that practically all the great heroes of the Old West were on their own – or rather, 'lone'. The clues were right there in the titles: *The Lone Ranger, Lone Gun, Lone Rider, Lone Star.*

The Old West, as mythologised in the movies, was a time for the individual. A man couldn't rely on the law, or even his fellows, so he had to rely on himself – and his trusty six-shooter. For a certain kind of man, going it alone was the only way to survive.

But what made the lone Western hero so alluring was the mystery behind his solitude. Where has he come from, and where – if anywhere – is he headed? Has he committed some terrible crime that condemned him to a life on the run? Somewhere back there down the road, did he say goodbye to a home, a job, a family? Is he answering a call for help or seeking riches for himself?

More to the point, does the lone rider even *want* to be part of society, or is he happy outside it? Does he actively choose his solitude because he enjoys it, or is it simply a destiny that he can't control? Is he seeking spiritual truth, or merely drifting?

Good luck finding out, because lone riders ain't big on talkin'. They're strong and silent: men of few words who let their actions speak. They play into a classic masculine fantasy: awesome skill and strength, allied with impeccable honour and profound modesty. Like Preacher, Clint Eastwood's enigmatic character in *Pale Rider* (1985), the lone rider is a peerless marksman and lightning-quick on the draw – yet, with noble forbearance, he uses his abilities only reluctantly, and always in the cause of good.

In *Shane* (1953), Alan Ladd's hero rides into town, rights a few wrongs, and ultimately rides off again, a mystery to the last. Lacking an obvious motive or even a moral code, the only reason he can give is his own immutable nature. 'A man has to be what he is, Joey,' he drawls. 'Can't break the mold. I tried it and it didn't work for me.'[276]

For an introvert, it's the ultimate fantasy: doing what needs to be done, on your terms, without the need to explain, answer questions or even hold a conversation that lasts longer than ten seconds, while still commanding total respect. The lone rider needs nothing and nobody – sometimes, not even a name. He has taken both self-acceptance and self-isolation to truly heroic heights.

# running up that hill

> Work hard in silence; let your success be your noise.
>
> FRANK OCEAN

At the start of *Stranger Things 4*, Max Mayfield (Sadie Sink) is in a lonely place. Understandably distressed by the gruesome death of her brother Billy, she spends most of her time on her own, sullen and withdrawn, lost in music.

Like other young adults from Hawkins who are struggling with past traumas, Max soon finds herself targeted by the demonic Vecna, who tries to imprison her in the Upside Down, a hellish mirror-image of the real world. But it turns out that Vecna has one weakness. When Max's friends back in the real world play the music she loves most, it illuminates her past memories, opening up a portal that she can run back through and rejoin them.

Max's favourite song, and the soundtrack to that scene, is Kate Bush's mesmeric 1985 single 'Running Up That Hill'. The track struck such a chord with viewers in 2022 that it ascended to the UK number-one spot, 37 years after its release.

It was a fitting way to crown a career that has been solo in every sense. From the very beginning, Bush has insisted on making the music she wants to make, resulting in a body of work that is truly unique. She writes all her own songs – which was much rarer in the 1970s, when she emerged, than it is today – and was the first UK female artist to reach number one with a self-penned song, 'Wuthering Heights'. Since 1982, she's produced her own records, and has even bought back the rights to her recordings, making her the sole owner of her work (and bringing her an estimated $200,000 a week from the newfound success of 'Running Up That Hill').[277]

However, Bush has achieved all this in her own way – and that way is decidedly introvert. You'll search in vain for her personal profile on social media. She grants interviews at intervals of years rather than weeks. In her songs, she often draws inspiration from films, books and history rather than the events of her own life, speaking to a deep need for privacy. However, that doesn't make her a recluse or a shrinking violet; it's just the way she likes things.

> I go out of my way to be a very normal person, and I just find it frustrating that people think that I'm some kind of weirdo reclusive that never comes out into the world.[278]

Thanks to her guarded approach, misunderstandings about Bush's personality, her art and her life have flourished. But there's no real mystery. Like many creative introverts, she simply wants her work to speak on her behalf:

> People have a lot of conceptions about my image, which is something quite different from what I am… I really like the idea of my work speaking for me, not *me* speaking for me. I think my work says a lot more interesting stuff than I ever could; it's more eloquent. And that's what I feel I have to offer the world.[279]

Although Bush was delighted that *Stranger Things* brought 'Running Up That Hill' to a new audience, she insisted on knowing the context before she allowed it to be used.[280] And when you watch it, you can see why she agreed. It's one of those rare moments when a cultural work briefly transcends its own boundaries.

One way to read Max's flight from Vecna is as an entreaty not to let solitude overwhelm you, or to hang on to your friends, or just to stay with us. It's also a metaphor for how it feels sometimes to be a teenager, when everything looks black, most other people are distant or perplexing and only music makes any sort of sense. And it's a testament to the power of music itself: so fresh and luminous when you're growing up, but still bright decades later, when you're enjoying knowingly retro culture like *Stranger Things* with your kids. Songs of the past, made weirdly ever-present by the internet, reach across the years to say *yes, we felt that way too.*

However, 'Running Up That Hill' is more than period colour or a dramatic soundtrack. The song's lyric is about longing for a 'deal with God' to 'swap our places' – to see through someone else's eyes, and let them see through ours. If only that were possible, wires would be uncrossed and misunderstandings would disperse.

Max needs to 'swap places' because she's shutting out those who love her most – and so do her friends, so they can appreciate what she's going through. But she's not the only one; *Stranger Things 4* is full of secrets, misunderstandings and hidden knowledge. Everybody has things they can't see, or need to learn, but they're bogged down in the valley of not knowing instead.

I'm not sure what I made of the lyric of 'Running Up That Hill' when I first heard it, aged fourteen. These days, I read it as an introvert's plea for understanding. For comprehension without conversation. *Why can't people understand how I feel?* Well, maybe because you could never find the right words, or you never wanted to try, or you were afraid to. If only there was some way to *show* instead of tell, we'd be running up that hill with no problems.

## humbug

> If I could work my will, every idiot who goes about with 'Merry Christmas' on his lips should be boiled with his own pudding and buried with a stake of holly through his heart. He should!
>
> 'Ebenezer Scrooge'[281]

Could you enjoy being alone at Christmas, if you'd chosen it? Although I've never done it myself, I really don't see why not. You can eat turkey, watch TV and open presents just as well on your own. And you'd avoid the awkward family dinners and wine-fuelled political ding-dongs too.

What's more, you could avoid the lowest-common-denominator-ness of the occasion. Faced with the need to honour every tradition and please every guest, you can end up with a compromise that pleases nobody. In contrast, your radical solitary Christmas could be champagne at 7am, followed by a dip in the sea and four Sandra Bullock films on the bounce. Nobody will be there to judge.

From Scrooge on, it's been accepted that any character who chooses to be alone at Christmas must be lonely, crotchety or both. That certainly applies to Dr Seuss's Grinch:

> The Grinch hated Christmas! The whole Christmas
> season!
> Now, please don't ask why. No one quite knows the
> reason.[282]

The Grinch becomes so resentful of the townsfolk's sociable feasting and singing that he descends from his cave outside Who-ville and tries to steal the entire occasion. In the end, though, he sees sense and joins in the celebrations.

Obviously, the Grinch is a villain who takes his dislike of Christmas way too far. But still, his redemption makes for a profoundly extrovert fable. Instead of being tolerated, understood and allowed to enjoy Christmas in his own way, he winds up renouncing his own character and being co-opted into sociability.

A more positive introvert role model is Father Christmas (Santa Claus) as portrayed in Raymond Briggs' eponymous comic strip and the 1991 film adaptation.[283] Father Christmas lives alone at the North Pole – no elves here – with only his unnamed dog, cat and reindeer for company. (He's just one of several solitary characters Briggs created – like Gentleman Jim, an underground toilet attendant who spends his days imagining another life, or James, the only child who builds the famous Snowman.)

As the story unfolds, we follow Father Christmas' morning routine – feeding his pets, boiling the kettle, sitting on his outside toilet. Subverting the jolly 'Ho Ho Ho!' persona, Briggs gives his Santa the brusque demeanour of a grumpy old English curmudgeon – but it's clear that he likes his life just the way it is. (In the sequel, *Father Christmas Goes on Holiday*, we even see him tending his garden, although quite how he grows peas and carrots in the Arctic Circle is never explained.)

Back from his all-night present-delivering odyssey, Father Christmas embarks on a solo celebration that, to me, looks rather fun. He takes a deep, steaming bath and brushes out his magnificent beard. He opens the wine and peels the vegetables, singing along to carols on the radio. He gives gifts to his pets and opens his own. Finally, he dozes off in front of the TV nursing a cognac.

Like Dr Seuss, Briggs found a sly and entertaining way to show kids an adult character who might not enjoy every aspect of Christmas. As a parent, I now have to stage-manage the whole

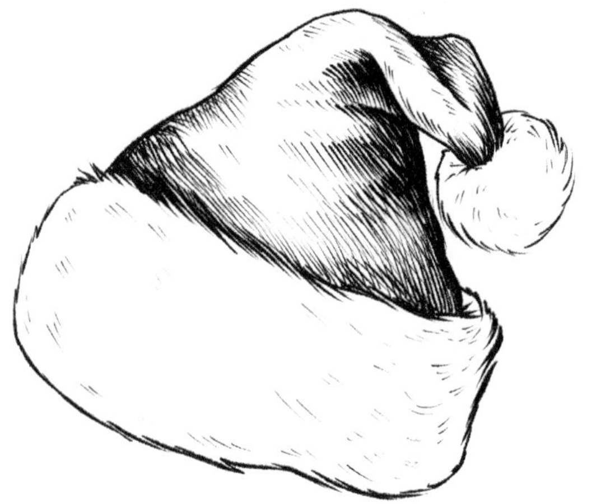

occasion, so I relate to that sentiment more than I used to. And I can also relate to Father Christmas' desire to make Christmas wonderful for others, while not necessarily wanting to play such an active part himself. Unlike Scrooge and the Grinch, Father Christmas doesn't resent anyone else's party season – he's just content to do at least some of his celebrating on his own.

TEN

# OUT ON YOUR OWN

On solitary journeys and endeavours of every sort.

# learning your lesson

> As a child I was in my own world a lot of the time. I was an imaginative kid, spending hours playing alone, lost in my creativity. It's where I was happiest.
>
> Charlotte Church[284]

When I was little, I never wanted to go to school. But I had a kind of solitude amulet to get me through the day. It was a round red reflector fixed to a wall beside the road, which I touched once on the walk to school and again on the way back home.

Maybe I was trying to invoke kind of sympathetic magic to spare me from the school day. If I linked these temporal bookends, perhaps I could slip across from one side of the day to the other. Failing that, the mere touch was reassuring. *This too shall pass*, the amulet seemed to say. *I will wait here and stand guard. By the time you return, it will be over.*

As you can tell, I didn't always have such a great time at school. And as with so many of the situations I've described in this book, the problem wasn't the people, but the experience. I liked plenty of the other kids, and the teachers too. But the classroom and the playground just weren't for me.

The playground options for six-year-old introverts are fairly limited. All too often, my sporty friends would be off playing football while I wandered around on my own. In classic introvert style, the best I could hope for was to link up with a single friend. (One heartening feature of modern playgrounds is the Friendship Bench, where you can sit and wait for someone to offer you some company.)

Was I really alone *that* much at school? Memories lie, but that's the way I remember it. I'm writing my story or painting my picture, absorbed in what I'm doing and ignoring the hubbub around me. I'm saying the Lord's Prayer in assembly, hands clasped together and eyes shut tight, enjoying a few seconds of abstracted solitude. I've been sent on an errand to a rarely opened store cupboard, or a deserted classroom next door, where I can linger for a moment on my own. I'm stuck on my own at a dining table, toying with some repulsive dinner that I've been told I have to finish before I can go out and play.

At school, we gain two types of knowledge. The first is explicit: the facts and figures that we're taught. But we also learn a deeper, more implicit lesson: how to wear a uniform, sit quietly in neat rows and listen to an authority figure. And it's this learning – as opposed to Pythagoras' theorem – that truly prepares us for the rest of life.

Along the way, we also get socialised. We learn to be with other people – all day, every day. We learn to make friends, read feelings, tell jokes, argue and make up. We learn to speak in front of our peers, ask questions and express ideas. We learn to work with others who are very different from ourselves.

Of course, that's an essential part of growing up, and a lot of the time it's fun. But when it's *all* that school can offer, less outgoing kids inevitably suffer. In fact, it's almost as if the inventors of school were trying to make introverts as uncomfortable as possible. 'OK, I want all-day company. Nine-to-five, wall-to-wall, always-on facetime. If they want solitude, I say we give them a few minutes in the bathroom – if they're lucky.'

In *Quiet*, Susan Cain documents the many problems faced by introvert children at school.[285] They're often regarded as being wrong or deficient in some way, and encouraged to overcome their 'shyness' or 'come out of their shell'. No matter how unappealing group activities may be, quiet kids still need to 'take part' or 'push themselves forward'.

By its nature, school is a collective, 'one size fits all' experience. Everyone does everything, and they do it together. But introverts and extroverts like to learn in different ways. For extroverts, group activities, assemblies, communal lunchtimes and team sports are all positive and energy-enhancing. But introvert kids need to work and think alone. For them, school is 'loud, crowded, superficial, boring, overstimulating, and focused on action, not reflection', as Jill Burruss and Liza Kaenzig put it.[286] As a result, introvert children are likely to come home from school feeling frazzled and strung out, yearning to lose themselves in a book or a film until dinnertime.

Getting used to school takes time. But introversion is a personality trait, not something a child will necessarily 'grow out of', like baby teeth. Indeed, as the social stakes increase, introversion may play a bigger role. All teenagers struggle with awkwardness and self-consciousness; for the introverts, high school is 'like an all-day cocktail party without any alcohol', in Cain's words.[287]

Teachers probably deserve some sympathy. After all, it's their job to motivate and engage the rows of kids staring back at them. They don't want to devote all their energy to cajoling some sullen, silent urchin who just stares out of the window. The ideal student is one with a cheerful demeanour who willingly volunteers in class and throws themselves into activities – so we can hardly blame teachers if they see introvert kids as 'difficult', friendless or even depressed. But whatever they think, they'll probably decide that the solution is to help the child 'fit in' and become more social and outgoing.

In reality, most introvert kids don't have any of these problems; they're just finding their own way. And there's probably a lot more going on with the quiet kids at the back than their teacher realises. OK, they're not speaking, but they may still be thinking very deeply about the things they see and hear. Introverts hate being pushed into a snap judgement or a quick reaction, so they're unlikely to raise their hands or share their thoughts in class. But later on, once they've had time to think things over, they might have something deeper to offer than someone who merely wants to impress teacher or be the first to speak.

Maybe things are improving over time. At my primary school, I would often glance longingly at the 'quiet corner' – the carpeted area where we would go to hear a story. The modern guidance seems to be that kids should always have the option of retreating to a 'cosy corner' or 'be-by-myself space' if they need to be in their feelings for a while.[288] It's like a little bit of home brought into school.

Eventually we grow up and leave school behind. But that 'don't want to go' feeling never really goes away; we just get better at hiding or suppressing it. In fact, that may be one of the most useful skills that school teaches introvert kids: how to put on a mask, play the game and get by, whatever you're feeling inside. At the same time, you get a clear sense of the sort of settings you *don't* enjoy, which might help you pick a career or role that suits your character in later life. By denying you the chance to work alone, school hints at ways you might be able to achieve it.

## alonework

> Without great solitude no serious work is possible.
>
> Pablo Picasso

When I was at school, I'd sometimes catch a glimpse of adults outside the playground, going about their daily business. As I now know, they must all have had a head full of worries. But all I could see was their freedom. Nobody was telling *them* where to go, or what to do. And they were alone. Perhaps I imagined them like the farmers and florists in children's TV programmes like *Trumpton* and *Camberwick Green*, who just kind of *did a job*, seemingly on their own.

If I was off school sick, I got to dip a toe in the adult world, and see what happened in it when I wasn't there. Now I work at home, I get to enjoy that same feeling all the time – and I do, very purposefully. I remind myself how much I wanted it, years ago, and I savour it. I look out at my garden and think, *I am here, at home. Not in an office or a meeting room or a school. Right here, on my own, and free.*

It's strange to think back on it now, but when I started out as a freelance writer and editor, I seriously questioned whether I would be able to work alone. Although I'd always loved solitude, I'd only ever worked in busy office environments. And while I generally envied the lifestyles of freelancers I had met, I'd also heard the horror stories of home-workers going crazy with loneliness, struggling for motivation or wasting hours on daytime TV.

Fifteen years on, the real question is whether I'd ever be able to work with others again. Working on my own just feels so natural, so enjoyable, that I wish I'd realised earlier that it would be best for me and actively sought it out, rather than passively falling into it.

It's not that I ever particularly *liked* the workplace; it was just the only thing I knew. Also, I'd been indoctrinated into what Susan Cain calls the 'New Groupthink': the idea that good work can only come from people working together:

> The New Groupthink elevates teamwork above all else. It insists that creativity and intellectual achievement come from a gregarious place.[289]

The New Groupthink is why so many firms now organise their workforces into teams and put them in open-plan offices. It's also why our ideal of a leader is usually someone who looks good, speaks confidently and networks like crazy – as opposed to someone who listens carefully, thinks deeply and prioritises the quality of connections over their quantity.

The internet gave the New Groupthink fresh impetus. Innovations like Wikipedia, open-source software and crowdsourcing suggested that the collective would always outperform the individual – so managers aspired to emulate their success in the real-world workplace. But while arm's-length, on-demand collaboration in a *virtual* space may be ideal for introverts, all-day face-to-face interaction most certainly is not.

As a freelance home worker, I'm one of the lucky ones. For every solitary worker who gets to choose a job they love, there must be many others who struggle through their working lives in group environments that jar with their personalities and prevent them from doing their best work – without them even being aware of it.

Think back to chapter one, when we looked at the characteristics of introverts. We love to work on things alone, and only reveal them to others when we're ready. We feel drained by company and need solitude to recharge. We communicate best one-on-one and feel cautious around new people.

Now contrast that with the modern office: noisy, crowded and obsessed with meetings, brainstorming and teamwork. It makes you wonder how much 'workplace stress' is really just square introvert pegs being stuck into round extrovert holes – and how much value is thrown away because they're forced to work in a way that just doesn't suit them.

The idea of open-plan office design is that more interaction helps co-workers communicate and support each other, making them happier and more effective. But one study found that when office occupants rate their indoor working environment, enclosed private offices clearly outperform open-plan layouts. In other words, the pros of open-plan don't actually outweigh the cons.[290]

Managers like open-plan because they're in love with teamwork. Teams are seen as the best way to come up with new ideas, solve difficult problems and allow everyone to play their part. It sounds good in principle – but the problem is that the experience of being on a team is not the same for everybody.

For extroverts, a team is a lively, buzzing environment where there's always something happening. For introverts, however, a team can be a perfect storm of inane chit-chat, perpetual distraction and pointless 'collaboration'. While the introvert worker is longing to be left alone to work on a problem, the team format obliges them to share and communicate when they really don't want to. For the introvert, teamwork is a diversion, not the way. That's why, rather than 'getting the best from everyone', teams actually have a levelling effect: they lift up and energise the extroverts while weighing the introverts down.

Since you're reading this book, I'm willing to bet you're not a big fan of meetings. Well, turns out the science is on your side. In a recent survey of seventy-six companies, when meetings were cut by forty percent, employee productivity leapt by seventy-one percent. People also felt more in charge of their work, which increased their job satisfaction by fifty-two percent. When meetings were reduced by one hundred percent – yes, that means *no meetings at all, ever* – stress plummeted by seventy-five percent.[291] Sounds like even the extroverts don't get as much value out of meetings as they think.

During a meeting, it's perfectly acceptable to seek a 'contribution' from everyone around the table. (Better pray it's not 'Tell us something funny about yourself.') But the opposite approach – requesting or demanding silence – would be a different matter entirely. Some meetings would be far more productive if certain people were told to *stop* talking – but of course, that would be seen as 'negative' or just rude. Meetings should be about listening and learning as well as talking and sharing – but those quieter aims are either taken for granted or just ignored.

The pernicious idea that talking is always good reaches its absolute nadir in the introvert's worst nightmare: the brainstorming session. Normally, introverts prefer to refine our ideas alone, then share the best ones when we're good and ready. A brainstorm forces us into the exact opposite: blurting out ill-considered, half-baked ideas for others to judge, distort or reject on the spot. Refuse to contribute and you risk being branded ineffective, obstructive or 'not a team player'. If this is a storm, bring me my umbrella.

Brainstorming is really *mouth*storming: a talkfest for its own sake. If I was a manager, I'd introduce *thoughtstorming*. Instead of shouting things out, we'd keep things in. My team would gather to spend ten minutes just quietly thinking about a project or a problem, in companionable silence, before sharing our ideas. And even if we didn't solve anything, the quiet time would still be bliss.

Most workplaces are profoundly *phonocentric*: they prize spoken communication over every other kind. That's rough on introverts, because staying quiet is *how* we think. It's not that we stubbornly refuse to think and speak at the same time; we just can't do it.

Phonocentricism manifests in workspaces too. We have meeting rooms, breakout areas, chillout zones and even playrooms. But where are the spaces to be alone? Where are the focus zones, the isolation pods, the soundproofed cubicles? Is the bathroom really to be our only escape?

The library at my university had little cubicles, known as 'carrels', that you could book out for a whole day of solo occupancy. Intended for study, they also functioned as introvert bolt-holes. Each one had an outward-facing window, so you could go inside, lock the door and stare out at the treetops, all the while kidding yourself that you were somehow preparing to write an essay.

As we saw in chapter four, our constantly connected world makes 'just thinking' difficult to imagine, let alone do. But it can be far more productive than calling another meeting. Here's how legendary investor Warren Buffett manages his team:

> I insist on a lot of time being spent, almost every day, to just sit and think. That is very uncommon in American business… I do more reading and thinking, and make less impulse decisions than most people in business. I do it because I like this kind of life.[292]

So there you have it: sitting quietly at your desk could make you as rich as the Sage of Omaha. Maybe you can point that out the next time someone drags you into a pointless meetup, accosts you at the watercooler or insists that they just want five minutes to 'pick your brain'.

## solo science

> Somewhere, something incredible is waiting to be known.
>
> CARL SAGAN

For a shining example of what someone can achieve while working on their own, I give you mathematician Sir Andrew Wiles, who proved Fermat's famous last theorem.

If I asked you to picture a solitary scientist, you might well imagine a lab-coated man, aged around sixty, with a shock of unruly white hair, working alone in the lab. That image is a composite portrait that draws on several sources – some real, some fictitious. In terms of real-world scientists, Isaac Newton was deeply suspicious of his fellow thinkers and kept his discoveries to himself for many years before finally publishing them. Albert Einstein fused the idea of genius with the image of white hair. And there's a long tradition of British 'boffins', like Patrick Moore and Magnus Pyke, who seemed so wildly eccentric you couldn't imagine them working with anyone else. Throw in a few mannerisms from made-up, possibly 'mad' scientists like Mary Shelley's Dr Frankenstein, Doc Brown in *Back to the Future* and Hubert Farnsworth of *Futurama* and your solitary scientist is complete.

In reality, few scientists can achieve very much on their own. They're always building on the work of those who went before – 'standing on the shoulders of giants', as Newton put it – and collaborating with those around them now. What's more, every new finding must be considered, critiqued and debated by other scientists before it can be generally accepted. So the chances of some lone genius secretly building a time machine, or creating a living being from body parts, are actually pretty slim. The myth of the lone scientist can even be dangerous, because it encourages people to seize on questionable findings from fringe thinkers as 'genius', making mainstream science seem dull and pedestrian.[293]

However, some sciences, like mathematics, are more amenable to solo work. And some thinkers, like Andrew Wiles, are more independent than others. The theorem that became his obsession states that no three positive integers $a$, $b$ and $c$ satisfy the equation $a^n + b^n = c^n$ for any integer (whole-number) value of $n > 2$. It was first stated in 1637 by French mathematician Pierre Fermat, who scribbled it in the margin of a book, adding, 'I have a truly marvellous demonstration of this proposition, which this margin is too narrow to contain.'

Fermat's successors had proven his other theorems with relative ease. But this last one proved a tougher nut to crack. Generations of mathematicians failed to find a proof, and it became the most famous unproven theorem in mathematics.

Wiles had been fascinated by Fermat since childhood. In 1986, aged 33, he heard of a new discovery that could open the door to a proof, and decided to start working on it. Fearing disruptive publicity, he resolved to keep his decision secret from everyone but his wife. For the next eight years, whether up in his study or out for a walk, he lived and breathed Fermat's last theorem.

> I carried this problem around in my head basically the whole time. I would wake up with it first thing in the morning, I would be thinking about it all day, and I would be thinking about it when I went to sleep.[294]

Three and a half centuries after Fermat had scribbled down the theorem, Wiles unveiled his proof.

> It was so indescribably beautiful; it was so simple and so elegant… I couldn't contain myself, I was so excited. It was the most important moment of my working life. Nothing I ever do again will mean as much.[295]

For his achievement, Wiles was made a knight and awarded the 2016 Abel Prize and the 2017 Copley Medal by the Royal Society. Reflecting on his achievement, he offers some wise words for scientists, mathematicians and, really, anyone at all:

> It is important to pick a problem based on how much you care about it. However impenetrable it seems, if you don't try it, then you can never do it. Always try the problem that matters most to you.

## one for the road

> I wondered why it was that places are so much lovelier when one is alone.
>
> Daphne du Maurier

A group or family holiday can be a stern test for the introvert or solitude-lover. Since holidays theoretically involve doing stuff you actually enjoy, you might be secretly hoping for a chance to sit quietly and read your book, or head out to explore the local scenery alone. But against that stands the concentrated and communal nature of the vacation. This particular confluence of place and people may only happen once, and in a few short days it will be over. Going solo, even for an hour or two, can feel wasteful, self-indulgent and downright rude. However, it may also be the only way to avoid overdosing on company and going quietly insane.

The alternative, travelling alone, can be difficult, confusing and downright scary. But on the positive side, successfully completing a solo trip does wonders for your self-confidence. What's more, when you plan a whole trip on your own, you can choose exactly where to go and what to do. And when you think about all the many decisions that must be made over the course of a trip, it's easy to see how solo travel saves a whole lot of heartache. You may be undecided about where to go for lunch, but at least you won't have an argument about it.

More importantly, travelling incognito gives a unique feeling of liberation – a bit like being invisible. And whatever thoughts you have along the way, you'll be able to follow them wherever they lead.

> The soul of a solitary journey is liberty, perfect liberty, to think, feel, do, just as one pleases… I want to see my vague notions float like the down of the thistle before the breeze, and not to have them entangled in the briars and thorns of controversy. For once, I like to have it all my own way; and this is impossible unless you are alone.
>
> William Hazlitt[296]

You can also explore your destination at your own pace, and connect with it more deeply as a result. If you want to linger in the town square, or return to that one café you really liked, you can. If you're in a relationship, many experts suggest that striking out on your own will actually strengthen the bond between you rather than weaken it. Sometimes it's good to get a reminder that you're both still individual people, who sometimes want different things – and that's perfectly OK. And whatever you do while you're apart, it will probably remind you why you want to be together.

The word 'adventure' comes from the Latin *adventurus*, which simply means 'about to happen'. That's how solo travel should make you feel – a sense of stepping over the threshold of the unknown. But adventure isn't some external standard that you have to live up to, and you don't have to travel to the other side of the world. If it feels like an adventure to you, that's what it is.

Whenever I travel on my own, I like to appreciate the other solitudes I pass along the way. I look out of the train window and wonder what it would be like to explore the places I see. There's a wood I could walk through, and a pond that no-one can see from the road. Here's a secluded garden surrounded by trees. Sometimes someone is there, being alone. Just for an instant, our two solitudes are connected.

Much of the appeal of a journey lies in its *in-betweenness*. You pass through transitional places that are neither here nor there – known as *liminal spaces*, from the Latin word *limen*, meaning 'threshold'. Entrance halls, corridors, lifts, staircases and bridges are liminal, and on a grander scale, so are stations and airports. They can feel stressful if you're stuck in them for too long, but they can also be restful, because the expectations around them are so low. Being nowhere, and with no-one, all you have to do is exist in this moment and wait for it to become something else.

# do not disturb

> I do love a hotel room: adore it. What's not to love about everything you need in one room? Would you have a kettle on a tea tray with biscuits in a packet in your bedroom at home?
>
> MIRANDA HART[297]

The feeling begins in the corridor – silent, windowless, unsettlingly long. You've negotiated the check-in desk and the lift, and the chances of meeting someone are dwindling with every softly carpeted step. Just a few more metres and you'll be home free.

Now the door is swinging shut and sealing itself with a forceful *shhchunk*. You have the delirious thought that only you can open it now. But then again, why would you want to?

Next up is the atmosphere – both gaseous and psychological. The air conditioner whirrs into action at your touch, and with the weather banished behind the double-glazing, time itself feels suspended, and normal life feels far away.

With the bathroom door securely locked, you now have *two* reassuringly solid slabs of wood between you and the rest of the world. This bathroom might be the most private, inviolate, impenetrable space you'll ever inhabit.

It's all for you: the kettle, the TV, the boring view, even the trouser press. When Christopher Marlowe wrote of 'infinite riches in a little room' in 1589, he was obviously anticipating the invention of the Travelodge four hundred years later.

I know people dislike beige, boring hotels. But for me, their very anonymity makes solitude more vivid and real. I don't want to be a discerning traveller staying in the most bijou boutique hotel. I don't want to express anything about myself with my choices. I want to be unknown and unknowing, with nothing to explain.

Before we check out, a word of warning. The communal spaces of most traditional hotels are amenable for the introvert guest – you simply select a table as far as possible from everyone else. But there are other, smaller establishments where guests are expected to sit *alongside each other at the same tables*.

We can only assume that the hosts wish to create some sort of 'community feel' or 'friendly vibe'. But for an introvert, the implications of this policy are truly terrifying. Before the day's first coffee has even passed your lips, you could be doing the one thing that every introvert detests above all else: talking about yourself. To a complete stranger! So do yourself a favour. Check Tripadvisor before you book, and make sure your holiday isn't spoilt by the very worst hazard you can encounter on your travels: other people.

## solitary steps

> Thus did I steal along that silent road,
> My body from the stillness drinking in
> A restoration like the calm of sleep,
> But sweeter far. Above, before, behind,
> Around me, all was peace and solitude,
> I looked not round, nor did the solitude
> Speak to my eye, but was heard and felt.
>
> WILLIAM WORDSWORTH[298]

According to some estimates, Wordsworth walked a whopping 180,000 miles (290,000km) in his lifetime. No wonder his poetry is so full of the pleasures of walking – up hills and mountains, through valleys and forests and along paths and roads. And as the lines above suggest, he was never happier than when walking alone.

Writers such as Jean-Jacques Rousseau, James Joyce and Virginia Woolf all used walking as a way to free up their thoughts. Philosopher Søren Kierkegaard thrived on city strolls, and even claimed to have done his writing while walking around. Walking can also be a means of pilgrimage, or a way to protest.

Despite these many valuable sides to walking, we sometimes see it as nothing more than a basic mode of transport. Or we might regard it as an unavoidable hiatus between places, tasks or activities, which we would probably fast-forward if we could. In fact, walking is one of the best activities for both body and mind – not to mention a golden chance to enjoy some almost perfect solitude.

Walking, particularly through nature, is extremely healthy. Being in a natural environment helps to lower blood pressure, heart rate, muscle tension and stress hormones, calming anger and fear. Because we're genetically programmed to be absorbed by nature, it helps us cope with pain. Such is the power of nature that just adding a pot-plant to a room helps to reduce anxiety.[299]

Walking is a whole-being activity: it reunites body, mind and spirit. The outer and inner worlds meld together: the things you hear and see shape the things you think and feel. The speed of your thinking matches the pace of your walking: to dwell on a thought, linger and dawdle; to push things forward, stride out.

> Walking, ideally, is a state in which the mind, the body, and the world are aligned, as though they were three characters finally in conversation together, three notes suddenly making a chord.
>
> Rebecca Solnit[300]

Walking is woven into everything we do. It's how we listen to the music of the world, note by note, as we move forward and the scenery changes around us. In contrast, travelling in a vehicle interrupts our experience, cutting us off from the world.

Walking gives you both time and space to think. Set out from your front door with a problem, and there's a good chance you'll have an answer by the time you get home. Researchers have found that walking is excellent for promoting creative thought – although intriguingly, it's better for generating lots of ideas than for choosing the single best one.[301]

Of course, you could just sit there on the sofa, or even lie in bed, to do your thinking. But your brain isn't a computer. When you walk, your heart rate rises, pumping oxygen to all your organs – including the brain. People who've been for a short walk perform better on tests of memory and attention, and regular walking fights the effects of ageing, boosts memory and stimulates the growth of new neurons.[302] 'How vain it is to sit down to write when you have not stood up to live!' wrote Henry David Thoreau in his journal. 'Methinks that the moment my legs begin to move, my thoughts begin to flow.'

For introverts, home is where we surround ourselves with the things that give meaning to our lives, and retreat to regain energy when life gets too much. But if you spend too long at home, it can become stifling. You can even start to feel oppressed by your own character or memories. Walking takes you out of yourself, either into nature or abstracted solitude among the crowd. On the other hand, if your home is noisy or crowded, 'going for a walk' is the perfect excuse to grab some precious solitude.

As you walk, you can slip into a liminal stage of in-between time, when normal life is suspended and you're free to follow your thoughts. And yet, despite these ideal solitude conditions, there's still nothing self-indulgent about what you're doing. You're attending to the business of the day while taking fresh air and exercise. And who could criticise you for that?

# *vive la flânerie*

A *flâneur* ('stroller' or 'lounger') is a solitary wanderer through a crowded city. The word comes to English from French, but it's originally from the Old Norse *flana*, 'to wander with no purpose'.

The *flâneur* is not really a traveller, because they have no destination. The point of *flânerie* is that it has no point. It's the physical equivalent of daydreaming. However, this lack of purpose allows the *flâneur* to absorb life and feeling from those around them:

> The crowd is [the *flâneur*'s] element, as the air is that of birds and water of fishes. His passion and his profession are to become one flesh with the crowd. For the perfect *flâneur*, for the passionate spectator, it is an immense joy to set up house in the heart of the multitude, amid the ebb and flow of movement, in the midst of the fugitive and the infinite.
>
> CHARLES BAUDELAIRE[303]

The *flâneur* is a connoisseur of the city, savouring its sights, sounds and smells like a smörgåsbord. Honoré de Balzac called *flânerie* 'the gastronomy of the eye'.[304]

The *flâneur* is a figure of contradictions. They are in the city, but apart from it, standing always 'at a slight angle to the universe'.[305] They take in the busyness of modern life, but without getting caught up in it. They are often to be found in a crowd, yet usually alone. While they love to look, they prefer not to be seen. And while their minds may be engaged, physically they're pretty idle. Indeed, since the original *flâneurs* were usually wealthy, educated men, you could argue that there's something patronising about them – floating smugly above the fray on a cloud of male privilege, polishing their *aperçus* while others toil below.

In her book *Flâneuse*, Lauren Elkin redresses the imbalance by celebrating the female spirit of idle strolling.[306] She defines a *flâneuse* as 'a determined resourceful woman keenly attuned to the creative potential of the city, and the liberating possibilities of a good walk'. In the time of the original *flâneurs*, women 'lacked access to the city streets that their male counterparts took for granted, reduced instead to mere objects upon which the *flâneur*'s gaze alighted and delighted'.[307] Elkin points out that creative women from authors Virginia Woolf, George Sand and Jean Rhys to artist Sophie Calle and filmmaker Agnès Varda were all devoted *flâneuses*, and argues that the freedom to wander is just as vital for women today.

When you're a *flâneur*, getting lost isn't really a problem – in fact, it's rather pleasant. Time is not of the essence, so the day can be shaped by the route rather than vice versa. Since no-one else is around, there will be no argument over navigation. In fact, since you have no particular place to go, you're not really getting lost at all – just finding a new, unanticipated destination.[308]

Thanks to Google Maps, the experience of getting lost has been pretty much erased. However, it has an antithesis in Randonautica, 'the first ever quantumly generated adventure game that takes you on a journey of true randomness'. All the app actually does is send you to a random location nearby, so you can break out of your 'probability tunnel' and discover something genuinely new. Arriving with no sense of what you might find, you're free to simply *observe what's there*, just as a child would. And when you let go of the need to evaluate or explain, you discover the poetry and meaning that has been here all along, waiting for you to see it.[309]

# running solo

> Running and meditation are very personal activities. Therefore they are lonely. This loneliness is one of their best qualities because it strengthens our incentive to motivate ourselves.
>
> SAKYONG MIPHAM[310]

You wake up and check the clock: almost six. You slip quietly out of bed, change into your kit and make your way downstairs. As the kettle boils, you check the weather outside: fine and dry. Everything is as it should be.

A few minutes later, coffee drunk and trainers tied, you close the front door softly behind you and step into the silent street. The sun is rising, the streetlamps still aglow. And you're going running.

The first mile or so is hard work, but you're used to that. You run through it. After ten or fifteen minutes, your muscles loosen up, your breathing evens out and you settle into your pace. It's going to be another good run. And you're *so* glad you made the effort.

The main reason to run is for physical fitness. But the other benefits, which may be even more important, are emotional and mental. Running stimulates a release of 'happy chemicals' in your body, triggering the 'runner's high'. Over the next few hours, the process of neurogenesis will build new cells and blood vessels in your brain, boosting both your mood and your cognitive performance.[311]

Best of all, though, you get to enjoy solid-gold solitude on tap. In fact, that's why I got into running in the first place. I'd been a fat, unfit kid who predictably grew into a fat, unfit adult. I hated team sports and competition. Yet I knew I had to get fit – so I looked for a way to exercise alone.

You don't need to spend a lot of money or time. All you need is shoes, shorts and the willingness to give it a go. This wonderful solitary experience is waiting, quite literally, right outside your door.

> The hour or so I spend running, maintaining my own silent, private time, is important to help me keep my mental well-being. When I'm running I don't have to talk to anybody and don't have to listen to anybody. All I need to do is gaze at the scenery passing by. This is a part of my day I can't do without.
>
> HARUKI MARUKAMI[312]

The solitude you experience while running is almost perfect. For the duration of the run, you're safe in a solitary bubble that nobody – not even you – can burst. Your phone is out of reach, and you can't avoid your own thoughts by turning to some not-really-urgent household task. Running puts you right inside your head, and in your body, in a way that nothing else quite can. Your run is a time outside time, which you're pretty much obliged to spend in your own company.

Running thought is different from regular, everyday thought. I think that's because the physical experience is fairly all-consuming

– unlike walking, you can never quite forget that you're doing it. That keeps your attention on what your body is doing from moment to moment, leaving rational thought in the background. But at the same time, your thinking still carries on – just in a different, more abstract and allusive way.

For me, this 'runner's mind' has a quality that I just can't get anywhere else. My thoughts are clear, but they take some unexpected turns. When I run first thing in the morning, my state of mind feels closer to dreaming than full wakefulness. During the run, I'll often get many ideas for writing, which I have to capture as soon as I return before they fade away.

> The thoughts that occur to me while I'm running are like clouds in the sky. Clouds of all different sizes. They come and they go, while the sky remains the same sky as always. The clouds are mere guests in the sky that pass away and vanish, leaving behind the sky.
>
> HARUKI MURAKAMI[313]

## one on two wheels

> The bike provides a means of escape… It is about self-reliance and independence… It is about recapturing a sense of childlike wonder, and turning back the clock to simpler, more innocent days.
>
> NICK MOORE[314]

The bicycle as we know it today is a surprisingly recent invention. Early iterations like the aptly named bone-shaker and the dauntingly elevated penny-farthing were strictly for sporting daredevils; it wasn't until the advent of the reassuringly named 'safety bicycle' in the late nineteenth century that cycling became a popular pursuit.

A bike confers instant independence, allowing you to travel wherever and whenever you want, subject to the limits of your leg muscles (and even that problem is addressed by modern e-bikes). In its early years, cycling make mobility a possibility for many who'd never enjoyed it before. Women could ditch the billowing skirts, break free of the drawing-room and male chaperones and go wherever they wished. This minor liberation paved the way for far bigger ones, as the suffragettes turned to bikes to mobilise, group together and protest to claim votes for women.

Today, bikes can mean almost anything to anybody. As a means of transport, a bike could indicate poverty – someone who only cycles because they can't afford a car. Yet a more expensive bike can also be a status symbol, and even a cheap one is a way to wear your environmental credentials with pride.

As a solitary experience, cycling has a unique flavour that, to my mind, sets it apart from either walking or running. First, the sheer speed of movement means you get further from your home, and therefore see more of the area around it, in far less time.

Gliding along the road, you are in the world, yet apart from it: not partitioned off in a metal box on wheels, yet distinct from pedestrians at the same time. You'll also find that your fellow cyclists are generally friendly, and helpful in a crisis too, but will unfailingly respect your desire to ride alone.

Try a longer ride and you might surprise yourself with how far afield you've managed to venture, giving a proud sense of solitary adventure and accomplishment. For as long as you're out on your ride, no-one can reach you, and when you return, you really do feel like you've voyaged out in the world on your own.

Are you really alone on a bike? If you cover enough miles together, your trusty steed can come to seem like an old friend. But at the same time, bike and rider can sometimes seem to meld into a single hybrid bike-being. The relationship is one of co-dependence: neither of you can move at speed on your own, but together, you fuse into a super-efficient, environmentally friendly vehicle. In fact, as a cyclist, you become the driver, engine and passenger all at once.

In Flann O'Brien's fantastical novel *The Third Policeman*, rural copper Gilhaney has spent so long pounding up the Irish hills that he and his bicycle have begun to intermingle. He is already twenty-three percent bike, while his bike, conversely, is twenty-three percent him. If his 'number' were to increase much further, he would start to display the characteristics of a bike himself:

> 'When a man lets things go so far that he is half or more than half bicycle, you will not see him so much because he spends a lot of his time leaning with one elbow on walls or standing propped by one foot at kerbstones...'[315]

That hasn't happened to me yet, as far as I know. But there's no doubt that cycling will get under your skin if you let it. One person, one bike – it's solitary freedom on two wheels.

## wave hello

> My soul is full of longing
> for the secret of the sea,
> and the heart of the great ocean
> sends a thrilling pulse through me.
>
> HENRY WADSWORTH LONGFELLOW

Swimming encompasses both the good and the bad extremes of introvert experience. At the lower end of the scale is battling through an overcrowded indoor pool as some horrible beefy man ploughs past you, puffing like a walrus and shoving a wave of chlorine directly into your face. But at the other extreme is the solitude of swimming in open water, with no-one around for miles.

Ocean swimming could be my favourite thing in the world. I love the sensory transition of 'going in': from sight and sound to touch, taste and smell. Ashore, the ocean starts out as a distant panorama and a vague susurration. As you approach, it gets gradually louder and closer, before becoming an unavoidable, in-your-face reality. The waves you saw from the clifftop now surround you, their sun-glints right before your eyes. The physical immediacy is overwhelming – but at the same time you feel adrift in the vastness, a tiny dot under the big sky.

Because I love sea swimming so much, I take every opportunity to do it. Admittedly, what constitutes an 'opportunity' in UK waters is open to debate. Swimming off the North Norfolk coast in May, I've glanced back at the beach to see walkers still wearing hats and scarves, and wondered which one of us is crazy.

Even in summer, it's a strange feeling to survey a crowded beach resort from the sea. Back there on land, everyone's having the most uproarious time – eating ice cream, playing frisbee, basking in the sun. Meanwhile, just a few metres offshore, I'm in an altogether deeper, colder and less forgiving world, treading water to preserve body heat as my fingertips inexorably turn blue.

To take my mind off the cold, I further embellish my elaborate fantasy life based on sea swimming. Briefly, I somehow end up as a bald, gnarly old gent with a Captain Webb moustache living in a small coastal town. Every morning without fail, the locals see me perched on a groyne, wrapped in a faded, threadbare towel and smoking a roll-up, having braved the icy waters under a leaden sky.

In this very alternative reality, I live alone but happy in some tiny, humble dwelling like a static caravan or a beach-hut, warmed by a venerable gas stove and entertained by a few paperbacks and a transistor radio. In contrast to real life, I did not earn my living by editing Word documents while wearing a scarf indoors and sipping on a latte, but toiling at some worthy, muscular, elemental trade like stonemason or blacksmith. I rarely speak beyond a terse exchange with a fishmonger while purchasing a crab.

If that sounds elaborate, it's because swimming, like walking and running, is excellent for engaging the brain. Maybe it's because there's so little opportunity for distraction – even less than on foot. You can't really listen to music, and your view of your surroundings changes only gradually. All you can do is get on your train of thought and see where it goes.

Fitness writer Nicola Joyce has swum the English Channel several times. As she explains, she never gets bored, even on the longest swim:

> I love it. I like my own company. You know how sometimes you just want to get away from it all? Well, there's no better way to do that than to be face down in cold water miles away from anyone else... You can't hear anything except your own breathing and the sound of the water. You can't see anything except the colour of the water and glimpses of the sky. You can't talk to anyone... I love that.[316]

For some, wild swimming becomes a ritual, a compulsion or an addiction. Tamsin Calidas' memoir *I Am An Island* tells of her radical rehoming from London to a remote island in the Scottish Hebrides, where she lived for sixteen years – the first ten with her husband, and then with just her two dogs.

Hoping for a new start on the island, Calidas finds the quiet that she's looking for, but must also deal with disappointment and despair. However, her love of nature and the sheer simplicity of island life pull her through. In the process, sea swimming – alone, and in all weathers – becomes an essential part of her day:

> I never used to like cold water, yet here I have grown to love its shocking, icy embrace … Above all, the sea teaches me to trust… I know that if I can stand bare-skinned in the freezing cold, hurl myself into the waves and keep swimming, then I am winning.[317]

Living alone in her remote island croft and sometimes struggling to connect with her fellow islanders, Calidas' solitude threatens to tip over into isolation. Hers is a raw, powerful solitude, and one that must be handled with care. As she observes, 'Solitude helps you to redraw your own parameters, but its navigation takes skill and practice.' Over time, she learns how to thrive on it, and to find a different kind of kinship in the natural world:

> It was freezing, the depths of winter. I stripped off and dived into the waves. Out in the channel, the wind had dropped and snow, long promised, started to fall. Then something happened that changed my life. A wilder voice called my name with love and changed me forever. Afterwards, all it takes is a breath to reconnect to the pulse and beat of the universe. Once that feeling is experienced, it is impossible ever to feel alone.[318]

## art of solitude

Art galleries are one of a select group of public spaces, along with libraries and places of worship, where conversation is usually discouraged. They are places to be quiet and alone – but with others, in public. And they are oases of calm in busy urban centres.

Why, then, do people in movies so often meet in galleries? I guess they get to stand in front of some baffling modern artwork and have an arch, allusive conversation about it, symbolising or foreshadowing some aspect of the plot. But in real life, I can't really see why anyone would want to visit a gallery with anyone else, no matter how well they know them. It sounds good in theory, but in practice there are multiple issues.

First, you probably won't to look at the same things. So you'll be moving at different speeds the whole time – either lingering by a piece that you find entrancing, or tapping your foot while your gallery-mate gazes lovingly at some unsightly lump of bronze.

When you're alone, however, the itinerary is down to you. Up bright and early for an eight-thirty start? Want to walk round in the wrong direction? Feel like breezing right by an entire room of nineteenth-century portraits, then spending twenty minutes in front of that abstract that you just can't get enough of? *Go right ahead.* No-one can judge you now.

On a more intellectual plane, it's good to just experience an artwork without feeling the need to explain it, discuss it or work out what it 'means'. When you're alone, you can simply allow the art to work on you directly, on an emotional level, without casting around for an interpretation or an opinion. The meaning of the work is what you feel.

## table for one

There's definitely a thing about going to a restaurant alone, isn't there? It must be because there are so many happy occasions where two or more people eat together, while eating alone has overtones of loneliness and sadness. TV dinners, the instant meals hailed in the 1950s as a revolution in cooking convenience, eventually came to symbolise divorced dads and miserable, enforced nights in – just because they were made for one person.

OK, you *can* enjoy company when you go out to eat. But that's not what restaurants are mainly about. What's on the menu is not conversation and interaction, but food. On top of that, the hour you spend in a restaurant or café could be your only downtime in a busy day. So why shouldn't you make the most of it?

I guess people think eating alone is awkward somehow. But there's plenty to feel awkward about when you're dining with someone else. There's being watched while you eat, for a start, and the struggle to sustain conversation as you tackle something far too chewy. With no-one else there, you don't have to talk at all. You can even do something else, like read a book or tackle today's Wordle.

The idea that eating alone is sad has been reinforced by countless film and TV scenes set in cafeterias, usually in high school, where a character's solo eating is a signal that they're a miserable outcast. To intensify their dramatic isolation, other characters can ostentatiously move away, call out unkind remarks or even hurl a scrap of food. For full-on bullying, you can't beat tipping the loner's tray out of their hands as they walk by.

The layout of spaces like canteens implicitly encourages sociability. You can see why it's done – group seating denotes friendship and inclusion, while a solo chair screams 'friendless' and might even encourage bullying, like a modern version of the village stocks. That's presumably why, even in grown-up bars and cafés, most tables have at least two chairs. The very format implies that solo diners aren't quite enough in themselves – although some restaurants will thoughtfully remove the extra chair when they realise nobody else is joining.

As an alternative, the Moomin Café in Japan started providing giant soft-toy Moomins to sit opposite solo diners and keep them company.[319] (If you're not familiar with Moomins, they look rather like big, cuddly hippos in pastel shades.)

Personally, I can see a lot of upsides to dining with an inanimate Moomin. They won't steal your fries like a gannet, having previously assured you that they didn't want any of their own. They won't judge what you're ordering, or try to inveigle you into ordering something that *they* want to try. They won't interrupt your train of thought or tell you off if your attention wanders to the people on the next table. The only downside is that they're unlikely to contribute very much to the bill.

## the one badge

For situations like eating alone, there should be some way to signal to others that yes, you are on your own and no, you're not remotely bothered about it. To meet this need, I propose what I call the One Badge. It's a simple metal pin badge bears a simple, universally recognised symbol, such as the numeral '1' or a stylised human figure standing alone. Like those children's birthday badges that proudly declare *I am 5*, the One Badge makes a simple, factual statement about the wearer themselves. It's neither a challenge nor a provocation, and nor is it ironic or sarcastic. It simply says that the wearer is alone, and happy that way.

If someone is wearing this badge, they should not be spoken to. Whatever you have to say to them, short of an actual emergency, will have to wait. The One Badge is rather like those t-shirts that shop assistants have saying 'happy to help', but with precisely the opposite sentiment: 'unhappy to talk'.

We have to be mindful that historically, badges have been used as instruments of oppression. So the One Badge is never used to enforce silence or solitude on another, but only ever chosen by the wearer themselves. Therefore, it's a sign of freedom.

In theory, such a badge would be open to misinterpretation. Some might not understand how anyone could want to be alone. And others might decide that the wearer must be aloof, arrogant, standoffish, passive-aggressive, superior, snooty or any of the other negative attributes that introverts routinely attract.

But this is my fantasy, not reality – and here, miraculously, the One Badge has managed to avoid every one of these traps. Thanks to an extensive programme of public education, generously funded by the taxpayer, its full meaning is universally understood. It means, 'I don't hate you. I don't hate anyone! I just want to be alone right now, even in this warmly sociable setting, and I'd really appreciate it if you respected that. And yes, this does still apply to you even though you're my colleague, best friend, parent or spouse.'

As a result of these efforts, society has taken the One Badge to heart, embracing the spirit as well as the letter of the law. Wherever you go, it will always be quietly noted and respected. It's like the white stick of the visually impaired, or the yellow collar of the nervous dog – an outward signal of an otherwise unseen need. So instead of arousing hostility, it merely draws a sympathetic smile, an understanding nod or perhaps a wry expression of envy. 'Enjoying solitude? Sounds great. Mind if I join you?'

# ELEVEN

# HOME ALONE

On being alone
behind closed doors.

# lockdown

> I'd watch three seasons passing by, and then
> When winter came with dreary snows, I'd pen
> Myself between closed shutters, bolts, and doors,
> And build my fairy palaces indoors.
>
> CHARLES BAUDELAIRE[320]

Home is pretty important to introverts. It's where we take refuge from the world, in an environment that we control, surrounded by the objects that reflect our characters and our lives. So when lockdown was imposed during the pandemic, it's no wonder many introverts were ready with a smug response. 'Spending day after day all alone indoors?' we scoffed. 'Welcome to my world!'

Researchers have found that lockdown did feel more natural to introverts.[321] However, it still tested our love of solitude to destruction. As we quickly realised, voluntary alone time is one thing, but feeling isolated or confined is something else entirely. While chosen solitude is refreshing, the unchosen kind can quickly become oppressive.

If you shared a household with others, you were spared utter isolation. You were not alone because other people were physically present. But you may still have experienced a weird, topsy-turvy cocktail of loneliness and aloneliness (the longing to be alone from chapter six). On the one hand, you were missing the friends, family and colleagues you couldn't see. But on the other, you were craving true solitude because you were cooped up with your cohabitants.[322] Lockdown shone a light on the difference between presence and connection: how you can easily have either one without the other, and how most of us – even introverts – need at least some of both.

It's easy to forget now, but in its early stages, the pandemic really did feel like the end of the world. I vividly remember going out for my government-sanctioned run through deserted streets, hearing sirens in the distance and feeling like an extra from *28 Days Later*.

The impact of lockdown on people's mental health was very real, with the less advantaged in society suffering more than most. As the UK's Mental Health Foundation puts it, we were all in the same storm, but not necessarily in the same boat.[323]

I freely admit that I was one of the luckiest ones. Our daughter was old enough to regulate her own schoolwork at home. Both of us adults had been working at home anyway. So even though I gradually became more and more fed up, I had to admit that lockdown wasn't all that different from my normal life.

In fact, if your lockdown was bearable, it could even be quite comforting. There were no difficult choices to make about where to go or who to see, and no guilt about staying in and seeing no-one. Suddenly, solitude wasn't antisocial – it was altruistic.

As I write this, a few years on, people are beginning to realise that lockdown was a truly once-in-a-lifetime experience (or so we hope). Some are even ready to admit to lockdown nostalgia. For instance, two-thirds of fourteen to twenty-three-year-olds in the UK now say they miss lockdown.[324]

Sent home from work, educated in their bedrooms and banished from bars and clubs, young people had their freedoms curtailed more severely than anyone else's. But for the introverted among them, being grounded was the mother of self-discovery. Lockdown meant a break from social anxiety and comparing themselves to others. It also gave them a welcome opportunity to slow down the pace of life, reflect on their beliefs and focus on passion projects.[325]

Lockdown also introduced the world to the dubious pleasures of the Zoom call. Family catch-ups that had previously been done on the phone suddenly went visual, taking on the daunting overtones of a job interview or police interrogation. I didn't want to stare right into everyone's face, asking them what they'd been up to. And I certainly didn't want to talk to everyone present about my own life, which frankly had been boring enough *before* lockdown.

When I attended my first and only virtual pint, I chose a background image of the interior of a pub we used to like. But that merely highlighted how profoundly *un*-pub-like the experience was. It couldn't replicate the appeal of social spaces for introverts, which is just to *be there* – off to one side, throwing in the odd word, listening more than talking. I wanted everybody to be there, and I wanted to be with them – but I didn't want, or need, to be visible or centred all the time. Now we're mostly back to in-person socialising, I'm back in the background where I belong.

## sole occupants

On one level, *The Lord of the Rings* is about the struggle between good and evil for control of Middle-Earth. But on another level, it's about going for long walks in the countryside with a few good friends before returning to a cosy home for a good meal, a frothing tankard of ale by a roaring fire and a nice long sleep. Both Bilbo and Frodo begin their journeys living alone in the domestic haven of Bag End, a hobbit-hole deep in The Shire:

> In a hole in the ground there lived a hobbit. Not a nasty, dirty, wet hole, filled with the ends of worms and an oozy smell, nor yet a dry, bare, sandy hole with nothing in it to sit down on or to eat. It was a hobbit-hole, and that meant comfort.
>
> J.R.R. TOLKIEN[326]

Bag End must be one of the most appealing introvert bolt-holes ever imagined. Outside, it features 'a perfectly round door like a porthole, painted green'. This opens on to a round, wood-panelled tunnel with rooms leading off to either side, the left-hand ones with windows looking out over Hobbiton. Gollum, the hobbits' nemesis, lives alone too, but in far less salubrious surroundings that reflect his character: on a rock in the middle of an underground lake, deep under the Misty Mountains. Gollum had friends once, but then he was 'driven away, alone, and crept down, down, into the dark under the mountains'. In Middle-Earth as elsewhere, if you want to gauge someone's character, just look at the place they call home.

When you're out exploring some lonely place, it's only natural to wonder what it would be like to live there permanently. See that cottage over there across the valley, with just one window lit. What cosy reading room lies inside? Who is in there, right now, with a good book, a mug of tea and a panoramic view of the landscape you're standing in? Like aloneliness (chapter six), I always think this feeling should have a serious-sounding German name, like *Fensterwundern* ('window-wondering').

And then there are lighthouses. Surely every introvert who has seen one on the horizon has fantasised about living there alone. Part of the appeal is the stark, almost insurmountable separation from the rest of humanity. Perched up there on the cliff, or out on a rock among the waves, no-one can possibly reach you. But then, why would anybody try? The whole point is that you're out on your own, a solitary sentinel, looking out for everybody else and asking nothing in return. For Joe Moran, it's this combination of severance and service that makes lighthouses so compelling:

> Perhaps there is something about lighthouses that appeals to introverts, who need to make regular withdrawals from the social world but still retain a link with it. For lighthouses are a concrete expression of our common humanity. Their beacons turn and blink eternally because we accept that people we may never meet, whom we may do no more than flash our lights at in the dark, are also our concern.[327]

This seems like a perfect metaphor for how introverts generally relate to the world. We don't dislike others, or wish them any harm – in fact, we may care for them very deeply. We just want to be apart from them right now.

In *Journal of a Solitude*, May Sarton draws a parallel between the lighthouse keeper's life and her own life as a writer, carrying a torch on behalf of her readers and all womankind:

> The fact that a middle-aged, single woman, without any vestige of family left, lives in this house in a silent village and is responsible only to her own soul means something. The fact that she is a writer and can tell where she is and what it is like on the pilgrimage inward can be of comfort. It is comforting to know there are lighthouse keepers on rocky islands along the coast.[328]

The writer sends out her words like a beam of light, bringing comfort to those others she does not know and will never meet. And even if she doesn't write, her mere existence is a beacon in the dark.

A cosier attraction of lighthouse life is the thought of being safe amid the storm. The waves may crash, the thunder roar, the lightning strike, and even though you are right there in the middle of it, you're still safe at home, sipping your tea beside the gas heater while the tempest rages outside. It's as if the danger were merely a dream, and you the dreamer.

If all this is making you want to move to a lighthouse right now, I should emphasise that none of these whimsical musings are based on my own lighthouse-keeping experience. Most modern lighthouses have no human operator at all – and historically, the conditions of employment were pretty grim. Many lighthouse keepers succumbed to mental illness and even thoughts of suicide, which gave rise to a myth that they 'all went mad' as a result of employment that amounted to solitary confinement. The real reason was more prosaic, though just as sad: keepers were poisoned by the mercury used as a lubricant to help the huge light rotate on its base.[329]

Actually, it seems that those who take charge of lighthouses are fairly down-to-earth, practical types – not swooning introverts who yearn to be far from the madding crowd. That makes sense when you consider that they oversee a vital element of coastal infrastructure. A lighthouse may *look* like an ivory tower, but when you actually take charge of one, there's serious work to be done.

To get a dose of realism, let's hear from Doug Laugher, one of two keepers who take turns to do 28-day solitary shifts at the lighthouse on Machias Seal Island, between Canada and Maine:

> You're only bored out here if you want to be bored. If you're gonna be bored out here, you're gonna be bored anywhere... I think one of the nicest things is you just come out here and you kind of escape from reality for a while. This is your little piece of reality, and you can make it whatever you want it to be.[330]

If a single building just isn't enough room to be alone, how about a whole village? For the last twenty-five years, seventy-four-year-old Giuseppe Spagnuolo has been the sole inhabitant of Roscigno Vecchia, a tiny mountain hamlet in Italy that was abandoned in the 1960s due to the risk of landslides. Born in the new town that was built to replace Roscigno Vecchia, Spagnuolo moved into a deserted house in the old village in 1997, when his marriage broke down and he struggled to find work. Over the years, his fame has spread; today, visitors bring him gifts from around the world in return for his skills as a tour guide. 'If you've experienced the school of life like I have, then you can easily live this way,' says Spagnuolo. 'I have everything I need here, and I take things one day at a time.'[331]

## party of one

> We solitary drinkers – we prefer to be called solo drinkers – have always been stigmatised. Drinking on your own is seen by the medical profession as a sign of such mental health problems as depression and alcoholism. And the public at large regard solo drinking with suspicion, particularly when it comes to men. It's what sad, lonely men do.
>
> COSMO LANDESMAN[332]

Why is drinking alone regarded in such a bad light? Maybe it's because alcohol is such a useful social lubricant, so we imagine that's the only use for it. But if solitude is a conversation with yourself, maybe alcohol will break the ice. A drink or two puts you at your ease, brightens your mood and gets the thought processes going. Why shouldn't you make that pleasant transition by yourself, and follow it wherever it leads?

What's more, it needn't be a low-key affair. Neighbours and sleeping kids permitting, you can make it as rowdy as you like. I'm sure every introvert, at some point, has wished they could separate out the bits of a party they liked from those they didn't. Let me keep the drinking, the music and even the dancing; the sweaty bodies, shouted conversations and bathroom queues I can do without. Get the party started on your own and you can dance like nobody's watching – because nobody *is* watching. (An intriguing, 'alone in a crowd' twist on this is the silent disco, where people get together to dance to their own chosen music on headphones.)

So much for drinking at home. But what about in a bar or pub? How would you feel about drinking alone in public?

As Cosmo Landesman's quote above suggests, taking your solo drinking public is not without its risks. But if you decide that you don't care what anyone thinks, the world is your oyster. If it helps, you could adopt the demeanour of one who is merely waiting for a companion to arrive, or engaged in some elevated pursuit outside of the drinking, like browsing a slim volume of poetry.

I've found my own attitudes have changed markedly over time. In my twenties, I'd probably have been mortified if my friends had discovered me drinking alone. But now, in my fifties, the thought of a solo pub trip is like some magical dream. I could just *sit there*, chilling out and having a drink! As Jamie Carson puts it, 'Do not pity those lonesome bar drinkers, for they are kings of the pub.'[333]

## the solitude room

> Alone had always felt like an actual place to me, as if it weren't a state of being, but rather a room where I could retreat to be who I really was.
>
> CHERYL STRAYED[334]

The metaphor of solitude as a room makes a lot of sense. Roman emperor Marcus Aurelius wrote of an 'inner citadel': 'It is in thy power whenever thou shalt choose to retire into thyself,' he said.[335] Michel de Montaigne argued that 'a man must keep a little back shop where he can be himself without reserve'. And John Lennon expressed similar sentiments in 'There's a Place'.

But why should the room be only in our heads? Why can't we build it in the real world?

After all, we have plenty of rooms for being together – meeting rooms, dining rooms, sitting rooms, auditoriums, stadiums. Bedrooms, studies and bathrooms may be designed for sole occupancy, but they're intended for other purposes. What about a space whose sole function is solitude?

Such a space becomes even more vital when you're obliged to socialise. At times like Christmas and Thanksgiving, there should be a tradition that families provide just one room where introverts can recharge their social batteries. (Extroverts seeking 'good listeners' will not be admitted.) And depending on who you live with, a solitude room might be welcome even in your own home.

The solitude room would be designed solely and specifically for solitude. First, it would be proportioned for one person – somewhere between a bathroom and a box bedroom. This is not just somewhere you *can* be alone, but somewhere you *can only* be alone. I guess we can't really prevent multiple occupancy, but it would be strongly discouraged.

Also, like a bathroom, the door could be firmly bolted from the inside, probably with some sort of outside indication that the occupant has checked out of society for a while and has no wish to be disturbed. A sign saying 'disengaged' might do.

How would it look inside? Well, you can decorate yours however you want – pastel shades, a cat cushion, an acoustic guitar. Personally, I envisage something unashamedly old-school: deep red walls or wood panelling, a single chair (comfortable, yet upright), a reading lamp, a discreet sound system (plus soundproofing) and a round window with a view over trees. A small radiator keeps things cosy, and a quietly ticking clock lets you keep an eye on the time.

At the risk of overcomplicating things, you could also add a minibar, a fridge and a modest en suite bathroom. That would allow you to maintain an uninterrupted stay for as long as you wanted, with no sense of being forced out against your will.

Crucially, no-one can see, hear or otherwise monitor your activities in the solitude room. Not that you're planning to do anything untoward in there, of course. But perfect solitude depends on being unobserved, and you'd want the reassurance that nobody was listening in.

If you want to spend time in the solitude room, your wish must be respected. No-one is allowed to accost you as you enter, to ask what the weather's like outside or when you're going to sort out that insurance. And knocking on the door is *absolutely forbidden* – in fact, the outside of the door is covered in plush fabric that makes it impossible. In return for that forbearance, you undertake to use the room in a responsible way, only entering when you genuinely need an escape and exiting if you're genuinely needed elsewhere.

What introvert's life would not be transformed by such a room? What difference could those few moments of solitude make? How much calmer, saner and more serene could we emerge, if only we were allowed to feed our souls with ten or twenty minutes' precious time alone?

## unspeaking friends

The great thing about pets is they give you company on your own terms. They don't live with you so much as *alongside* you – pursuing their own natural lifestyles as best they can around your home, while you get on with your life. Each of you is alone in your nature, but together in life. For people who are lonely as opposed to just alone, pets fill the hole where people can't be, forging a vital missing link between solitude and company.

The presence of a pet acts as a frame around your solitude, throwing it into sharper relief and reminding you that in human terms, you're still very much alone. You can allow animals into your most intimate spaces and situations, and they won't judge you or even pass comment. If you've decided to spend the whole weekend watching *Friends* in your sweatpants, that's absolutely fine by them.

However, even though pets can't speak, they can still dispel the sense of solitude at times. Or at least, some can. A goldfish eyeing you from its bowl is only one step up from the gaze of a painted portrait or a cuddly toy. But when my Labrador is piercing me with a laser-like stare that very clearly says 'Walk me' or 'Pay me some attention' or 'I want a peanut', it's almost more intrusive than a talkative human. Dogs have enough intelligence to identify humans

who can meet their need for fun, but not *quite* enough to realise when they just don't want to.

To have a pet is to be needed, which is a big part of the attraction. Some give a reassuring rhythm to the day – feeding, cleaning, sleeping, petting. And maintaining a daily schedule of care is probably character-building somehow – at least, that's the effect we hope it will have on kids. But as we've seen, to experience true solitude, you sometimes want to break the ties of day-to-day obligations and demands. By tethering you to their time, animals prevent you from drifting off into your own.

On the plus side, an energetic dog will get you out for a *lot* of solo walks. Meeting other dog owners gives you a nicely bounded dose of human contact, as well as a reliable topic of conversation: dogs. If even that's too much, there seems to be an unwritten rule that if you exude a strong 'walking on my own' vibe, other walkers will generally respect it. At times like this, a dog is the perfect solitude companion, giving you both a reason to be out on your own and the space in which to enjoy it.

Pets, like plants, also give you the chance to engage in a 'conversation' that's entirely on your own terms. You can talk whenever you want, change the subject at will and even break into improvised nonsense verse or song. Your dog will tilt her head in puzzled enquiry, your cat will tolerate your burbling with icy disdain and your goldfish will have no reaction at all – or at least, none that you can see. And if you decide that you prefer silence, that's fine too. If only humans were so accommodating…

## collecting

> Is it so wrong, wanting to be at home with your record collection?
>
> NICK HORNBY[336]

Collecting stuff is a natural fit for the introvert. It requires deep concentration, which we're good at. It allows us to stay at home, which we enjoy. And it has long time horizons – potentially lifelong – which suits our instinct to follow through.

The actual object of collection hardly matters. It could be stamps, coins, first editions, rare vinyl, comics, railway engine numbers, buried ancient artefacts or wine. More recently, digital pastimes like Pokémon Go and Munzee expressly appeal to the collecting impulse ('Gotta catch 'em all!').

Through your collection, you gradually build up a one-person world that only you, and other collectors, understand. Sometimes, collecting is aggressively solitary, because it actively excludes others. But when it's shared, it can be a form of networked solitude, placing the collector at the heart of an extended family of fellow hobbyists.

Collecting can also be a way to hang on to something you remember from your childhood, or never had back then. If you feel that your self has become scattered over time, collecting brings it back together and makes it whole. The collection is an ordered realm within a chaotic world. There's perhaps also something inherently childlike and reassuring about the activity– whatever adult ingenuity it demands, it's a simple and knowable task at heart.

However, collecting also has its dark side. Psychologists have linked it to obsessive-compulsive disorder, hoarding and problems with decision-making. They've also noted that it's based on an 'erroneous' emotional attachment to objects, including feeling responsible for them somehow, and concerns over hanging on to memories (which is why older people tend to hoard more).[337]

Bizarrely, Freud linked collecting to toilet training in our early years. Apparently, we're so traumatised by our 'possessions' disappearing down the pan that we seek out an 'object of desire' to cling on to.[338] More plausibly, Carl Jung traced it to our ancestors' hunter-gatherer lifestyles. Just as they stored up foraged foodstuffs for the long, dark winter, so we store up the Star Wars figures we found in a charity shop. There's even a chance that our collections will pass on to the next generation – unless they just stick the whole lot on eBay the moment we're gone.

## page one

> Reading is solitude. One reads alone, even in another's presence.
>
> ITALO CALVINO[339]

To read is to escape. Simply by picking up an inanimate chunk of paper and ink, you can be transported into other places, other times and other lives. And yet wherever you go, and whoever you meet, there you are: sat snugly in your armchair, completely alone.

> What an astonishing thing a book is. It's a flat object made from a tree with flexible parts on which are imprinted lots of funny dark squiggles. But one glance at it and you're inside the mind of another person, maybe somebody dead for thousands of years... A book is proof that humans are capable of working magic.
>
> CARL SAGAN[340]

As Rebecca Solnit observes, a book in itself is merely an inert object that only becomes its true self through the act of reading:

> The object we call a book is not the real book, but its potential, like a musical score or seed. It exists fully only in the act of being read; and its real home is inside the head of the reader, where the symphony resounds, the seed germinates.[341]

Reading is a dance between writer and reader, conducted across space and time. So reading alone is a form of networked solitude, where you're in touch with another person – the author – but still physically alone. You allow their voice to enter your consciousness, yet you still retain full control. As long as you stay focused on these words, I keep talking – but lift your eyes and I fall silent.

Since reading takes you away from the here-and-now, you could argue that solitary reading is not true solitude. When you open a book, you transport yourself to the author's inner world of thought and imagination. You also strike up a kind of dialogue with them, as you 'reply' in thought to the things they're 'saying' on the page. Of course, that's exactly what close, attentive reading is all about. But by opening yourself to the text, you're closing yourself off to the here-and-now. To read is to choose the word over the world, and the author's consciousness over your own.

Why would you do that? One reason, paradoxically, is 'to know we are not alone', as William Nicholson put it.[342] Although you may want to be physically alone in this moment, that doesn't mean you crave isolation. As introverts, we often feel that the world isn't really made for people like us. And yet we still want to know that we belong – even if it's only to an idea, or a feeling, or some invisible fellowship of the quiet. Whatever we're going through, we want to know that others have been the same way before. Reading alone gives us the solitude we need and the validation we long for, all at the same time.

> There's this part that is redemptive and instructive, [so that] when you read something, it's not just delight— you go, 'Oh my god, that's me! I've lived like that, I've felt like that, I'm not alone in the world…'
>
> DAVID FOSTER WALLACE[343]

Marcel Proust argued that solitary reading was the only way to ignite the creative spark that lies dormant within us all. The 'lazy mind' is 'incapable of putting its creativity into motion', and other people's speech is not enough to rouse it. Only solitary reading, with its mix of reflection and receptiveness, can break the spell:

> What is needed is an intervention that, while coming from another, takes place deep within ourselves. Although [it is] the impulse of another mind, we receive it within our own solitude. And we have seen that this is precisely the nature of reading; that reading alone has this capacity.[344]

I loved books when I was growing up, and spent many hours reading, up in my bedroom alone. When real life is confusing, hurtful or just plain dull, books are the perfect escape. However many times you re-read them, they will reliably work their alchemy time and time again.

The stories I liked best were those of fantastical escapes – like Edmund stepping through the back of the wardrobe into Narnia, Charlie disappearing into Willy Wonka's chocolate factory or James sailing off on the giant peach to New York. Stories like these paint a picture of a world where change is possible. They say that everything passes, for better or worse. They also show that reading itself can be an escape – not just now, but for the whole of life. Yet, at the same time, just by being what they are, they impart the truth that books are not where we live. The story must end, the book must be closed and life must recommence – until next time.

## sole author

> If you are a writer, or want to be a writer, this is how you spend your days—listening, observing, storing things away, making your isolation pay off. You take home all you've taken in, all that you've overheard, and you turn it into gold.
>
> ANNE LAMOTT[345]

Sometime in 1797, Samuel Taylor Coleridge awoke from a vivid dream with an entire poem already formed in his mind. Springing to his writing desk, he hurried to capture it on paper – but then a 'person from Porlock' knocked at his door, detaining him for over an hour. When Coleridge was finally alone once more, 'all the rest had passed away like the images on the surface of a stream into which a stone has been cast', and the poem – *Kubla Khan* – was never finished.

Did 'Porlock' really shatter Coleridge's fruitful solitude? Or were they a fabrication to excuse his writer's block? Stevie Smith thought so, suggesting slyly that 'he was already stuck'. Moreover, she longed for a friendly Porlock of her own:

> I am hungry to be interrupted
> For ever and ever amen
> O Person from Porlock come quickly
> And bring my thoughts to an end.[346]

Whatever the truth, it's easy to sympathise with both poets, because writing can be a lonely business. Whatever your thoughts on solitude, you can only ever write on your own. While there might be some collaboration around the edges to ease the burden, the essential act of choosing words and putting them down is something you can only do alone.

Writing is the other half of the networked solitude experienced by the reader. From within your solitude, you send your words out into the world to speak on your behalf. Like reading, writing can be a form of escapism too. Physically, you're just sitting there at home, drinking tea in front of your laptop. But mentally, you're far away, lost in the world you're creating with your words. Here's Leïla Slimani, author of *Adèle* and *Lullaby*:

> *When were you happiest?*
> Once a year I go away alone to write for a fortnight. I don't talk to anyone, I don't leave my office, I don't shower, I don't get dressed. Nothing makes me happier than these moments of solitary writing, where I live only for my characters.[347]

Such solitary writing feels very different at different times of the day. For me, early morning is the time of peak energy and focus, and I can enjoy an hour of fleet-footed, almost effortless writing as soon as I get up. Edna O'Brien wrote in the morning 'because one is nearer to the unconscious, the source of inspiration.'[348] Maya Angelou, who wrote alone in a hotel room from seven in the morning until two in the afternoon, enthused, 'It's lonely, and it's marvellous.'[349]

Sometimes, an hour of morning writing is worth two or more later in the day. That's certainly how Anthony Trollope saw it: he would habitually rise at five-thirty sharp and write for three hours (producing ten pages) before going off to work at the post office.[350] To discipline himself, he kept his watch in front of him, cranking out 250 words per quarter-hour without fail. Personally, that's the sort of hack I'd be more likely to use in the afternoon, when energy levels plummet and writing feels like more of a trudge.

To choose solitude is to create your own space for writing. The words will never appear while others are watching; you have to be alone. You need a place where you won't be disturbed – which isn't always so easy in a shared or family household.

> One does not find solitude, one creates it. Solitude is created alone. I have created it. Because I decided that here was where I should be alone, that I would be alone to write books... This house became the house of writing.
>
> MARGUERITE DURAS[351]

During lockdown, novelist Jennifer Egan took to writing outside – in all weathers.

> ...I would sit on a deckchair with my binoculars and electric blanket – sometimes two electric blankets – hats and gloves. I looked like a nut. But it was incredibly quiet. I was the only one out there. It was this really deep state of concentration.[352]

And then there is night writing – probably the most intimate, most solitary way to write alone. Not only are you alone with your text, but you also feel alone in the world, as if you're the only one who is awake and aware. Dylan Thomas portrays this brilliantly:

> In my craft or sullen art
> Exercised in the still night
> When only the moon rages
> And the lovers lie abed
> With all their griefs in their arms,
> I labour by singing light…[353]

'Sullen art' evokes writing that stubbornly resists being put to bed, keeping its creator awake. The poet rages in silence, like the moon above him and his synaesthetically 'singing' lamplight, as he tries to put the feelings of the lovers into words. They have no thought of his craft and are asleep elsewhere – but the sly pun on 'lie' suggests that it's the poet who knows the truth. Sometimes, the comfort of solitude is its refusal to deceive.

For Franz Kafka, the best time to see clearly was after darkness fell. Bustling diurnal life was superficial, distracting and ultimately false; the only way to truth was through solitude and silence:

> Writing that springs from the surface of existence – when there is no other way and the deeper wells have dried up – is nothing, and collapses the moment a truer emotion makes that surface shake. That is why one can never be alone enough when one writes, why there can never be enough silence around one when one writes, why even night is not night enough.[354]

Such intense seclusion raises the tension between the process of writing and its content. For some writers, human interaction provides the raw material, while solitude converts it into words. As we saw in chapter five, Ralph Waldo Emerson was a fan of solitude and a fierce proponent of self-reliance – but he was equally bullish that writing was a social process:

> If you would learn to write, 'tis in the street you must learn it. Both for the vehicle and for the aims of fine arts you must frequent the public square. The people, and not the college, is the writer's home.[355]

Emerson's view presupposes that writing is a tool for communication. But just as you can sing, play or dance without an audience, so you can write for no reader but yourself, and with no aim beyond the sheer joy of writing.

The classic form of private writing is the diary. Keeping a diary can help you organise your thoughts, record ideas and reflect on what's going on. It's also a powerful aid to memory: capturing happy and fulfilling experiences in writing helps you keep a hold of them, so you can return to them in future – like Wordsworth's daffodils from chapter two.

If you want, you can also set yourself targets for the future – just writing down goals can help in achieving them, and a diary is the perfect place to do it. Conversely, putting your achievements into words makes them more solid and real, compiling a 'greatest hits' that you can review to remind yourself of your talents in the future.

Writing can also activate the incubation effect, which is where our unconscious minds keep pondering on a task or problem while we're thinking about something else. Your reticular activating system will become attuned to resources and opportunities that you might otherwise have missed.[356]

If you do decide to share your writing, you'll need to make it ready for the world. The word 'edit' comes from the Latin *edere*, meaning 'bring forth', evoking how careful, patient effort helps your writing to gradually emerge. And for the introvert, the unfolding of this process raises the dilemma of when to show the work to someone else.

I'm sure all introvert creators share a strong desire to keep their work private, where they have full control. Just about *any* feedback, no matter how tactful or well-intentioned, can take root in the dark soil of the introvert's mind. What did they *mean* by that? Should I change something – or everything? Does the work actually have any worth at all?

I've self-published all my books on Amazon, and what I love about this model is that nobody comes between me and my reader. In my here-and-now, which is your past, I can write whatever I want, and be sure that you will read it in your here-and-now, which is my future. I'm speaking straight from my solitude to yours.

## headphone head

> Music is the wine that fills the cup of silence.
>
> ROBERT FRIPP

When Thomas Edison invented the phonograph (vinyl record player) in 1877, he changed music for ever. Until then, there had only been two ways to listen to music: listening to musicians perform, or performing it yourself. So a lot of music was inherently social – singing around the piano, for example, or going to a concert. But with the advent of the record, music went from being a one-off event, here today and gone tomorrow, to being fixed in amber, locked down, repeatable. You could listen to a song over and over again, until you knew it down to the tiniest detail. Records became a fixed point against which you could measure changes in yourself. And last but not least, you could listen on your own.

However, not everyone welcomed that. Critics argued that solo listening was narcissistic and would atrophy 'mental muscles', sinking the listener's mind into 'a complete and comfortable vacuum'. But devotees countered that the format brought them closer to the work: 'You are alone with the composer and his music. Surely no more ideal circumstances could be imagined.'[357]

Moral panics will always be with us; only the topic changes. I'm much happier to see my daughter lost in Apple Music than scrolling aimlessly through junk content on TikTok. In fact, I often think the greatest gift her generation enjoys is their easy, instant access to the universe of music – every artist, every era, every style.

When I was growing up, in a time when records got spins rather than streams, listening to music was *way* harder. The best you could hope for was a tinny cassette tape player or a hand-me-down turntable in your bedroom. If you wanted hi-fi, you had to go to the lounge and play your records on the family stereo (or 'music centre'). Whenever I got the chance, I used to love putting on my

dad's big, white plastic headphones and disappearing into an all-enveloping audio cocoon.

With the advent of the Walkman, music became an amulet that you could carry all day long. Your own private music-world was always there, ready to be escaped into at a moment's notice. And once the iPod brought us 'a thousand songs in your pocket', you didn't even have to choose which songs to take.

Sometimes, I've played the music I love to friends, to see if they feel what I feel. That's no small thing for an introvert, because sharing your music is like opening your heart. And the stakes are high: if they don't like it, you could end up resenting them for their honesty, berating yourself for your naïveté or even vindictively turning against the music itself. On the other hand, even a positive reaction feels inadequate and hollow. OK, they said they liked it – but do they *really* hear what you hear?

As it turns out, there's a good reason for this: our listening experience changes when other people are around. While collective listening increases music's stress-busting power, solo listening intensifies its emotional content – happy or sad.[358] If we're *already* feeling sad, private listening helps us repair our mood and fosters a sense of connection. By harmonising with our own mood, the music acts as a 'social surrogate' – a stand-in for an empathetic friend.[359] As with reading, we want to *be* alone, but not necessarily *feel* alone.

When it comes to playing music for yourself, some instruments are better suited to solitude than others. I learned the piano, which lets the solo player make a full sound – but also a fairly loud one. If you're like me, the sense of being overheard will slightly taint the experience. Playing music lets people hear a little bit of your soul.

These days, I play an electronic keyboard that lets me hide inside headphones. During the 1980s and 90s, the technical development of electronic instruments reached the point where aspiring musicians could put together ambitious productions completely on their own, their sounds limited only by their imaginations.

> I like making music on my own. I work well when it's just me in a room. That was the thing that first attracted me to a sampler back in the 90s. Here was a grey box that allowed me to do everything on my own. Suddenly, I didn't need to be in a band.
>
> SI GREEN (BONOBO)[360]

It's not just electronic albums that can be made by one person. Bruce Springsteen initially recorded his bleak acoustic opus *Nebraska* as intimate home demos. When he came to re-record them with the E Street Band, he realised that the group couldn't match the intimacy of his solo tape – so he released that instead. 'I was carrying that cassette around with me in my pocket without a case for a couple of weeks, just dragging it around,' he recalls. 'Finally, we realized, "Uh-oh, that's the album."'[361]

In pop today, lone musicians are on the rise. Forming a band means recruiting friends, buying instruments, rehearsing and playing live – all hard work, and expensive, too. With digital music-making tools so readily available, and social media so strongly oriented towards individuals, it's no wonder today's young musicians are taking to their home studios to create alone.[362]

## friends in your phone

Podcasts are one of my favourite forms of digital networked solitude. They're like a friendship group, but without the friends. They provide what psychologists call *parasocial interaction*: when we feel we know real or fictional figures from culture, the media or the internet, even when we've never interacted with them.[363]

As our parasocial relationship unfolds, we elaborate an illusory intimacy, using whatever facts we discover to fill in the details of our 'friendship'. Some people even *prefer* parasocial relationships, because the object of their affections will never let them down.

I wouldn't go that far about *Test Match Special*. But what podcasts do give me is the feeling of conversation without the need to speak; the sense of camaraderie while I'm actually alone. That impression is encouraged by the format itself, where people who really are friends in real life chat away like they're meeting for a coffee.

As described earlier, I often stay silent in company – but it can come across as stand-offish or even selfish, particularly with people who don't know you that well. With the right podcast, you can have the full wallflower experience without the guilt. Your 'friends' will talk about a subject you love while you stay snugly in the background, listening in with the blessing of your hosts, secure in the knowledge that no-one is going to ask you what you think, or why you're so quiet tonight.

I often listen in bed, last thing at night. I drift off to sleep as the conversation flows on, floating into the night on a cloud of friendly words. It's like sitting in a crowded bar towards the end of the evening, realising I'm feeling a bit tired, and then being magically spirited away to my bed. Which, let's be honest, is something we've all fantasised about at some point.

During the pandemic, when all our relationships went digital anyway, podcasts offered happiness on demand. We couldn't meet up to hang out – and even when we did, we often found that the mood was less celebratory than we hoped. But podcasts never disappointed. They were like a Zoom call you could dance to.[364]

The other great thing about pods is they can give you the trivial yet somehow indispensable chat you only get when you see people all the time. Most of my closest friends are people I once hung out with every day, but now see rarely. That makes it hard to slip straight into easy-going conversation, because we have so much vital stuff to catch up on. Sometimes I wish we could skip what really matters and get down to the small talk. And podcasts give me that on tap.

# seeds of solitude

> Fair quiet, have I found thee here,
> And Innocence thy Sister dear!
> Mistaken long, I sought you then
> In busie Companies of Men.
> Your sacred Plants, if here below,
> Only among the Plants will grow.
> Society is all but rude,
> To this delicious Solitude.
>
> ANDREW MARVELL[365]

Gardening must be the perfect introvert hobby. First of all, it's the perfect form of alonework: in pretty much any garden, any time of the year, there's always *something* that needs doing. If home is feeling hectic, or you just need some time to recharge, you always have the perfect excuse to slip outside and pull some weeds.

A garden is the ideal artefact to proclaim an introvert's talents on their behalf. While you may pour many hours into nurturing its glory, most of the credit will still go to nature. Even though others may look at the garden every day, they're still unlikely to realise how many tasks and decisions you went through, all alone, to bring it to this point. Only your fellow gardeners, who've travelled the same road, will appreciate how much you've done.

When you think about it, it's not strictly accurate to talk about being 'alone in a garden'. Sure, there are no other *people* present, but you're still surrounded by living beings, all quietly going about their biological business. There you stand among your many subjects, monarch of a grateful nation who still cannot thank you for your care. Like people, plants sometimes do well and sometimes badly – but unlike people, they can never tell us why. As May Sarton puts it, 'Plants do not speak, but their silence is alive with change.'[366]

Because I work in my office most of the time, I love the different flavour of solitude the garden provides: outdoors instead of indoors, using tools instead of words and hands instead of brain. The garden is a great place to think things through – yet it's also a place to *not* think, to lose yourself in handiwork.

> A garden offers the opposite of the disembodied uncertainties of writing. It's vivid to all the senses, it's a space of bodily labor, of getting dirty in the best and most literal way, an opportunity to see immediate and unarguable effect.
>
> REBECCA SOLNIT[367]

Gardeners are always looking forward. Every year is a new start, with the chance to dig over past mistakes and begin afresh. Bare earth is the blank page of the garden. As we make our plans for it, we have high hopes for what we might achieve – but it's a mellow, earthy sort of ambition, with nothing brash or avaricious about it.

> Expectation is what gives us the face of contentment as we work in it through sun and rain. We labour in accordance with the needs of the garden, and our life joins there with the life of nature. The garden has a future, and so have we.
>
> DOUGLAS SWINSCOW[368]

Through that shared future, we can rediscover a connection to nature that would have been second nature to our ancestors, but is distant and neglected today. As a gardener, you can't help but become attuned to the turning of the seasons, the angle of the sun, the frequency of rain and the unalterable consistency of soil. You observe, and slowly learn, the many interlocking and overlapping timescales of the garden – measured in days, seasons or years.

And if you're lucky enough to have space to grow some fruit or veg, you can witness the wonder of something with the power to sustain life – *your* life – coming into being from a tiny seed. Pulling a carrot from the earth, rather than a supermarket shelf, is a humbling reminder of how much we take for granted.

> Kneeling between the scale of seeds and the scale of stars, touching evolutionary time and the cycle of seasons at once, you find yourself rooted more deeply into your own existence — transient and transcendent, fragile and ferociously resilient — and are suddenly humbled into your humanity.
>
> MARIA POPOVA[369]

My own garden is overlooked by a towering oak that must be several hundred years old. Before our street was even thought of, that tree was already old. It may stand on 'my' land, but as I obediently clear its drifts of leaves every autumn, I know that it is the master, and I the servant.

That's how gardening is. You think you're working on your garden, when in fact it's working on *you*. Some choices are made, and they feel like they're yours, but nature is always pushing back. You aspire to self-expression, but the garden has something of its own to say. Like writing, the garden falls short of the creator's vision because it reflects their character all too well, with its weeds as well as its flowers.

> Gardens are a paradox. They reflect their owners; they are totally dependent; and yet in no time at all they are breathing with their own lungs, growing at their own pace, behaving with either wilful disregard or subjugation.
>
> MIRABEL OSLER[370]

Every garden is both inheritance and bequest. Rather than designing the whole thing from scratch, as glossy books suggest, you usually just look after it for a while, tending your predecessor's plants and maybe adding a few of your own. A magnolia I plant today might not flower until I'm in my seventies – or in the ground myself.

In these lines, Emily Dickinson reflects on those who will enjoy her garden after she has left:

New feet within my garden go—
New fingers stir the sod—
A Troubadour upon the Elm
Betrays the solitude.

New children play upon the green—
New Weary sleep below—
And still the pensive Spring returns—
And still the punctual snow!

In Frances Hodgson Burnett's *The Secret Garden*, Mary Lennox is an unloved and unloving ten-year-old, raised in British India, who is sent to live in a country house on the Yorkshire moors following the death of her parents. Stuck indoors on her own, Mary feels confined and fed up. 'People never like me and I never like people,' she sulks. But then she discovers the key to a long-locked secret garden in the grounds of the house – 'the sweetest, most mysterious-looking place any one could imagine'.

The secret garden has the power to help Mary's reclusive cousin, Colin, return to health. In the process, it also helps Mary become less selfish – growing as a person along with the flowers. Having originally been locked up and neglected as an act of mourning for Mary's aunt Lilias, the rejuvenated garden becomes an emblem of rebirth. It's a place of solitude that offers solace, natural wonder, friendship and, above all, tranquillity.

> In secret places we can think and imagine, we can feel angry or sad in peace. There is something to be said for just being, without worrying about offending anyone.[371]

Gardens that feel modest to an adult can seem vast to a child, with their open spaces and secret corners. The garden is a space that is at home, yet also apart from it– somewhere you can explore without risk. And there's always something new to discover.

> One day Sally found a secret house which nobody knew about. It was in a bush at the bottom of the garden. There was a hole in it just right for a front door, and inside were leafy walls and room in the middle for Sally to stand up straight. The floor was of earth and it smelt lovely.
>
> SHIRLEY HUGHES[372]

Sally also likes to make her houses around her home, but they often get tidied away by mistake. The home is subject to the tyranny of adult rationality: the rigid regimes and dull discipline of parents. But the garden, even though it's just outside the back door, is a place where rules are relaxed and imagination can run free.

I would very much like to see my garden through Sally's eyes – to see leaves as walls and earth as a fragrant floor. Unfortunately, the older you get, the harder that becomes. 'The things which I have seen I now can see no more,' as Wordsworth put it.[373] The best I can do is leave a few untended corners that retain their mystery and surprise. Maybe 'new feet' will come in the future to explore them.

# player one

There's a lot to be said for playing games alone. You choose the rules, and when to break them. You decide when play starts, and when it ends. And if you walk away from the game halfway through, nobody really minds.

Card games for multiple players have been around for centuries, but as middle-class households found more free time during the nineteenth century, solo games became more popular. In patience, the single player tries to arrange a pack of cards in some systematic order. There are hundreds of variants, some with enticingly poetic names – *The Gathering of the Clans*, *The Beleaguered Castle*, *The House on the Hill*. I guess with a bit of imagination, you could picture yourself as a Highland warrior or a medieval monarch as you played. After all, you didn't have to convince anyone else.

Patience has a pleasantly meditative quality. Once you've learned the rules, you can easily think of something else while you play it. It also has a gratifying sense of restoring harmony out of chaos. As the pack is brought back into order, so is your mind.

To play patience is to become both player and referee. You must observe the rules, or suffer the private shame of cheating yourself. You *can* play in company, but if you've ever tried, you know that having someone looking over your shoulder and pointing out mistakes will sorely test your own patience.

I used to play quite a bit of patience as a teenager. Once I twigged that the outcome was pretty much predestined as soon as the cards were dealt, I would furiously shuffle the pack beforehand, as if I could generate a winning configuration through sheer effort.

Another of my teenage time-sinks was the Fighting Fantasy series: 'choose your own adventure' gamebooks 'in which YOU become the hero!' These were ordinary paperbacks comprised of numbered sections that you navigated by making choices or rolling dice and following instructions. Thus, they combined traditional fictional narratives with player agency and a slice of luck. And they were solitary in every sense: you were a lone reader and a lone player, and you became a lone character and adventurer too.

Critics pointed out that chance played an unfairly large part in the outcome – and I have to say, I shared their concerns. One unlucky dice-roll could see you skewered by some malignant goblin or plunging into an inescapable pit through no fault of your own. As with patience, there was always a strong temptation to bend the rules, rewind time and try again. After all, no one was watching.

The first title in the series, *The Warlock of Firetop Mountain*, sold two million copies.[374] That's astonishing in itself, but even more so when you consider that these books were competing for teenage eyeballs with early video games, played in arcades and also on home computers. Like Fighting Fantasy, most of these cast you as a lone hero on a million-to-one mission. Whether you were controlling a plumber, a frog, a paperboy or a spaceship, it was you against the world, no turning back. Tasked yet again with single-handedly saving humankind, as you were in *Space Invaders* or *Missile Command*, you could be forgiven for wondering why you never got any help with your missions. Where *was* everybody?

Due to the limitations of the technology, game design was necessarily basic and abstract – usually, a plain black playfield populated by colourful, darting sprites. But these barren, empty spaces still felt strangely comforting, because they were a place you could escape to where no-one could find you and nothing unexpected could happen.

With the advent of home computers (as they were then known), you could not only play games at home, but potentially create your own. Machines like the ZX Spectrum and Commodore 64 were pitifully weak by today's standards, but their simplicity meant that an entire program could be conceived, written and tested by just one person. Learning to program made you the undisputed ruler of a finite and perfectly logical universe under your absolute control.

> The first time I used a computer was the first time the world really went dim – the outside world, that is – and it was just me and the computer.
>
> PETER MOLYNEUX[375]

In those days, talented self-taught programmers could create commercially viable games completely on their own. From their unruly imaginations sprang madcap creations like *Attack of the Mutant Camels* and *Manic Miner*, drawing on the antic humour of *Monty Python* and *The Hitch-Hiker's Guide to the Galaxy*. Authored by one individual and played by another, these games were like a digital letter from the programmer's solitude to the player's.

Today, games are multi-million-pound affairs created by hundred-strong teams. They offer the solo player immersive experiences with absorbing stories, set in game-worlds in which the player can get lost for hundreds of hours. Thanks to astronomical increases in computing power, these worlds are now populated with almost-human non-player characters that the player can battle, befriend or betray as they wish. Modern games are not just escapism, but a fully-fledged escape; in the words of novelist and gamer Tom Bissell, they offer us an 'extra life'.[376]

Games can also admit dozens of other human players – something that would have been completely impossible in my youth. But although multiplayer gaming is a form of networked solitude, it's a fairly scrappy and frenetic one. Wandering round the icy wastes of single-player *Skyrim* has a pleasingly solitary flavour, no matter how many in-game characters you meet. (You can even visit a town called Solitude.) But getting trounced and insulted by a twelve-year-old at online *Call of Duty* feels like being stuck in a soft play area and pelted with multicoloured plastic balls. Maybe I'm getting too old for this…

# in the bathroom

> If I want to be alone, some place I can write, I can read, I can pray, I can cry, I can do whatever I want—I go to the bathroom.
>
> Alicia Keys

Sanitation is socially sanctioned solitude. Using the bathroom alone is not only desirable, but entirely appropriate. The whole of civilised society actively encourages you to be in there on your own.

And once you are in the bathroom, you can remain there as long as you want, within reason. Everyone understands implicitly that there's something sacred about the space itself, and the time you spend there. It's the inner sanctum of hygiene.

I've rarely been in a British bathroom that didn't have a lock on the door. If your experience is the same, you may be alarmed to learn that American bathrooms never used to have locks. You were just supposed to infer occupancy from the door being closed, which may be logical but feels reckless nonetheless. The thought of trusting this system to safeguard my privacy makes me feel a little dizzy.

Do you lock the bathroom door when you're already at home on your own? *Of course you do.* Because it makes you feel even more secure, even more alone, with even more walls and doors between you and those who would disrupt your solitude. It's a sort of domestic motte-and-bailey affair, with you as the solitary monarch on your throne and the vandal hordes kept at bay by layers of stone.

No bathroom, however luxurious, can ever really compare to your own. But even a bathroom outside the home provides the opportunity for a solitude mini-break.[377] If a family gathering or night out is proving too intense, you can always retreat to the loo for a time-out. Nobody will question whether you really need it – and the older you get, the more plausible your absence becomes.

What about a public toilet/bathroom? Here, your solitude is balanced on a knife-edge. Assuming we're not talking about a lockable, single-occupancy cubicle, as found on a train or a plane, just to enter the space is a gamble. Unless you've been discreetly staking out the entrance from across the room, you push that door open with literally *no idea* how many people are inside. You could be in for anything from a blissful solo experience to a hectic jostle involving queuing for a cubicle, awkward two-steps around the hand dryer and, at worst, even *speaking to another person.* (I'm a man, remember. Toilet chit-chat, even when standing side by side at the urinals, isn't really the done thing.)

Psychologically, your task is to somehow block out the cacophony and establish a sort of mental home-from-home. Researchers have found that bathroom-goers 'may lay claim to any unoccupied stall in the bathroom,' but 'once such a claim is laid, once the door to the stall is closed, it is transformed into the occupying individual's private, albeit temporary, retreat'.[378] Once you convince yourself, against the odds, that this facility is as warm and welcoming as the one you have at home, you'll be able to do what you came to do.

## only sleeping

> Alone one is never lonely: the spirit adventures, waking
> In a quiet garden, in a cool house, abiding single there;
> The spirit adventures in sleep, the sweet thirst-slaking
> When only the moon's reflection touches the wild hair.
>
> MAY SARTON[379]

At the end of the day, what could be more solitary than sleep? Whoever you share your bed with, and whatever you do with them while you're there, you still go into sleep alone. As Paul Martin puts it, 'When we are awake we all inhabit a common world, but when we sleep each of us occupies a world of our own.'[380]

Of all the solitary activities in this book, sleeping is one you're almost certain to have done. In fact, you'll spend a third of your life doing it – far more than you spend walking, reading, listening to music or any other solitary pursuit. And yet it's also the activity that you probably know the least about. All the action takes place inside your mind, and most of it is forgotten by morning. And if anyone else is present, their observations are likely to be limited to complaints that they can't sleep themselves or irritable requests for you to *please* stop snoring because they've got to be up in four hours.

Sleep, like solitude, is often seen as a blank space, an interlude or a pause, rather than a thing in itself. But just as solitude is more than the absence of people, so sleep is more than the absence of consciousness and movement. It's an active brain state, as essential to life as food and water – yet we often neglect it, and many of us are chronically sleep-deprived throughout our lives.

Provided you're physically able to do it, sleeping is hugely pleasurable. It's easy to do and supremely refreshing once you've done it, with lavish in-flight entertainment in the form of dreams. And yet, in comparison with other activities that are essential to our survival, like eating and sex, there's much less sybaritic culture around sleeping. In response to an enquiry about weekend plans, the reply 'I'm going to do some sleeping' is likely to sound facetious, sullen or even nihilistic. And it's a brave jobseeker who lists 'sleeping' as an interest on their cv.

That might be because sleeping is seen as mere downtime, or because it's considered to be solitary in the 'wrong' way. Eating, drinking and indeed having sex on your own are sometimes frowned on, or regarded as inferior to their more sociable equivalents. Somehow, sleeping gets lumped in with those sensual pleasures, rather than with elevated pursuits like reading that are acceptable to do solo. In its way, a good sleep could be as salubrious as a run or as edifying as a symphony. But in society's eyes, it's just lounging in your pit.

Talking of pits, maybe all these downwardly mobile metaphors are part of the problem. For example, we 'lie down' or 'crash', then 'fall asleep' or 'drop off'. Sound sleep is an attribute of earthbound objects like rocks or logs. Emerging from it, we 'wake up', 'get up' or 'rise and shine'. Why can't going to sleep be more of an ascension – drifting up to the stars, or sleeping like a cloud? After all, sleep is where we dream – and fantastical visions must surely be of the heavens, not the earth. When we envision or imagine, we cast our eyes upwards rather than down.

Most of us spend around two hours a night dreaming, or six years over our whole lives. We sometimes think of dreams as the opposite to 'real life', when really, they're an integral part of it. Just like solitude, they're an experience on a par with all the other experiences of our lives – the ultimate solitary experience, in fact.

Dreaming and wakefulness are more like similar shades than contrasting colours. After all, they both come from the same origin: your ever-active brain. They differ only in their raw material – your senses with eyes open, your memories with them closed – and how rationally you process it.[381] And they influence each other all the time: waking life is a rich source for dreams, and while many dreams melt away on waking, others can have a profound and lasting impact. In fact, dream events can be just as instructive or insightful as waking ones, as Cathy Linton observes in Emily Brontë's *Wuthering Heights*:

> I've dreamt in my life dreams that have stayed with me ever after, and changed my ideas; they've gone through and through me, like wine through water, and altered the colour of my mind.[382]

Dreams are a great leveller – or a great elevator, I should say. We all travel to the same unbounded dreamworld, and we all enjoy the same freedoms once we're there. Whatever your brain takes a fancy to, it can bring into your nocturnal drama. Money is no object, and neither is permission: everyone must play their part whether they want to or not.

Nearly all dreams take place in the present and involve ourselves. Regarding the rest of the cast, researchers at Harvard found that these other 'characters' are roughly half people we know from waking life, and half generic walk-on parts like 'teacher', 'policeman' and so on. Fewer than one in six people are specially created for the dream. Non-human elements are usually drawn from everyday life, but juxtaposed in extraordinary ways – the raw material of surrealist art.[383]

When we say something is 'a dream', we usually mean it's good or even perfect. But around two-thirds of dreams involve fear, confusion, helplessness or just low-grade embarrassment or hassle. Personally, my least favourite dreams aren't outlandish nightmares – they do, at least, speak to a fertile imagination – but those of deskbound drudgery, where I'm fixing punctuation or fiddling with a spreadsheet. A dream that's different from my waking life seems like the very least I can expect.

At the other extreme, dreams can be a powerful creative force. As we saw earlier in this chapter, Coleridge's *Kubla Khan* came from a dream. 'Yesterday' came to Paul McCartney in a dream, so fully formed that he had trouble believing he'd really written it – although he still struggled with the lyric, making do with 'scrambled eggs' until he arrived at 'yesterday'.[384] But before we fantasise about dreaming a number one of our own, we should bear in mind that McCartney had already written dozens of hits when his head hit the pillow – just as Coleridge already had some first drafts of *Kubla Khan*. The dreamer matters, not just the dream.

Thanks for reading, and goodnight.

# NOTES

[1] Defining solitude: Philip Koch, *Solitude: A Philosophical Encounter*, chapter 1 'Dimensions'. Open Court, 1994.

[2] Philip Koch, op. cit., chapter 2.

[3] The Extrovert Ideal: Susan Cain, *Quiet: The Power of Introverts in a World That Can't Stop Talking*. Crown Publishing Group, 2012.

[4] 'It is possible to be solitary…': Benedicta Ward, *The Sayings of the Desert Fathers: The Alphabetical Collection*. Cistercian Publications, 1975.

[5] Networked vs abstracted solitude: David Vincent, *A History of Solitude*. Polity Press, 2020. Chapter 1

[6] 'Shake off the village': Henry David Thoreau, *Walden, or Life in the Woods*. Ticknor and Fields, 1854.

[7] 'A solitude of space': Emily Dickinson, 'There is a solitude of space'. In *The Complete Poems of Emily Dickinson*, Back Bay Books, 1976.

[8] Buddha on solitude: Dharmawiki, 'Solitude'. https://www.dhammawiki.com/index.php/Solitude

[9] Reasons to seek solitude in Buddhism: University of Idaho, 'Buddhist Practice of the Solitude'. https://www.webpages.uidaho.edu/~rfrey/PDF/101/101_Solitude.pdf

[10] 'Helpful everywhere': Dharmawiki, 'Right Mindfulness'. https://www.dhammawiki.com/index.php?title=Right_Mindfulness

[11] 'Mind weeds' and 'no gaining idea': Shunryū Suzuki, *Zen Mind, Beginner's Mind*. Weatherhill, 1970.

[12] Prefer anything to doing nothing: Timothy D. Wilson, David A. Reinhard Erin C. Westgate, Daniel T. Gilbert, Nicole Ellerbeck, Cheryl Hahn, Casey l. Brown and Adi Shaked, 'Just think: The challenges of the disengaged mind'. *Science*, Vol 345, Issue 6192. 4 July 2014. https://www.science.org/doi/10.1126/science.1250830

[13] Contemplation as exercise: Carmen Acevedo Acevedo, *The Cloud of Unknowing: A New Translation*. Shambhala Publications, 2011.

[14] Quintilian, an inner sanctuary: Quoted in Aaron J. Kachuck, *The Solitary Sphere in the Age of Virgil*. Oxford University Press, 2021. p. 9.

[15] Erosion of solitude: Vincent, op. cit.

[16] Crusoe enjoying solitude: Daniel Defoe, *Serious Reflections during the Life and Surprising Adventures of Robinson Crusoe: with his Vision of the Angelick World. Written by Himself*, 1720.

[17] Networked solitude: Vincent, op. cit. Chapter 3.

[18] Recalling conversations: Laura Stafford, Cynthia S. Burggraf and William F. Sharkey, 'Conversational Memory The Effects of Time, Recall, Mode, and Memory Expectancies on Remembrances of Natural Conversations'. *Human Communication Research*, 1987. https://doi.org/10.1111/j.1468-2958.1987.tb00127.x

[19] Remembering our own reactions: Anthony G. Greenwald, 'On Defining Attitude and Attitude Theory', in Anthony G. Greenwald, Timothy C. Brock and Thomas M. Ostrom (eds.), *Psychological Foundation of Attitude*, 1968.

[20] Imagined conversations: Margaret Arnd-Caddigan, 'Imagining the other: The influence of imagined conversations on the treatment process'. *American Journal of Psychotherapy*, 66(4), 2012. https://doi.org/10.1176/appi.psychotherapy.2012.66.4.331

[21] 'While here I stand': William Wordsworth, 'Lines Composed a Few Miles above Tintern Abbey, On Revisiting the Banks of the Wye during a Tour. July 13, 1798'. https://www.poetryfoundation.org/poems/45527/lines-composed-a-few-miles-above-tintern-abbey-on-revisiting-the-banks-of-the-wye-during-a-tour-july-13-1798

[22] 'A host, of golden daffodils': William Wordsworth, 'I Wandered Lonely as a Cloud'. https://www.poetryfoundation.org/poems/45521/i-wandered-lonely-as-a-cloud

[23] 'We all need space': Sam Knight, 'Britain's idyllic country houses reveal a darker history.' *New Yorker*, 23 August 2021.

https://www.newyorker.com/magazine/2021/08/23/britains-idyllic-country-houses-reveal-a-darker-history

[24] True solitude in wild spaces: Wendell Berry, *What are People For?: Essays*. Counterpoint, 2010.

[25] Harriet Sherwood, 'Getting back to nature: how forest bathing can make us feel better'. *The Observer*, 8 June 2019. https://www.theguardian.com/environment/2019/jun/08/forest-bathing-japanese-practice-in-west-wellbeing

[26] 'I am sitting at my desk': Oliver Morgan, 'Music for the Dance: Some Meanings of Solitude'. *Journal of Religion and Health*, 25, No. 1 (Spring 1986).

[27] 'Solitudes are not to be measured…': Alice Meynell, 'Solitude'. In *The Spirit of Place, and Other Essays.* Lane, 1899. https://www.hermitary.com/solitude/meynell.html

[28] 'We are one…': May Sarton, *Journal of a Solitude*. Norton & Co, 1973.

[29] 'Each day, each month…': Terry Waite, *Solitude: Memories, People, Places* SPCK, 2017. Chapter 3.

[30] Time seems to pass more quickly for adults and parents: Marc Wittman, 'Having Children May Make the Years Seem to Pass More Quickly'. *Psychology Today*, 28 January 2021. https://www.psychologytoday.com/gb/blog/sense-time/202101/having-children-may-make-the-years-seem-pass-more-quickly

[31] 'Flowing personal time': Koch, op. cit., chapter 1.

[32] Temporal bandwidth: Thomas Pynchon, *Gravity's Rainbow*. Viking, 1973.

[33] 'All the world's a stage': From the 'seven ages of man' speech by Jaques in *As You Like It*, Act 2 Scene 7. https://www.rsc.org.uk/as-you-like-it/about-the-play/famous-quotes

[34] How we interact face to face: Erving Goffman, *The Presentation of Self in Everyday Life*. Doubleday, 1959. Translated editions use alternative titles including *We All Play-Act* and *The Self and the Masks*.

[35] 'Behind Closed Doors': Jean-Paul Sartre, *Huis Clos*. 1944.

[36] *The Good Place*: 'Chapter 1: Mike Schur' (from 18m 50s). *The Good Place: The Podcast*. https://www.nbc.com/the-good-place/exclusives/tgp-podcast

[37] 'A man can be himself…': Arthur Schopenhauer, *The World as Will and Representation*, 1818.

[38] 'Freedom is the possibility of isolation': Ferdinand Pessoa, *The Book of Disquiet*. Penguin, 2002.

[39] 'You do not have to be good': From Mary Oliver, 'Wild Geese' in *Wild Geese: Selected Poems*. Bloodaxe, 2004.

[40] Pig consciousness: Marion Woodman, *The Maiden King*. Dorset, 1999. p. 179

[41] 'You talk when you cease to be at peace with your thoughts': Khalil Gibran, *The Prophet*. Alfred A. Knopf, 1923.

[42] Mary Oliver, 'How I Go to the Woods'. In *Swan: Poems and Prose Poems*. Beacon Press, 2010.

[43] 'Withholding of information': David Hare, 'New Britain, same as the old one: the legacy of the second Elizabethan era'. *The Guardian*, 9 September 2022. https://www.theguardian.com/uk-news/2022/sep/09/queen-elizabeth-ii-legacy-david-hare

[44] Mr Rental: Michelle Ye Hee Lee and Julia Mio Inuma, 'Meet the Japanese man paid to do nothing'. *The Independent*, 23 March 2022. https://www.independent.co.uk/life-style/japan-do-nothing-man-rent-pay-b2040364.html

[45] Truth attained in silence: Iris Murdoch, *Under the Net*. Chatto & Windus, 1954.

[46] Health benefits of silence: L. Bernardi, C Porta and P. Sleight, Cardiovascular, cerebrovascular, and respiratory changes induced by different types of music in musicians and non-musicians: the importance of silence'. *Heart* (BMJ), Volume 92, Issue 4. https://heart.bmj.com/content/92/4/445

[47] Health hazards of noise: F. Lederbogen and A. Meyer-Lindenberg, 'Erhöhte Stressvulnerabilität bei Großstadtbewohnern [Increased stress vulnerability in big city dwellers]'. *Die Psychiatrie*, 2016. https://www.thieme-connect.com/products/ejournals/abstract/10.1055/s-0038-1670121

[48] Silence and solitude are linked: Sara Maitland, *A Book of Silence*. Granta Books, 2009. Chapter 1.

[49] Premiere of '4' 33"': Alex Ross, 'Searching for Silence'. *New York Times*, 27 September 2010. https://www.newyorker.com/magazine/2010/10/04/searching-for-silence

[50] 'A new way of hearing music': From Eno's sleeve notes for *Discreet Music*, 1975. http://music.hyperreal.org/artists/brian_eno/discreet-txt.html

[51] 'As ignorable as it is interesting': From Eno's sleeve notes for *Music for Airports*, 1978. http://music.hyperreal.org/artists/brian_eno/MFA-txt.html

[52] Effects of prolonged exposure to silence: Maitland, op cit., chapter 2.

[53] 'We're drawn to identity-markers…': David P. Levine and Matthew H. Bowker, *A Dangerous Place to Be: Identity, Conflict, and Trauma in Higher Education*. Routledge, 2018.

[54] 'Immeasurable solitude of self': Resignation speech from the National American Woman Suffrage Association, of which she was the first president. Included in Zachary Seager, *The Art of Solitude*, Pan Macmillan, 2020.

[55] 'Uncontradicting solitude': Closing lines from 'Best Society' (c1951), in *Philip Larkin: Collected Poems*. Faber, 1988.

[56] 'How you speak to yourself': Michel de Montaigne, 'On Solitude' in *The Complete Essays*. Penguin, 2013.

[57] 'That inner world…': *Thomas de Quincey, Confessions of an English Opium-Eater*. 1821.

[58] Gary Lupyan and Daniel Swingley, 'Self-directed speech affects visual search performance'. *Quarterly Journal of Experimental Psychology*, Volume 65, 2012 – Issue 6. https://doi.org/10.1080/17470218.2011.647039

[59] Ethan Kross, Emma Bruehlman-Senecal, Jiyoung Park, Aleah Burson, Adrienne Dougherty,

Holly Shablack, Ryan Bremner, Jason Moser and Ozlem Ayduk, 'Self-Talk as a Regulatory Mechanism: How You Do It Matters'. *Journal of Personality and Social Psychology*, 2014, Vol. 106, No. 2, 304–324. http://selfcontrol.psych.lsa.umich.edu/wp-content/uploads/2014/01/KrossJ_Pers_Soc_Psychol2014Self-talk_as_a_regulatory_mechanism_How_you_do_it_matters.pdf

[60] 'To understand the world': Albert Camus, 'The Minotaur (or, the Stop in Oran)', in *The Myth of Sisyphus*. Hamish Hamilton, 1955. Retranslated from the French ('*Pour comprendre le monde, il faut parfois se détourner*').

[61] 'When people take these moments…': Brent Crane, 'The Virtues of Isolation'. *The Atlantic*, 30 March 2017. https://www.theatlantic.com/health/archive/2017/03/the-virtues-of-isolation/521100/

[62] 'There is a you…': Pádraig Ó Tuama, 'How to ~~Belong~~ Be Alone'. https://onbeing.org/poetry/how-to-be-alone/

[63] 'I find it wholesome…': Thoreau, op. cit.

[64] An opportunity for rest: Claudia Hammond, 'How being alone may be the key to rest', BBC News, 27 September 2016. https://www.bbc.co.uk/news/magazine-37444982

[65] 'At this moment I allow the quiet…': Matthew Sharpe, 'Why philosophers say solitude can be helpful (even if you didn't choose it)'. *The Conversation*, 21 October 2020. https://theconversation.com/why-philosophers-say-solitude-can-be-helpful-even-if-you-didnt-choose-it-147440

[66] 'Thin, sort of stretched…': J.R.R. Tolkien, *The Fellowship of the Ring*, Chapter 1. George Allen & Unwin, 1954.

[67] 'Melancholy can be overcome…': Robert Burton, *The Anatomy of Melancholy*, 1621.

[68] 'I am here alone…': Sarton, op. cit.

[69] Solitude reduces 'high-arousal effects': Thuy-vy T. Nguyen, Richard M. Ryan and Edward L. Deci, 'Solitude as an Approach to Affective Self-Regulation'. *Personality and Social Psychology Bulletin*, 2017. https://doi.org/10.1177/0146167217733073

[70] 'Coming to terms with loss…': Storr, op.cit. Chapter 3.

[71] *Inside Out* (2015). dir. Pete Docter. Original screenplay by Peter Docter, Meg LeFauve and Josh Cooley. https://www.dailyscript.com/scripts/inside-out-screenplay.pdf

[72] 'Solitude has been the greatest gift…': Terry Waite, op. cit. Chapter 4.

[73] 'We cannot find ourselves…': Thomas

Merton, *No Man Is an Island*, 1955.

[74] 'Once you value a relationship with yourself…': Francesca Specter, *Alonement*. Quercus Books, 2021.

[75] 'Society is commonly too cheap': Thoreau, op. cit.

[76] 'Save yourself first': Amod Lele, 'The Buddhist oxygen mask'. Love of All Wisdom, 15 August 2021. https://loveofallwisdom.com/blog/2021/08/the-buddhist-oxygen-mask/

[77] Christ made himself nothing: Philippians 2:7. 'rather, he made himself nothing by taking the very nature of a servant, being made in human likeness'.

[78] 'Something to bring into a relationship': Carl Jung, *Letters*. Vol. II, p. 610.

[79] 'Why, words, did I let you out?': Ward, op. cit.

[80] The unexamined life: https://en.wikipedia.org/wiki/The_unexamined_life_is_not_worth_living

[81] David M. Levy: see his web page at https://dmlevy.ischool.uw.edu/no-time-to-think/

[82] 'The system will come first': Frederick Winslow Taylor, *The Principles of Scientific Management*. Harper and Brothers, 1911.

[83] More free time than our parents: Esteban Ortiz-Ospina, Charlie Giattino and Max Roser, 'Time Use'. Our World in Data, 2020. https://ourworldindata.org/time-use

[84] Personal productivity: Oliver Burkeman, 'Why time management is ruining our lives'. *The Guardian*, 22 December 2016. https://www.theguardian.com/technology/2016/dec/22/why-time-management-is-ruining-our-lives

[85] Fast and slow time: Thomas Hylland Eriksen, *The Tyranny of the Moment: Fast and Slow Time in the Information Age*. Pluto Press, 2001.

[86] 'Just thinking' isn't as hard as we think: Kate Connolly, 'Contemplation can help problem-solving and boost creativity, study claims'. *The Guardian*, 5 August 2022.

[87] 'The fight is won or lost': https://www.brainyquote.com/quotes/muhammad_ali_145945

[88] Cain, op. cit. Chapter 3.

[89] 'We just concentrate…': Suzuki, op. cit.

[90] 'There's this focus…': Mihaly Csikszentmihalyi, 'Flow, the secret to happiness'. TED Talk, 2004. https://www.ted.com/talks/mihaly_csikszentmihalyi_flow_the_secret_to_happiness

[91] 'Great form of mindfulness': Knit Rowan, Interview with Tom Daley. https://knitrowan.com/fr/blog/rowan-blog-or-tom-daley

[92] 'Secret weapon': Nick Hope, 'Olympic Secrets: Knitting is Tom Daley's Tokyo 2020 "secret weapon"'. BBC, 16 July 2020. https://www.bbc.co.uk/sport/diving/53421329

[93] 'She could be by herself…' Virginia Woolf, *To The Lighthouse*. Grove Press, 1961.

[94] 'The designer's dream': Quoted in Armando Gallo, *Peter Gabriel*. Omnibus Press, 1986. Gabriel is discussing the lyrics to 'Mercy Street' (from *So*, 1986).

[95] 'Without time and space…': Maria Popova, 'Artist Louise Bourgeois on How Solitude Enriches Creative Work'. The Marginalian, 15 April 2016. https://www.themarginalian.org/2016/04/15/louise-bourgeois-solitude/

[96] 'They return in memory…': Elizabeth Cobb, *The Ecology of Imagination in Childhood*. Columbia University Press, 1977.

[97] 'I carry my thoughts about with me…': Elliot Forbes (ed.), *Thayer's Life of Beethoven*. Princeton University Press, 1967.

[98] Kekulé's ouroboros dream: Andrew Robinson, 'Chemistry's visual origins'. *Nature*, 5 May 2010. https://www.nature.com/articles/465036a

[99] Philosophical arguments: Barbara Taylor, 'Philosophical Solitude: David Hume versus Jean-Jacques Rousseau'. *History Workshop Journal*, Volume 89, Spring 2020, Pages 1–21. https://doi.org/10.1093/hwj/dbz048

[100] *Secum loqui*: Aaron J. Kachuck, 'Cicero Speaking With Solitudes'. In *The Solitary Sphere in the Age of Virgil*, New York Oxford University Press, 2021.

[101] A special state of being: David Vincent, 'Lockdown lessons from the history of solitude'. *The Conversation*, 9 April 2020. https://theconversation.com/lockdown-lessons-from-the-history-of-solitude-134611

[102] 'For the god-like few': Taylor, op. cit.

[103] Lonelinesses: Amelia Worsley, 'A history of loneliness'. *The Conversation*, 19 March 2018. https://theconversation.com/a-history-of-loneliness-91542

[104] 'They did not talk…': Ward, op. cit.

[105] Solitary Bible figures: Richard Blakaby, 'Elijah: Navigating Your Wilderness'. https://preachitteachit.org/articles/detail/elijah-navigating-your-wilderness/

[106] 'A locale for intense experiences': Holmes Roston, 'Midbar, Arabah and Eremos—Biblical Wilderness'. Environment & Society Portal, 2020. https://www.environmentandsociety.org/exhibitions/wilderness-babel/midbar-arabah-and-eremos-biblical-wilderness

[107] Surviving anchorite's cell in Chester: https://en.wikipedia.org/wiki/Anchorite%27s_Cell,_Chester

[108] Charles Hamilton's garden hermit: Catherine Caulfield, *The Emperor of the United States of America and Other Magnificent British Eccentrics*. Routledge & Kegan Paul, 1981.

[109] Zhongnan hermits: Lin Qiqing, 'The Hermit Culture Living On in China's Misty Mountains'. *Sixth Tone*, 4 May 2019. https://www.sixthtone.com/news/1003932/the-hermit-culture-living-on-in-chinas-misty-mountains

[110] Master Hou: Agence France-Presse, 'China's Mountain Hermits Seek a Highway to Heaven'. NDTV, 16 December 2014. https://www.ndtv.com/world-news/chinas-mountain-hermits-seek-a-highway-to-heaven-713600

[111] 'No man is an island': John Donne, Meditation XVII, from *Devotions upon Emergent Occasions*, 1624.

[112] 'From the 1660s…': Barbara Taylor, op. cit.

[113] The atomic self: Peter Abbs, 'The Development of Autobiography in Western Culture: from Augustine to Rousseau'. Unpublished thesis, University of Sussex, 1986. Quoted in Anthony Storr, *Solitude: A Return to the Self*. Flamingo, 1988.

[114] Self is more than memories: C.J. Rathbone, C.J.A. Moulin and M.A. Conway, 'Autobiographical memory and amnesia: using conceptual knowledge to ground the self'. *Neurocase*, 15 (5), 2009. https://doi.org/10.1080/13554790902849164

[115] People don't know why they do things: Richard Nisbett, and Timothy Wilson, 'Telling more than we can know: Verbal reports on mental processes'. *Psychological Review*, 84(3), 231–259, 1979. https://doi.org/10.1037/0033-295X.84.3.231

[116] 'The wild man is alone at will': Meynell, op. cit.

[117] 'Now since we are undertaking to live…': De Montaigne, op. cit.

[118] Rousseau not really alone: Gavin McCrea, 'What Rousseau Knew about Solitude'. *The Paris Review*, 27 April 2020. https://www.theparisreview.org/blog/2020/04/27/what-rousseau-knew-about-solitude/

[119] Bentinck-Scott, Cavendish and Dering: Caufield, op. cit.

[120] 'A sin against nature': Bridget Hill, 'A Refuge from Men: the Idea of a Protestant Nunnery', *Past and Present* 117, 1987, p. 128.

[121] 'The solitary woman': Eileen Manion, 'All Alone Feeling Blue? Women's Experience of Solitude'. In *Women and Men*, 1987.

[122] Loneliness as a failing: Eleanor Wilkinson, 'Loneliness is a feminist issue'. *Feminist Theory*, 20 February 2022. https://doi.org/10.1177%2F14647001211062739

[123] The power of naming: Andrea Dworkin, *Pornography: Men Possessing Women*. Plume, 1991.

[124] The quest to become feminine: Susan Brownmiller, *Femininity*. Linden Press/Simon & Schuster, 1984. Quoted in Yvonne Roberts, 'Fab abs, Nicole Kidman. But this frantic effort to look half your age is frankly demeaning'. *The Guardian*, 28 August 2022. https://www.theguardian.com/commentisfree/2022/aug/28/fab-abs-nicole-kidman-frantic-effort-to-look-half-your-age-demeaning

[125] Alonement defined: Specter, op. cit.

[126] 'The greatest misery of sickness': John Donne, *Devotions on Emergent Occasions*, 1623. V. Meditation. https://ccel.org/ccel/donne/devotions.iv.iii.v.i.html

[127] 'Laborious webs': Francis Bacon, *The Advancement of Learning*, 1605.

[128] 'Disease of learning': Robert Burton, *The Anatomy of Melancholy*, 1621.

[129] 'Solitude produces ignorance…': John Evelyn, *Publick Employment and an Active Life Prefer'd to Solitude*, 1667. https://quod.lib.umich.edu/e/eebo/A38809.0001.001?view=toc

[130] 'Candle in foul air': Hester Lynch Piozzi, *Anecdotes of Samuel Johnson, LL.D. During the Last Twenty Years of His Life*. Sagwan Press, 2018.

[131] 'Apt to feel too strongly…': Adam Smith, *The Theory of Moral Sentiments*, Part III. Andrew Millar, 1759.

[132] 'Greatest punishment…': David Hume, *A Treatise of Human Nature*, 1739.

[133] 'Stupify the understanding': David Hume, *An Enquiry Concerning the Principles of Morals*, 1751.

[134] 'It is necessary…': Jean-Jacques Rousseau, *Reveries of a Solitary Walker*, 1778.

[135] 'The feeling infinite': Lord Byron, 'Childe Harold's Pilgrimage', 1812.

[136] 'Beauty is truth': John Keats, 'Ode on a Grecian Urn', 1820.

[137] Emotions flow from nature: 'Romanticism and solitude'. Hermitary – Hermit's Thatch, 11 February 2008. https://www.hermitary.com/thatch/?p=425

[138] *Amour-propre*: Jean-Jacques Rousseau, *Judge of Jean-Jacques: Dialogues*, CW, vol. 1, pp. 99–100

[139] 'There is a charm…': John Clare, 'There is a charm in Solitude that cheers', written before 1856 and published 1949.

[140] 'Enough of Science…': William Wordsworth, 'The Tables Turned'.

[141] 'Unfenced existence': 'Here', in *The Whitsun Weddings*. Faber, 1964.

[142] 'A pleasure in the pathless woods': Lord Byron, op. cit. (stanza 178).

[143] 'And I have felt…': William Wordsworth, 'Lines Composed a Few Miles above Tintern Abbey, On Revisiting the Banks of the Wye during a Tour. July 13, 1798'. https://www.poetryfoundation.org/poems/45527/lines-composed-a-few-miles-above-tintern-abbey-on-revisiting-the-banks-of-the-wye-during-a-tour-july-13-1798

[144] 'I never found…': Thoreau, op. cit.

[145] 'Slavedrivers of themselves': *Stanford Encyclopedia of Philosophy*, entry for 'Transcendentalism'. https://plato.stanford.edu/entries/transcendentalism/

[146] 'Standing on the bare ground': Ralph Waldo Emerson, *Nature*. James Munroe and Company, 1836. https://archive.vcu.edu/english/engweb/transcendentalism/authors/emerson/nature.html

[147] 'While I was in the next room…': Sigmund Freud, *Mourning and Melancholia*. 1917.

[148] 'Against the suffering…': Sigmund Freud, *Civilization and Its Discontents*. Internationaler Psychoanalytischer Verlag Wien, 1930.

[149] 'It seems to me…': Storr, *op. cit.* p. xiv.

[150] 'I think, therefore I am': René Descartes, *Discourse on the Method*, 1637.

[151] 'There is very often less perfection…': Ibid.

[152] 'Everything depends on relationship': Cited in Paul Halmos, *Solitude and Privacy*. Greenwood Press, 1953.

[153] John Muir, *Nature Writings*. Library of America, 1997.

[154] 'The profoundest fact': Octavio Paz, 'The Dialectic of Solitude'. In The Labyrinth of Solitude, 1985. https://archive.org/details/labyrinthofsolit0000pazo/

[155] 'Only when the soul is alone…': John Cowper Powys, *A Philosophy of Solitude*. Jonathan Cape, 1933.

[156] 'Society everywhere…': Ralph Waldo Emerson, 'Self-Reliance', 1841. https://archive.vcu.edu/english/engweb/transcendentalism/authors/emerson/essays/selfreliance.html

[157] 'No such thing as society': Margaret Thatcher, interview for *Woman's Own*, 1987. https://www.margaretthatcher.org/document/106689

[158] Lone stars vs cells: for a full discussion of these ideas, see chapter 9 of Koch, op. cit.

[159] 'A fount of healing': Carl Jung, letter to Gustav Schmaltz, 30 May 1957. http://jungcurrents.com/jung-solitude-

healing-silence

[160] 'Highest and most decisive experience…': Carl Jung, *Collected Works* 12, 1943.

[161] Do for ourselves: Sue Mehrtens, 'The Value of Isolation, Loneliness and Solitude'. Jungian Center for the Spiritual Sciences. https://jungiancenter.org/the-value-of-isolation-loneliness-and-solitude/

[162] Diminishing utility of company: Kostadin Kushlev, Samantha J. Heintzelman, Shigehiro Oishi and Ed Diener, 'The declining marginal utility of social time for subjective well-being'. *Journal of Research in Personality*, Vol. 74, June 2018. https://doi.org/10.1016/j.jrp.2018.04.004

[163] 'Animated but not broken': Sarton, op. cit.

[164] 'All solitude is selfish': Philip Larkin, 'Vers de Societé', from *Collected Poems*. Faber, 2001. (https://www.poetryfoundation.org/poems/48420/vers-de-societe

[165] Pursuit of happiness can make us lonely: Iris B. Mauss, Nicole S. Savino, Craig L. Anderson, Max Weisbuch, Maya Tamir and Mark L. Laudenslager, 'The pursuit of happiness can be lonely'. *Emotion*, 2012. https://psycnet.apa.org/doi/10.1037/a0025299

[166] '*L'enfer, c'est les autres*' ('Hell is other people'): Jean-Paul Sartre, *Huis Clos* ('No Exit'), 1944.

[167] Motivations for solitude: Robert J. Coplan, Will E. Hipson, Kristen A. Archbell, Laura L. Ooi, Danielle Baldwin and Julie C. Bowker, 'Seeking more solitude: Conceptualization, assessment, and implications of aloneliness'. *Personality and Individual Differences*, Vol. 148, 1 October 2019. https://doi.org/10.1016/j.paid.2019.05.020

[168] Negative degenerative cycle: Virginia Thomas, 'Are You Lonely… or Alonely?' *Psychology Today*, 12 February 2021. https://www.psychologytoday.com/gb/blog/solitude-in-social-world/202102/are-you-lonely-or-alonely

[169] Doing something purposeful: Robert J. Coplan, Will E. Hipson and Julie C. Bowker, 'Social Withdrawal and Aloneliness in Adolescence: Examining the Implications of Too Much and Not Enough Solitude'. *Journal of Youth and Adolescence*, 2021. https://link.springer.com/article/10.1007/s10964-020-01365-0

[170] 'I never wish to offend…': Jane Austen (as 'A Lady'), *Sense and Sensibility*. Thomas Egerton, 1811.

[171] 'Shy people unsettle others': Joe Moran, *Shrinking Violets: The Secret Life of Shyness*. Profile Books, 2016.

[172] 'Bob nodded his head…': Stephen Chbosky, *The Perks of Being a Wallflower*. Simon & Schuster, 1999.

[173] 'Slipfast': John Koenig, *The Dictionary of Obscure Sorrows*. Simon & Schuster, 2021.

[174] 'Why don't I know much about you?': Excerpt from interview with Frank Ocean transcribed from *Dissect* podcast, Series 3, Episode 7. https://open.spotify.com/episode/2EQze8VpQOZvUipOCOu0Kc

[175] 'Humans are social beings': Richard Layard, *Happiness: Lessons from a New Science*. Penguin, 2005, p. 225.

[176] 'When we are happy…': Martin Seligman, *Authentic Happiness*. Free Press, 2002.

[177] , 'If the new science of happiness…': Sara Ahmed, *The Promise of Happiness*. Duke University Press Books, 2010.

[178] 'The happiness of others': Simone de Beauvoir, *The Second Sex* (*Le Deuxième Sexe*). 1949.

[179] 'We assume other people…': Emma Brockes, 'I've learned to say no and not care what other people think: why did it take so long?' *The Guardian*, 21 July 2022. https://www.theguardian.com/commentisfree/2022/jul/21/learned-say-no-people-think-assertive-briton-us-age-pandemic

[180] Animals alone: Daniel Marston PhD, 'We Are Meant to Spend Time Alone'. *Psychology Today*, 6 June 2020. https://www.psychologytoday.com/us/blog/comparatively-speaking/202006/we-are-meant-spend-time-alone

[181] 'Each individual is an isolate': D.W. Winnicott, *The maturational processes and the facilitating environment: Studies in the theory of emotional development*. International Universities Press, 1965.

[182] 'Other people's expectations': D.W.

Winnicott, quoted in Josephine Klein, *Our Need for Others*, 1994, p. 241.

[183] 'The strongest person': Alice Harmon is the main character of the TV drama *The Queen's Gambit*. Taken from Season 1 Episode 5, 'Fork'. https://subslikescript.com/series/The_Queens_Gambit-10048342/season-1/episode-5-Fork

[184] 'Through desire…': Adam Phillips, 'On risk and solitude' in *On Kissing, Tickling, and Being Bored: Psychoanalytic Essays on the Unexamined Life*. Harvard University Press, 1994.

[185] Adolescent individuation: Reed W. Larson, 'The solitary side of life: An examination of the time people spend alone from childhood to old age'. *Developmental Review*, June 1990. https://doi.org/10.1016/0273-2297(90)90008-R

[186] Relief from self-consciousness: Virginia Thomas, '4 Reasons Your Teenager Wants to (and Needs to) Be Alone'. *Psychology Today*, 1 July 2019. https://www.psychologytoday.com/gb/blog/solitude-in-social-world/201907/4-reasons-your-teenager-wants-and-needs-be-alone

[187] Benefits of time alone for young people: Jessica Kasamoto, 'Study shows solitude can be good for mental health'. *The Johns Hopkins News-Letter*, 4 April 2019. https://www.jhunewsletter.com/article/2019/04/study-shows-solitude-can-be-good-for-mental-health

[188] Eight traits of people who get the most from solitude: Virginia Thomas, '8 Ways to Embrace Solitude'. *Psychology Today*, 8 February 2022. https://www.psychologytoday.com/gb/blog/solitude-in-social-world/202202/8-ways-embrace-solitude

[189] 'It is not when he is working…': Lin Yutang, *The Importance of Living: The Noble Art of Leaving Things Undone*. 1937.

[190] 'Time torn off unused': From 'Aubade', published in *Collected Poems*. Faber, 2001. https://www.poetryfoundation.org/poems/48422/aubade-56d229a6e2f07

[191] 'A writer could get more ideas…': Lin Yutang, 'On Lying in Bed', in op. cit.

[192] 'Entangled in a culture': Madeleine Dore, *I Didn't Do the Thing Today: On letting go of productivity guilt*. Murdoch Books, 2022.

[193] 'Boredom is the dream bird…': Walter Benjamin, *Illuminations: Essays and Reflections*. Schocken, 1969.

[194] 'The unhappy person': Søren Kierkegaard, *Either/Or: A Fragment of Life*. Penguin, 2004.

[195] Boredom can stimulate creativity: Karen Gasper and Brianna L. Middlewood, 'Approaching novel thoughts: Understanding why elation and boredom promote associative thought more than distress and relaxation'. *Journal of Experimental Social Psychology*, 52, 50–57. https://psycnet.apa.org/doi/10.1016/j.jesp.2013.12.007

[196] 'Shells and dust': Epictetus, *Discourses*, book 3, chapter 13: 'What solitude is; and what a solitary person'. http://www.perseus.tufts.edu/hopper/text?doc=Perseus%3Atext%3A1999.01.0237%3Atext%3Ddisc%3Abook%3D3%3Achapter%3D13

[197] 'We are less bored than our ancestors…': Bertrand Russell, *The Conquest of Happiness*. Routledge, 1930.

[198] 'I personally love being alone': *Women of the Hour* podcast, Season 2 Episode 3. https://podcasts.apple.com/gb/podcast/women-of-the-hour/id1049452428?i=1000378464620

[199] 'Even in our best lives…': Leslie Jamison, 'Dreamers in Broad Daylight: Ten Conversations'. *Astra*, Issue 1 (The Ecstasy Issue). https://astra-mag.com/articles/dreamers-in-broad-daylight-ten-conversations/

[200] Daydreaming is adaptive: J.L. Singer, *Daydreaming: An Introduction to the Experimental Study of Inner Experience*. New York: Random House, 1966.

[201] James Thurber, 'The Secret Life of Walter Mitty'. *New Yorker*, 18 March 1939. https://www.newyorker.com/magazine/1939/03/18/the-secret-life-of-walter-james-thurber

[202] Loren Bouchard, Jim Dauterive and Holly Schlesinger, dialogue from *Bob's Burgers*, season 2 episode 8, 'Bad Tina', 2012.

[203] 'Past events exist…'L Ursula le Guin, *Tales from Earthsea*. Harcourt Brace &

Company, 2001.

[204] 'No one who cooks…': Laurie Colwin, *Home Cooking*. Knopf, 2016.

[205] 'And soon, mechanically…': Marcel Proust, *À la Recherce de Temps Perdu* ('In Search of Lost Time'). Grasset and Gallimard, 1913–1927.

[206] 'The records we liked…' and 'During that time…': David Hepworth, *A Fabulous Creation: How the LP Saved Our Lives*. Bantam Press, 2019, p. xii.

[207] 'Ongoing connection…': Sherry Turkle, *Alone Together: Why We Expect More from Technology and Less from Each Other*. Basic Books, 2011.

[208] A part of the self: Lily Carollo, 'Some People See Their Phones As Extensions of Themselves'. *The Cut*, 3 August 2017. https://www.thecut.com/2017/08/some-people-see-their-phones-as-extensions-of-themselves.html

[209] 'Mixes presence and absence': Iain MacRury and Candida Yates, 'Framing the Mobile Phone: The Psychopathologies of an Everyday Object'. *CM: Communication and Media*, 11 (38), pp. 41–70. https://doi.org/10.5937/comman11-11517

[210] Checking phone fifty-two times a day: Deloitte, *2021 Connectivity and Mobile Trends Survey*. https://www2.deloitte.com/us/en/insights/industry/telecommunications/connectivity-mobile-trends-survey.html

[211] Interrupting interaction: Sherry Turkle, op. cit.

[212] Smartphone Addiction Scale: Min Kwon, Joon-Yeop Lee, Wang-Youn Won, Jae-Woo Park, Jung-Ah Min, Changtae Hahn, Xinyu Gu, Ji-Hye Choi and Dai-Jin Kim, 'Development and Validation of a Smartphone Addiction Scale (SAS)'. *PLOS ONE*, 27 February 2013. https://doi.org/10.1371/journal.pone.0056936

[213] 'And yet our dear self…': Abraham Cowley, 'Of Solitude'. From *Essays*, 1668. https://www.gutenberg.org/files/3549/3549-h/3549-h.htm

[214] 'We desire to be seen…': L.M. Sacasas, 'Attending to the World'. The Convivial Society, Vol. 3, No. 2. 20 February 2022. https://theconvivialsociety.substack.com/p/attending-to-the-world

[215] 'The tragedy is that the strolll…': Nicholas Carr, 'Online, Offline, and the Line Between', in *Utopia is Creepy*. W.H. Norton & Company, 2016.

[216] 'In solitude…': Sherry Turkle, *Alone Together: Why We Expect More from Technology and Less from Each Other*. Basic Books, 2011.

[217] Corroding body image: Jasmine Fardouly and Lenny R. Vartanian, 'Social Media and Body Image Concerns: Current Research and Future Directions'. *Current Opinion in Psychology*, Volume 9, June 2016. https://doi.org/10.1016/j.copsyc.2015.09.005

[218] 'Society is growing ever more skeptical…': Nicholas Carr, 'The Dreams of Readers' in *Utopia is Creepy*. W.H. Norton & Company, 2016.

[219] 'When offered something…': Sherry Turkle, op. cit.

[220] 'We are drowning in information': Michael H. Goldhaber, 'Attention Shoppers!' *Wired*, 1 December 1997. https://www.wired.com/1997/12/es-attention/

[221] 'They're coming for every second of your life': Transcribed and edited for clarity from filmed panel discussion of Bo Burnham's film *Eighth Grade*, hosted by the Child Mind Institute. https://www.youtube.com/watch?v=SUTbnjIHfkg

[222] 'The most sophisticated software…': Hank Green, *A Beautifully Foolish Endeavor*. Trapeze, 2020.

[223] 'I thought at first…': Harris, op. cit.

[224] 'When I am on Twitter': Moya Lothian-McLean, 'Twitter is strictly for the birds: never am I more disconnected than when plugged in'. *The Guardian*, 3 April 2022. https://www.theguardian.com/commentisfree/2022/apr/03/twitter-birds-battles-digital-real-life

[225] You already have enough attention: L.M. Sacasas, 'Your Attention Is Not a Resource'. *The Convivial Society*, Vol. 2, No. 6. 1 April 2021. https://theconvivialsociety.substack.com/p/your-attention-is-not-a-resource

[226] 'Everything Waits to Be Noticed', from the album of the same name by Art Garfunkel With Maia Sharp & Buddy

Mondlock. Manhattan Recods, 2022.

[227] 'Where is it virtue comes from…': Horace, Epistle XVIII, 'To Lollius: He treats at large upon the cultivation of the favour of great men; and concludes with a few words concerning the acquirement of peace of mind.' Quoted in Alan Jacobs, 'Seeking a More Tranquil Mind? Take Horace's Advice'. *Literary Hub*, 13 September 2021. https://lithub.com/seeking-a-more-tranquil-mind-take-horaces-advice/

[228] Choosing something instead of smoking: Gillian Riley, *How to Stop Smoking and Stay Stopped for Good*. Vermilion, 2007.

[229] Crusoe as British colonist: James Joyce, *Daniel Defoe*. State University of New York, 1964.

[230] 'One soul saved': Defoe, op. cit.

[231] Defoe on solitude: Barbara Taylor, 'Robinson Crusoe and the morality of solitude'. Wellcome Collection, 20 September 2018. https://wellcomecollection.org/articles/XA44NhEAALf5xtU2

[232] 'Certain portions of the earth's crust erode…': Victor Sage, 'Crusoe', in *Dividing Lines*. Chatto & Windus, 1984.

[233] Being cast away as healing: Vicente Bicudo de Castro and Matthias Muskat, 'Inverted Crusoeism: Deliberately marooning yourself on a desert island'. *Shima*, Vol. 14 No. 1. https://shimajournal.org/issues/v14n1/16.-Bicudo-de-Castro-and-Muskat-Shima-v14n1.pdf

[234] 'Bare island': William Shakespeare, *The Tempest*, Act 5 Epilogue. First Folio, 1623.

[235] 'Rhythms of tides…': Philip Conkling, 'On islanders and islandness'. *Geographical Review*, Vol. 97 issue 2, April 2007, 191–201. https://doi.org/10.1111/j.1931-0846.2007.tb00398.x

[236] Urban interzone: J.G. Ballard, *Concrete Island*. Jonathan Cape, 1974.

[237] 'No film I've seen…': David Thomson, *How to Watch a Movie*. Alfred A. Knopf, 2015.

[238] 'Quiet… occupies the same space': Elvis Mitchell, 'A Train Depot, More Dream Than Destination'. *New York Times*, 3 October 2003. http://movies2.nytimes.com/2003/10/03/movies/03AGEN.html

[239] 'It's about things being disconnected…': Anne Thompson, 'Tokyo Story'. *Filmmaker*, Fall 2003. https://filmmakermagazine.com/archives/issues/fall2003/features/tokyo_story.php

[240] Extra meaning in language: Todd McGowan, 'There is Nothing *Lost in Translation*'. *Quarterly Review of Film and Video*, 24:53–63, 2007. https://doi.org/10.1080/10509200500486023

[241] Was Boo Radley autistic?: Lindsey Horn, 'Boo's Superpower: An Exploration of To Kill a Mockingbird's Boo Radley on the Autism Spectrum'. *EKU Libraries Research Award for Undergraduates*, 2020. https://encompass.eku.edu/ugra/2020/2020/3?utm_source=encompass.eku.edu/ugra/2020/2020/3&utm_medium=PDF&utm_campaign=PDFCoverPages

[242] 'In principle a party member had no spare time…': George Orwell, *Nineteen Eighty-Four*. Secker & Warburg, 1949.

[243] 'Much better than things were in the old days': Horace B. Fyfe, 'Manners of an Age'. First published in *Galaxy Science Fiction*, 1952.

[244] Grisly twist on the Crusoe formula: Stephen King, 'Survivor Type'. In *Skeleton Crew*, Putnam, 1985.

[245] 'Goes a little bit far': Charles L. Grant, 'Interview with Stephen King'. *Monsterland Magazine*, May/June 1985.

[246] Symbolism of Annie Wilkes: Wikipedia, 'Misery (novel)'. https://en.wikipedia.org/wiki/Misery_(novel)

[247] 'To sail on a dream…': From a 'filk' (mock folk) version of 'Calypso' by John Denver, with lyrics adapted to the voyages of the starship *Enterprise*. Diane Duane, *Star Trek: The Wounded Sky*. Pocket Books, 1983. Chapter 8.

[248] 'In space…': The tagline from *Alien* (1979).

[249] Drew Goddard, script for The Martian, based on the novel by Andy Weir. https://imsdb.com/scripts/Martian,-The.html

[250] 'Must get lonely…': John Carpenter and Dan O'Bannon, script for *Dark Star: A Science Fiction Adventure*. https://www.dailyscript.com/scripts/dark-

star_short.html

[251] Vader's *Qabbrat*: Donald F. Glut, *The Empire Strikes Back* (special young readers' edition), chapter 10. Sphere, 1980.

[252] In *Star Wars: The Empire Strikes Back (Episode V)* (1980), dir. Irvin Kirshner.

[253] 'Solitude – the very condition of our lives…': Paz, Ibid.

[254] 'It is true that I never leave my house…': Jorge Luis Borges, 'The House of Asterion'. In *Labyrinths*. Penguin, 1970.

[255] 'I am the sea…': From 'What shall I do today?', the theme song of the animated adaptation *Pippi Longstocking* (1997). Available to view at https://www.youtube.com/watch?v=Cl2Fao763ms

[256] 'She had neither mother nor father…': Astrid Lindgren, *Pippi Comes to Villekulla Cottage*. In *Pippi Longstocking*, 1945.

[257] 'But you could never do it…': Ibid., *Pippi Goes to the Circus*.

[258] Pippi's personality: Jaya Saxena, 'Jaya Catches Up: Actually Pippi Longstocking Is Really Depressing'. *The Toast*, 7 December 2015. https://the-toast.net/2015/12/07/jaya-catches-up-actually-pippi-longstocking-is-really-depressing/

[259] 'Astrid's child self': Sandra E. Cohen, 'BECOMING ASTRID: Lonely Girl's Superhuman Strength & Pippi Longstocking Too'. Characters on the Couch. https://charactersonthecouch.com/becoming-astrid-abandoned-girls-strength/

[260] Pippi grown up: Malin Rising, 'Swedish Crime Writer Finds Fame After Death'. *Washington Post*, 17 February 2009. https://www.washingtonpost.com/wp-dyn/content/article/2009/02/17/AR2009021700184.html

[261] Stieg Larsson, *The Girl with the Dragon Tattoo*. Quercus, 2008.

[262] 'Part of my exile…' and 'At night I went…': Madeline Miller, *Circe*, chapter VII. Little, Brown, 2018.

[263] Camus, op. cit.

[264] 'I am no bird…' and 'I can live alone…': Charlotte Brontë (as 'Currer Bell'), *Jane Eyre*. Smith, Elder & Co, 1847.

[265] First historian of the private consciousness: Daniel S. Burt, *The Literature 100: A Ranking of the Most Influential Novelists, Playwrights, and Poets of All Time*. Infobase Publishing, 2008.

[266] 'I am you': *Dark* (2017), season 2, episode 4.

[267] 'Have you ever had a dream…': Script for *The Matrix* by The Wachowskis. https://www.dailyscript.com/scripts/the_matrix.pdf

[268] 'The world as it had been shown to him…' and 'It is necessary…': Robert A. Heinlein, *They* (1941). Included in *The Unpleasant Profession of Jonathan Hoag*. New English Library, 1976.

[269] 'He feels trapped…': Michael Brearley and Andrea Sabbadini, 'The Truman Show: How's it going to end?'. *International Journal of Psychoanalysis*, 2008. https://doi.org/10.1111%2Fj.1745-8315.2008.00030.x

[270] 'We all know that art is not truth…': Originally spoken in Spanish in a 1923 interview. See https://quoteinvestigator.com/2019/10/29/lie-truth/

[271] Burnham play-acting at isolation: Lili Loofbourow, 'The Problem With Bo Burnham's *Inside*'. *Slate*, 23 June 2021. https://slate.com/culture/2021/06/problem-with-bo-burnham-inside.html

[272] A frontiersman in San Francisco: Tony Macklin, 'The Values in Dirty Harry'. http://tonymacklin.net/content.php?cID=202

[273] Sarah Lund on the autistic spectrum: John Winterson Richards, 'The Killing/Forbrydelsen'. *Television Heaven*, no date. https://televisionheaven.co.uk/reviews/the-killing-forbrydelsen

[274] 'Lund isn't married to the job…': Natalie Haynes, 'Sarah Lund: Natalie Haynes's guide to TV detectives #22'. *The Guardian*, 10 December 2012. https://www.theguardian.com/tv-and-radio/tvandradioblog/2012/dec/10/sarah-lund-guide-tv-detectives

[275] Ultimate comfort watch: Eleanor Morgan, 'The person who got me through 2021: Sofie Gråbøl as Sarah Lund felt like a brilliant old friend'. *The Guardian*, 26 December 2021. https://www.theguardian.com/lifeandstyle/2

021/dec/26/the-person-who-got-me-through-2021-sofie-grabl-as-sarah-lund-felt-like-a-brilliant-old-friend

[276] Lone stars: some themes and quotes adapted from 'The Lone Cowboy' by Jeff Arnold, no longer available online.

[277] $200,000 a week: Tim Ingham, 'Kate Bush is the world's biggest independent artist right now. She's owning it.' *Music Business Worldwide*, 16 June 2022. https://www.musicbusinessworldwide.com/kate-bush-is-the-worlds-biggest-independent-artist-right-now-shes-owning-it/

[278] 'I go out of my way…': Tom Doyle, 'I'm not some weirdo recluse' (interview with Kate Bush). *The Guardian*, 28 October 2005. https://www.theguardian.com/music/2005/oct/28/popandrock

[279] 'People have a lot of conceptions about my image…': Interview to promote *The Red Shoes* (1993) with Canadian TV Show *The New Music*. Available at https://www.youtube.com/watch?v=ppWXRwatpFc

[280] Dramatic context: Rebecca Nicholson, 'I'll be happy to be running up that hill with Kate Bush for ever'. *The Guardian*, 4 June 2022. https://www.theguardian.com/commentisfree/2022/jun/04/ill-be-happy-running-up-that-hill-with-kate-bush-for-ever

[281] 'If I could work my will…': Charles Dickens, *A Christmas Carol*. Chapman & Hall, 1843.

[282] 'The Grinch hated Christmas!': Dr. Seuss, *How the Grinch Stole Christmas*. Random House, 1957.

[283] Raymond Briggs, *Father Christmas*. Hamish Hamilton, 1973.

[284] 'As a child I was in my own world…': Michael Segalov, 'Charlotte Church: "Each time I put my head above the parapet I'm made to feel stupid"'. *The Guardian*, 8 October 2022. https://www.theguardian.com/lifeandstyle/2022/oct/08/this-much-i-know-charlotte-church-when-i-put-my-head-above-the-parapet-i-am-mocked

[285] Problems faced by introvert children: Cain, *op. cit.* pp. 252–258.

[286] 'Loud, crowded, superficial…': Jill D. Burruss and Liza Kaenzig, 'Introversion: The often forgotten factor impacting the gifted'. *Virginia Association for the Gifted Newsletter*, 1999 Fall 21(1). https://australiangiftedsupport.com/ccmword/wp-content/uploads/2014/12/1352289746.pdf

[287] 'An all-day cocktail party': Susan Cain, 'How Do Teachers Feel about Their Quiet Students?' https://susancain.net/how-do-teachers-feel-about-their-quiet-students/

[288] Be-by-myself space: Early Childhood Consultation Partnership, 'The Classroom Environment: Create a Quiet Space'. http://www.eccpct.com/Resources/Classrooms/Tips-for-Tots/Create-a-Quiet-Space/

[289] 'New Groupthink': Cain, op. cit. p. 75.

[290] Enclosed offices outperform open-plan: Jungsoo Kim and Richard de Dear, 'Workspace satisfaction: The privacy-communication trade-off in open-plan offices'. *Journal of Environmental Psychology*, vol. 36, December 2013. https://www.sciencedirect.com/science/article/abs/pii/S0272494413000340

[291] Fewer meetings, less stress: Ben Laker, Vijay Pereira, Ashish Malik and Lebene Soga, 'Dear Manager, You're Holding Too Many Meetings'. *Harvard Business Review :Ascend*, 9 March 2022. https://hbr.org/2022/03/dear-manager-youre-holding-too-many-meetings

[292] 'I insist on a lot of time being spent': https://www.goodreads.com/quotes/432412-i-insist-on-a-lot-of-time-being-spent-almost

[293] Myth of the lone scientist: Ken Clark, 'Myth of the genius solitary scientist is dangerous'. *The Conversation*, 21 November 2017. https://theconversation.com/myth-of-the-genius-solitary-scientist-is-dangerous-87835

[294] 'I carried this problem around…' and 'It is important to pick a problem…': 'Andrew Wiles on Solving Fermat'. *Nova*, 1 November 2000. https://www.pbs.org/wgbh/nova/article/andrew-wiles-fermat/

[295] 'It was so indescribably beautiful…': Condensed quotation from Simon Singh, *Fermat's Last Theorem*. HarperPress, 1997.

[296] 'The soul of a solitary journey is liberty…': William Hazlitt, *Table Talk*. Bell, 1889.

[297] 'Suddenly, the To Do list…': Miranda Hart, *Is It Just Me?* Hodder & Stoughton, 2012. Chapter 10.

[298] 'Thus did I steal…': William Wordsworth, *The Prelude*. Edward Moxon, 1851.

[299] Pot plants reduce anxiety: University of Minnesota, 'How Does Nature Impact Our Wellbeing?;' https://www.takingcharge.csh.umn.edu/how-does-nature-impact-our-wellbeing

[300] 'Walking, ideally…': Rebecca Solnit, *Wanderlust: A History of Walking*. Granta, 2014.

[301] Walking generates ideas: Marily Oppezzo and Daniel L. Schwartz, 'Give Your Ideas Some Legs: The Positive Effect of Walking on Creative Thinking'. *Journal of Experimental Psychology: Learning, Memory, and Cognition*. 2014, Vol. 40, No. 4. https://doi.org/10.1037/a0036577

[302] Mental benefits of walking: Ferris Jabr, 'Why Walking Helps Us Think'. *The New Yorker*, 3 September 2014. https://www.newyorker.com/tech/annals-of-technology/walking-helps-us-think

[303] 'The crowd is the flâneur's element': Charles Baudelaire, *The Painter of Modern Life*. New York: Da Capo Press, 1964. Originally published, in French, in *Le Figaro*, 1863.

[304] 'Gastronomy of the eye': Iqbal Mohammed, 'Flâneurs and the gastronomy of the eye'. FutureLab, 12 February 2012. https://www.futurelab.net/blog/2012/02/flâneurs-and-gastronomy-eye

[305] 'At a slight angle…': This is how E.M. Forster described the Greek poet C.P. Cavafy. E.M. Forster, *Pharos and Pharillon: A Novelist's Sketchbook of Alexandria Through the Ages*. 1923.

[306] 'A determined resourceful woman': Lauren Elkin, *Flâneuse: Women Walk the City in Paris, New York, Tokyo, Venice and London*. Chatto & Windus, 2016.

[307] Women lacked access to the city: Lucy Scholes, '*Flâneuse* by Lauren Elkin review – wandering women'. *The Guardian*, 25 July 2016.

[308] Monetisation opportunity: Michael Harris, *Solitude: In Pursuit of a Singular Life in a Crowded World*. Random House, 2017. Chapter 7.

[309] Randonautica: David Cain, 'How to Get the Magic Back'. Raptitude, May 2022. https://www.raptitude.com/2022/05/how-to-get-the-magic-back/

[310] 'Running and meditation': Sakyong Mipham, *Running with the Mind of Meditation: Lessons for Training Body and Mind*. Harmony, 2012.

[311] Runner's high: the 'happy chemicals' are usually considered to be endorphins, but are more likely to be endocannabinoids. David J. Linden, 'The Truth Behind 'Runner's High' and Other Mental Benefits of Running'. Johns Hopkins Medicine. https://www.hopkinsmedicine.org/health/wellness-and-prevention/the-truth-behind-runners-high-and-other-mental-benefits-of-running

[312] 'The hour or so I spend running…': Haruki Murakami, *What I Talk About When I Talk About Running*. Vintage, 2008.

[313] 'The thoughts that occur to me': ibid.

[314] 'The bicycle provides…': Nick Moore, Mindful Thoughts for Cyclists. Leaping Hare Press, 2017.

[315] 'When a man lets things go so far…': Flann O'Brien, *The Third Policeman*. Paladin, 1988. p. 89.

[316] 'I love it. I like my own company': Nicola Joyce, 'Channel swimming FAQs'. https://thefitwriter.wordpress.com/channel-swimming-stuff/channel-swimming-faqs/

[317] 'I never used to like cold water': Tamsin Calidas, *I Am An Island*. Doubleday, 2020.

[318] 'It was freezing…': Tamsin Calidas, 'I ran away to a remote Scottish isle. It was perfect'. *The Observer*, 26 July 2020. https://www.theguardian.com/lifeandstyle/2020/jul/26/i-ran-away-to-a-remote-scottish-island-it-was-perfect

[319] Moomins in the restaurant: Carmen Fishwick, 'Table for one? Restaurant offers giant stuffed animals for company'. *The Guardian*, 6 May 2014. https://www.theguardian.com/world/2014/may/06/table-for-one-restaurant-giant-stuffed-animals-loneliness-japan

[320] 'I'd watch three seasons passing by…': Original French: *Et quand viendra l'hiver aux neiges monotones / Je fermerai partout portières et volets / Pour bâtir dans la nuit mes féeriques palais*. From '*Paysage*' ('Landscape'), in Charles Baudelaire, *Les Fleurs du Mal*, 1857.

Translation: Roy Campbell, *Poems of Baudelaire*. Pantheon Books, 1952. https://fleursdumal.org/poem/219

[321] Lockdown felt natural to introverts: Indy Wijngaards, Sophie C. M. Sisouw de Zilwa and Martijn J. Burger, 'Extraversion Moderates the Relationship Between the Stringency of COVID-19 Protective Measures and Depressive Symptoms'. *Frontiers in Psychology*, 2 October 2020. https://doi.org/10.3389/fpsyg.2020.568907

[322] Cooped up with cohabitants: Simone M. Scully, 'Lockdown Taught Me That Loneliness Isn't Always About Being Alone'. *Healthline*, 12 May 2021. https://www.healthline.com/health/mental-health/loneliness-isnt-always-about-being-alone

[323] Same storm, not same boat: Mental Health Foundation, 'Coronavirus: The divergence of mental health experiences during the pandemic'. https://www.mentalhealth.org.uk/coronavirus/divergence-mental-health-experiences-during-pandemic

[324] Young people miss lockdown: Jade Wickes, 'Two thirds of the UK's young people miss lockdown'. *The Face*, 22 March 2022. https://theface.com/life/two-thirds-of-uk-young-people-miss-lockdown-nostalgia-mental-health-sexuality-relationships-covid-19-pandemic

[325] Break from social anxiety: Miya Chahal, '"It was quite a healing period": Young people are nostalgic about time spent in lockdown'. *The Tab*, February 2022. https://thetab.com/uk/2022/01/26/it-was-quite-a-healing-time-period-young-people-are-nostalgic-about-time-in-lockdown-pandemic-university-student-236938

[326] 'In a hole in the ground…': J.R.R. Tolkien, *The Hobbit, or There and Back Again*. George Allen & Unwin, 1937.

[327] 'Something about lighthouses': Moran, op. cit.

[328] 'The fact that a middle-aged, single woman…': Sarton, op. cit.

[329] Mercury poisoning in lighthouse keepers: Rick Spilman, 'Mad as a Lighthouse Keeper — Not the Solitude, but the Mercury'. The Old Salt Blog, 20 March 2014. http://www.oldsaltblog.com/2014/03/mad-as-a-lighthouse-keeper-not-the-solitude-but-the-mercury/. The same sickness affected milliners of past times, who used mercury to stiffen felt, providing the inspiration for the Mad Hatter in Lewis Carroll's *Alice's Adventures in Wonderland*.

[330] 'You're only bored…': Jungles in Paris, 'The Life of a Lighthouse Keeper in Eastern Canada'. https://www.junglesinparis.com/stories/the-life-of-a-lighthouse-keeper-in-eastern-canada

[331] Giuseppe Spagnuolo: Angela Giuffrida, 'How one man's love of isolation put an Italian ghost town on the map'. The Guardian, 6 March 2022. https://www.theguardian.com/world/2022/mar/06/how-one-mans-love-of-isolation-put-an-italian-ghost-town-on-the-map-giuseppe-spagnuolo-roscigno-vecchia

[332] 'We solitary drinkers': Cosmo Landesman, 'The joy of drinking alone'. *The Spectator*, 24 October 2020. https://www.spectator.co.uk/article/the-joy-of-drinking-alone

[333] 'Do not pity…': Jamie Carson, 'The joys of drinking alone: why solo drinking is the absolute best'. *ShortList*, 26 October 2016. https://www.shortlist.com/news/why-solo-drinking-is-the-absolute-best

[334] Cheryl Strayed, *Wild: From Lost to Found on the Pacific Coast Trail*. Knopf, 2012.

[335] 'It is in thy power…': Marcus Aurelius, *Meditations*, Book Four. http://classics.mit.edu/Antoninus/meditations.4.four.html

[336] 'Is it so wrong…': Nick Hornby, *High Fidelity*. Victor Gollancz, 1995.

[337] Honouring objects: Gail Sketekee, Randy O. Frost and Michael Kyrios, 'Cognitive Aspects of Compulsive Hoarding'. *Cognitive Therapy and Research*, 2003. https://psycnet.apa.org/doi/10.1023/A:1025428631552

[338] Freud and toilet training: Daniel Faris, 'The Problem with Using Psychology to Explain Collecting'. ZME Science, 5 September 2017. https://www.zmescience.com/other/feature-post/problem-using-psychology-explain-collecting/

[339] 'Reading is solitude': Italo Calvino, *Se una notte d'inverno un viaggiatore [If on a*

*Winter's Night a Traveller].* L&OD Key Porter, 1982.

[340] 'What an astonishing thing…': Carl Sagan, *Cosmos*, Part 11: The Persistence of Memory. Random House, 1980.

[341] 'The object we call a book…': Rebecca Solnit, 'Flight', in *The Faraway Nearby.* Viking, 2013.

[342] 'We read to know we are not alone': Spoken by the character of C.S. Lewis in Nicholson's play *Shadowlands.* , 1989.

[343] 'There's this part…': Maria Popova, 'David Foster Wallace on the Redemptive Power of Reading and the Future of Writing in the Age of Information'. *The Marginalian*, 19 September 2014. https://www.themarginalian.org/2014/09/19/david-foster-wallace-charlie-rose-interview/

[344] 'What is needed…': Marcel Proust, *Journées de Lecture* ('Reading Days'). Gallimard, 2017. Quote taken from English glosses by William Eaton in 'Proust, playthings, reading, solitude'. ZETEO, 19 September 2017. https://zeteojournal.com/2017/09/19/proust-playthings-reading-solitude-eaton/

[345] 'If you are a writer…': Anne Lamott, *Bird by Bird: Instructions on Writing and Life.* Penguin Random House, 1994.

[346] 'I am hungry to be interrupted': Stevie Smith, 'Thoughts about the Person from Porlock'. In *The New Selected Poems of Stevie Smith*, New Directions Publishing Corporation, 1988.

[347] 'Once a year…': 'Leïla Slimani's Q&A: "I smoke too much and I can't stand it any more"'. *New Statesman*, 11 May 2022. https://www.newstatesman.com/culture/qa/2022/05/leila-slimanis-qa-i-smoke-too-much-and-i-cant-stand-it-any-more

[348] 'Nearer to the unconscious': Chris White, 'Routine Matters: Edna O'Brien.' 20 December 2016. https://awritersden.wordpress.com/2016/12/20/edna-obrien/

[349] 'It's lonely, and it's marvellous': Naomi Pham, '6 Profound Benefits of a Morning Writing Routine (and How to Build One Yourself)'. *Craft Your Content*, 25 June 2020. https://www.craftyourcontent.com/benefits-morning-writing-routine/

[350] 'All those I think who have lived as literary men': Anthony Trollope, *Autobiography.* 1883. https://www.gutenberg.org/files/5978/5978-h/5978-h.htm

[351] 'One does not find solitude…': Marguerite Duras, *Writing.* Brookline Books, 1999.

[352] 'I would sit…': Emma Brockes, 'Jennifer Egan: "Twitter doesn't make me feel optimistic about human nature"'. *The Guardian*, 16 April 2022. https://www.theguardian.com/books/2022/apr/16/jennifer-egan-twitter-doesnt-make-me-feel-optimistic-about-human-nature

[353] 'In my craft or sullen art…': Dylan Thomas, 'In My Craft or Sullen Art'. https://poetrysociety.org.uk/poems/in-my-craft-or-sullen-art/

[354] 'Writing that springs…': Franz Kafka, *Letters to Felice.* Schocken Books, 1967.

[355] 'If you would learn to write…': Emerson, op. cit.

[356] Benefits of keeping a diary: Thai Nguyen, '10 Surprising Benefits You'll Get From Keeping a Journal'. *Huffington Post*, 6 December 2017. https://www.huffpost.com/entry/benefits-of-journaling_b_6648884

[357] 'You are alone with the composer…': Clive Thompson, 'How the Phonograph Changed Music Forever'. *Smithsonian Magazine*, January 2016. https://www.smithsonianmag.com/arts-culture/phonograph-changed-music-forever-180957677/

[358] Solo listening intensifies its emotional content: Neil Petersen, 'Listening Alone or With Others Changes the Effects of Music'. *AllPsych*, 9 October 2017. https://allpsych.com/listening-alone-or-with-others-changes-the-effects-of-music/

[359] Music as social surrogate: Katharina Schäfer, Suvi Saarikallio and Tuomas Eerola, 'Music May Reduce Loneliness and Act as Social Surrogate for a Friend: Evidence from an Experimental Listening Study'. *Music & Science*, 25 June 2020. https://doi.org/10.1177/2059204320935709

[360] 'I like making music on my own…': Computer Music, 'Bonobo on making music alone and the power of software'. 26 September 2014. https://www.musicradar.com/news/tech/bonobo-on-making-music-alone-and-the-

power-of-software-607467

[361] 'I was carrying that cassette…': Kurt Loder, 'The Rolling Stone Interview: Bruce Springsteen on "Born in the U.S.A."'. *Rolling Stone*, 7 December 1984. https://www.rollingstone.com/music/music-news/the-rolling-stone-interview-bruce-springsteen-on-born-in-the-u-s-a-184690/

[362] Young people making music alone: Dorian Lynskey, 'Why bands are disappearing: "Young people aren't excited by them"'. *The Guardian*, 18 March 2021. https://www.theguardian.com/music/2021/mar/18/why-bands-are-disappearing-young-people-arent-excited-by-them

[363] Parasocial interaction: Dara N. Greenwood and Christopher R. Long, 'Psychological Predictors of Media Involvement: Solitude Experiences and the Need to Belong'. *Communication Research*, 21 July 2009. https://doi.org/10.1177/0093650209338906

[364] Podcasts: Rachel Aroesti, 'Tragic but true: how podcasters replaced our real friends'. *The Guardian*, 7 June 2021. https://www.theguardian.com/tv-and-radio/2021/jun/07/tragic-but-true-have-podcasters-replaced-our-real-friends

[365] 'Fair quiet, have I found thee here…': Andrew Marvell, 'The Garden', 1651. First published 1681, London.

[366] 'Plants do not speak…': May Sarton, *Plant Dreaming Deep: A Journal*. 1968.

[367] 'A garden offers the opposite…': Rebecca Solnit, *Orwell's Roses*. Granta, 2021.

[368] 'Expectation is what gives us…': Douglas Swinscow, *The Mystic Garden*. Tiverton, 1992.

[369] 'Kneeling between the scale…': Maria Popova, '200 Years of Great Writers and Artists on the Creative and Spiritual Rewards of Gardening'. *The Marginalian*, 7 May 2022. https://www.themarginalian.org/2022/05/07/writers-artists-gardens/

[370] 'Gardens are a paradox…': Mirabel Osler, 'A Word about Boxes', *Hortus* (No. 16), 1990.

[371] 'People never like me…' and 'In secret places…': Frances Hodgson Burnett, *The Secret Garden*. William Heinemann, 1911.

[372] 'One day Sally found a secret house…': Shirley Hughes, *Sally's Secret*. The Bodley Head, 1973.

[373] 'The things which I have seen…': William Wordsworth, 'Ode: Intimations of Immortality from Recollections of Early Childhood'. https://www.bartleby.com/101/536.html

[374] *The Warlock of Firetop Mountain*: James Lowder (ed.), *Hobby Games: The 100 Best*. Green Ronin Publishing, 2007. pp. 362–364.

[375] 'The first time I used a computer…': 'In the chair with… Peter Molyneux'. *Retro Gamer*, load 71, p. 82.

[376] 'An extra life': Tom Bissell, *Extra Lives: Why Video Games Matter*. Vintage, 2010.

[377] Bathroom mini-break: Joe Pera, *A Bathroom Book for People Not Pooping or Peeing but Using the Bathroom as an Escape*. Forge Books, 2021.

[378] 'May lay claim to any unoccupied stall…': Spencer E. Cahill, William Distler, Cynthia Lachowetz, Andrea Meaney, Robyn Tarallo and Teena Willard, 'Meanwhile Backstage: Public Bathrooms and the Interaction Order'. *Journal of Contemporary Ethnography*, 1985. https://doi.org/10.1177%2F0098303985014001002

[379] 'Alone one is never lonely…': May Sarton, 'Canticle 6'. In *Inner Landscape: Poems*. Martino Fine, 2016.

[380] 'When we are awake…': Paul Martin, *Counting Sheep: The Science and Pleasures of Sleep and Dreams*. Flamingo, 2003.

[381] Dreaming and wakefulness have the same origin: R.R. Llinás and D Paré, 'Of dreaming and wakefulness'. *Neuroscience* 1991;44(3): 521–35. https://doi.org/10.1016/0306-4522(91)90075-y

[382] 'I've dreamt in my life…': Emily Brontë (as 'Ellis Bell'), *Wuthering Heights*. Thomas Cautley Newby, 1847.

[383] Cast of dream characters: Martin, op. cit.

[384] Paul McCartney writing 'Yesterday': Ian MacDonald, *Revolution in the Head: The Beatles' Records and the Sixties*. Fourth Estate, 1994.

*By the same author*

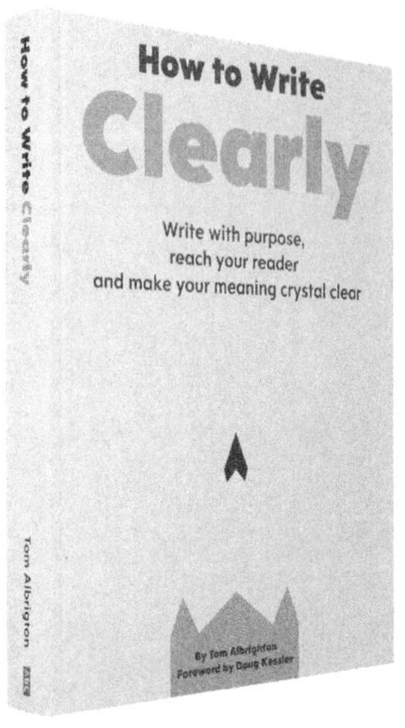


**How to Write**

**Clearly**

**Write with purpose, reach your reader and make your meaning crystal clear**

★★★★★ ‘One of the most focused writing guides I've ever come across’

★★★★★ ‘A must-read for professional writers’

★★★★★ ‘I really enjoyed it’

★★★★★ ‘Does exactly what it says’

★★★★★ ‘Worth its weight in gold’

★★★★★ ‘Heartily recommended’

*By the same author*

**Whatever you're writing, the clearer you make it, the better your results will be.**

*How to Write Clearly* is an authoritative yet easy-to-read guide that will make your non-fiction writing more colourful, expressive and precise.

It's ideal for marketers, businesspeople, journalists, educators and anyone who needs to communicate with the written word.

You'll learn...

- How to **understand your reader**
- How to use **plain language** to make your writing accessible, readable and relatable
- **Ten treacherous traps** you must avoid
- Proven techniques for **explaining new ideas**
- How to **captivate your reader** with storytelling, humour, intrigue, perspective and more
- What really **changes readers' minds**
- How to craft clear **sentences** and **paragraphs**
- Using **empathy** and **pacing** to put the reader at their ease
- How to choose the right **structure**, **length** and **title**
- Pages of pro tips for **drafting**, **editing** and using **feedback**.

Fully illustrated and referenced, with a wealth of examples throughout, *How to Write Clearly* is the definitive guide to non-fiction writing today.

Find it on Amazon in hardcover, paperback or ebook, or learn more at **tomalbrighton.com**

*By the same author*

# COPYWRITING MADE SIMPLE

How to write powerful and persuasive copy that sells

★★★★★ 'Excellent'

★★★★★ 'This book is gold'

★★★★★ 'So easy to read'

★★★★★ 'Clear, practical and encouraging'

★★★★★ 'I love this book'

★★★★★ 'Buy it!'

*By the same author*

**Copywriting is writing with purpose. It's about using words to reach people and change what they think, feel and do.**

This easy-to-read guide will teach you all the essentials of copywriting, from understanding products, readers and benefits to closing the sale.

It's packed with real-life examples that will show you exactly how the ideas and techniques will work in the real world.

Plus there's a whole chapter of handy tips on writing ads, websites, broadcast media, direct mail, social media and print.

What you'll learn...

- Understand the **product** and its **benefits**
- Get to know your **reader**
- Decide how your copy will change how the reader **thinks, feels or acts**
- **Talk to your reader** and make your copy more like a conversation
- **Bring the product to life** with rich, sensory language
- Learn eight proven formulas for **enticing headlines**
- Choose a rock-solid **structure**
- Create powerful **calls to action**
- Use 20 proven strategies for **creative copy**
- Make **persuasion and psychology** work for you
- Create a unique **tone of voice** for a brand.

*Copywriting Made Simple* is the perfect introduction to copywriting today.

Find it on Amazon in hardcover, paperback, ebook or audiobook, or learn more at **tomalbrighton.com**

*By the same author*

---

★★★★★

'This book changed my life'

★★★★★

'Insightful, easy to read and very enjoyable'

★★★★

'Loved this book... made me excited about the future'

★★★★★

'Great eye-opener'

★★★★★

'I felt it was written about me'

★★★★★

'Excellent book'

*By the same author*

**Are you an introvert?**

If you're happy in your own company most of the time, have just a few close friends and prefer to work alone, the answer is probably yes.

Modern working styles can be really hard on introverts. Freelancing offers a way out – but it also takes work. To make a success of it, you'll need to learn some new skills, overcome some challenges and build your confidence.

*The Freelance Introvert* shows you how to create and manage your freelance business, from taking the first steps to time management, working with clients and marketing.

What you'll learn...

- Why introversion is a strength, not a weakness
- How to decide what you want from freelance life
- How to find the right clients... and avoid the wrong ones
- How to set prices without self-sabotaging
- How to manage your time and set boundaries
- How to break through self-limiting beliefs.

Find *The Freelance Introvert* on Amazon in in hardcover, paperback, ebook or audiobook, or learn more at **tomalbrighton.com**.

*By the same author*

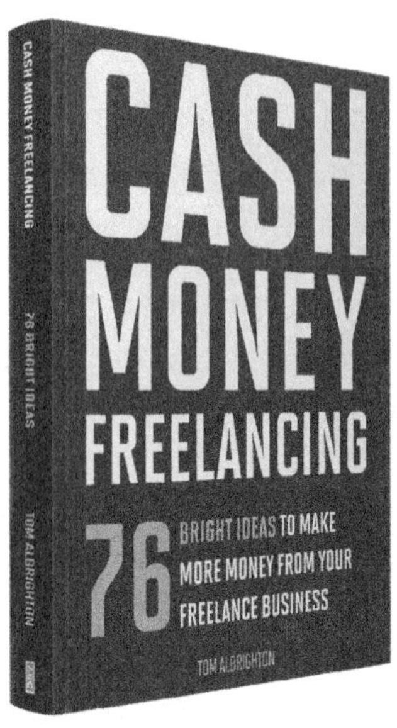


# CASH MONEY FREELANCING

## 76 BRIGHT IDEAS

**TO MAKE MORE MONEY FROM YOUR FREELANCE BUSINESS**

'Essential'

'Highly recommended'

'So much fun to read'

'Packed with good, solid advice'

'Every freelancer should own a copy'

'Refreshing, practical, and inspirational'

*By the same author*

**So, you've gone freelance. And you're making a living. But have you made yourself a life?**

Freelancing should set you free. But for some, it's more like a prison sentence – because they just don't make enough money.

*Cash Money Freelancing* will show you how to turn your freelance business into a bona fide money-making machine.

It's packed with ideas to turbo-charge your freelancing, from setting your goals through to making better deals, earning higher fees and exploring new ways to grow.

Here's what you'll learn...

- Why you need a 'money mind' as well as a 'work mind'
- How to understand the unique value you offer
- The best ways to charge – and what you should charge for
- How to present your prices more persuasively
- How to negotiate price deals like a pro
- Proven techniques for increasing your rates
- How to be less like a sole trader and more like a business.

If you've got the skills, the work and the clients, but your freelance business still isn't jumping the way it should, *Cash Money Freelancing* has the answers you need.

Find it on Amazon in in hardcover, paperback, ebook or audiobook, or learn more at **tomalbrighton.com**.

Printed in Great Britain
by Amazon

24053382R00185